D0218709

GAMES OF VENUS

The New Ancient World
a series published by Routledge

The Constraints of Desire
The Anthropology of Sex and Gender in Ancient Greece
John J. Winkler

One Hundred Years of Homosexuality
And Other Essays on Greek Love
David Halperin

Torture and Truth
Page duBois

GAMES OF VENUS

*An Anthology of Greek and Roman
Erotic Verse from Sappho to Ovid*

INTRODUCED, TRANSLATED AND ANNOTATED BY
PETER BING AND RIP COHEN

ROUTLEDGE NEW YORK AND LONDON

Published in 1991

Paperback published in 1993 by

Routledge
29 West 35 Street
New York, NY 10001

Published in Great Britain by

Routledge
11 New Fetter Lane
London EC4P 4EE

Copyright © 1991 by Routledge

Printed in the United States of America on acid free paper.

All rights reserved. No parts of this book may be reprinted or reproduced or utilized in any form
or by any electronic, mechanical or other means, now known or hereafter invented, including
photocopying and recording, or in any information storage or retrieval system, without permission
in writing from the publishers.

Library of Congress Cataloging in Publication Data

Games of Venus : an anthology of Greek and Roman erotic verse from
    Sappho to Ovid / introduced, translated, and annotated by Peter Bing
    and Rip Cohen.
        p.   cm.
    Includes bibliographical references.
    ISBN 0-415-90260-6 (HB)   ISBN 0-415-90261-4 (PB)
        1. Erotic poetry, Greek—Translations into English.   2. Erotic
    poetry, Latin—Translations into English.   I. Bing, Peter.
    II. Cohen, Rip.
    PA3624.E75G36   1991
    881'.0108'03538—dc20   91-26958

British Library cataloging in publication data also available

iv

TABLE OF CONTENTS

ACKNOWLEDGMENTS

This book was conceived a few years ago in a crowded bus winding along Lakeshore Drive in Chicago, and nurtured on our frustration at the lack of a collection we could use in courses on traditions of erotic poetry. As it grew, we subjected many students (at the Universities of Pennsylvania and Chicago, Case Western Reserve University, and Emory University), colleagues, and friends to our translations and interpretations, and also occasionally to some very heated arguments (collaborative translation, while enormously satisfying, is no picnic). They always responded with tact and good advice. Thanks, in particular, to Professors George Walsh of the University of Chicago, Ralph Rosen of the University of Pennsylvania, Tom Bishop of Case Western Reserve University, Louise Pratt, Cynthia Patterson, and Garth Tissol of Emory University; Alva Walter Bennett of the University of California at Santa Barbara, who suggested ideas long ago that have found their way into the introduction and into the translations; to Gail Levine, Jason Engel, and Mr. Martin David Cohen. Since we lived in far-flung places (first Cleveland and Chicago, then Atlanta and Madrid), we had to travel at various critical moments when it was necessary to work things out face to face. At such times we received generous assistance from Case Western Reserve University and Emory University. Finally, we'd like to thank our parents, whose understanding of eros made us possible. It is to them that we dedicate this book.

LIST OF ABBREVIATIONS

The abbreviations for journals are those used in the bibliographic annual, *L'Année Philologique*

Adams	J.N. Adams, *The Latin Sexual Vocabulary* (Baltimore 1982)
AP	*Anthologia Palatina* (the Greek Anthology)
CEG	P.A. Hansen, *Carmina Epigraphica Graeca Saeculorum VIII-V A. Chr. N.* (Berlin 1983)
Cunningham	I.C. Cunningham, *Herodas Mimiambi cum Appendice Fragmentorum Mimorum Papyraceorum* (Leipzig 1987)
Degani	E. Degani, *Hipponax. Testimonia et Fragmenta* (Leipzig 1983)
Gow	A.S.F. Gow, *Machon. The Fragments* (Cambridge 1965)
G-P	A.S.F. Gow and D.L. Page, *The Greek Anthology. Hellenistic Epigrams* 2 vols. (Cambridge 1965)
Henderson	J. Henderson, *The Maculate Muse: Obscene Language in Attic Comedy* (New Haven 1975)
Kroll	W. Kroll, *Catull* (Stuttgart 1980)
L-P	E. Lobel and D.L. Page, *Poetarum Lesbiorum Fragmenta* (Oxford 1955)
Page	D.L. Page, *Epigrammata Graeca* (Oxford 1975)
Pf.	R. Pfeiffer, *Callimachus* 2 vols. (Oxford 1941, 1953)
PMG	D.L. Page, *Poetae Melici Graeci* (Oxford 1962)
Powell	J.U. Powell, *Collectanea Alexandrina* (Oxford 1925)
SH	H. Lloyd-Jones, P. Parsons, *Supplementum Hellenisticum* (Berlin 1983)
SLG	D.L. Page, *Supplementum Lyricis Graecis* (Oxford 1974)
Snell-Maehler	B. Snell and H. Maehler, *Bacchylides* (Leipzig 1970) B. Snell and H. Maehler, *Pindar* 2 vols (Leipzig 1975)

Vetta   M. Vetta, *Theognis. Elegiarum Liber Secundus* (Rome 1980)

Voigt   E.-M. Voigt, *Sappho et Alcaeus* (Amsterdam 1971)

West   M.L. West, *Iambi et Elegi Graeci* 2 vols. (Oxford 1971)

West, *Studies*   M.L. West, *Studies in Greek Elegy and Iambus* (Berlin 1974)

A NOTE ON THE TRANSLATION

We have tried to make translations which are compelling and vigorous in English, which will engage and delight the general reader. At the same time, we attempt to stay as close as we can not just to the spirit, but to the letter of our originals. Wherever possible, we retain their structure, line-division, diction. When their language is low, so is ours; when elevated, ours attempts to match that tone as well. Teachers (and students) with knowledge of Greek and Latin—and resultant interpretations—should not constantly have to battle the translation.

Since we deal with both Greek and Latin verse in this translation, we have generally tried to render names as they would appear in their respective linguistic context. Thus Herakles and Odysseus appear in Greek texts, while those same heroes are called Hercules and Ulysses in Latin. There are, however, many names so well-known in English by their Latinized form that we have left them so throughout.

Man lernt das Spiel, indem man zusieht, wie Andere es spielen. Aber wir sagen, es werde nach den und den Regeln gespielt, weil ein Beobachter diese Regeln aus der Praxis des Spiels ablesen kann,—wie ein Naturgesetz, dem die Spielhandlungen folgen—Wie aber unterscheidet der Beobachter in diesem Fall zwischen einem Fehler der Spielenden und einer richtigen Spielhandlung?—Es gibt dafür Merkmale im Benehmen der Spieler.
—Wittgenstein, *Philosophische Untersuchungen* #54

Anderseits ändert sich das Sprachspiel mit der Zeit.
—Wittgenstein, *Über Gewissheit* #256

INTRODUCTION

Sexual desire, like most areas of human activity, is culturally determined. And modern readers who encounter it expressed in the poetry
of ancient Greece and Rome quickly see that it reflects certain cultural
assumptions very different from their own—many of which may surprise
them.[1] There is, for instance, a near total absence of conjugal passion,
pervasive differences in status between lover and beloved, the startling
prominence of homosexuality, etc. If readers are to account for such
surprising features, but also if they are to appreciate the poetry more
generally, they must be able to situate the poems within the larger
cultural system. It may be helpful, therefore, to sketch in the social
backdrop against which the various manifestations of sexual desire were
played out.

---

1. This section is much indebted to the pioneering work of many fine scholars, and
does not pretend to originality. Among the many works that have appeared on the
topic of ancient Greek sexual mores, we single out K.J. Dover, "Classical Greek
Attitudes to Sexual Behaviour," *Arethusa* 6 (1973) 59–73; *idem, Greek Popular Morality
in the Time of Plato and Aristotle* (Berkeley 1974) esp. 205–216; *idem, Greek Homosexuality*
(New York 1978); M. Foucault, *The Use of Pleasure: The History of Sexuality vol.2* (New
York 1985); J. Henderson, "Greek Attitudes toward Sex," in *Civilization of the Ancient
Mediterranean*, eds. M. Grant and R. Kitzinger (New York 1988) vol.2 pp. 1249–1263;
D. Halperin, *One Hundred Years of Homosexuality* (New York 1989); J. Winkler, *The
Constraints of Desire* (New York 1989); for the latter two cf. J. Griffin's sceptical review
in *The New York Review of Books* 37.5 (1990) 6–12; D. Halperin, J. Winkler, F. Zeitlin,
eds., *Before Sexuality* (Princeton 1990). For the erotic tradition in the visual arts, see J.
Boardman and E. La Rocca, *Eros in Greece* (London 1978); D. Mountfield, *Greek and
Roman Erotica* (New York 1982); C. Johns, *Sex or Symbol: Erotic Images of Greece and Rome*
(Austin 1982); A. Dierichs, "Erotik in der Kunst Griechenlands," *Antike Welt* 19
(Sondernummer 1988).

1

Greece:

Much of the ancient Greek poetry we have assembled in this anthology reflects the ideals of the wealthy and aristocratic.[2] Its perspective, moreover, is (with few exceptions) overwhelmingly male. Among the upper classes, at least during the Archaic period (ca. 800–480 B.C.) and Classical period (480–323 B.C.), women were not generally permitted easy contact with men outside of their immediate family. For the family unit (the *oikos*), was the basis for belonging, as a participating citizen, to the city-state (the *polis*). And within that unit, strictly conducted along bloodlines, one had to be sure of who a child's father was in order to establish its citizenship rights. We need not imagine that all Greek states put such stringent restrictions on females as did the Athenians of the Classical period, where women of citizen status were segregated from men even in their own households and allowed to go out unaccompanied only on special occasions such as funerals and religious festivals. Still, in a culture with no reliable means of contraception, many obstacles were thrown up to prevent unplanned unions, and the law inflicted severe punishment on males who committed "adultery." This was a term that covered a far broader range than it does today, since it could be used of a sexual offense against any citizen woman, whether she was another man's wife, his widowed mother, unmarried daughter, sister, niece, etc.[3]

Consequently, men were not encouraged to feel sexual desire for women of citizen status. And even for a wife, sexual passion (that strong appetite which the Greeks called *eros*) on the husband's part was not the norm. In his *Works and Days* Hesiod makes no mention of physical

---

2. This is due mainly to our decision to restrict ourselves to translating complete poems, rather than using excerpts. The literary forms which played to a much broader public (e.g. epic, tragedy, and comedy), while rich in erotic material, are thus necessarily excluded. A possible exception may be the poetry of Archilochus, which had (at least by the time of Plato's *Ion*) become part of the repertoire of the epic rhapsode. If we are to believe Plato, such a performer might, on occasion, perform before as many as 20,000 people.

3. I.e. any woman of whom a man might be the legal guardian. On segregation of females and adultery cf. Dover (1973) 61–62 and Henderson (1988) 1257–1258.

attraction as a factor in selecting a wife. On the contrary, he urges men to choose virgins (vv.695ff.) who know nothing of the works of Aphrodite (v.521), and who could be taught their duties from the ground up. Interest in sex on a wife's part was considered potentially dangerous and, thus, discouraged—for she might be capable of cuck-olding her husband and making him a laughing-stock to his neighbors.[4]

Even where conjugal passion existed—and there can be no doubt that it was a factor of daily life[5]—it was not something spoken of in public. A famous instance comparable, say, to that of the Brownings in modern times does not occur. And nowhere in Greek antiquity is love poetry addressed to a spouse.[6] On the contrary, we can see just how peculiar the public expression of conjugal passion was thought to be, how indecorous (even disastrous) its results might be, in Herodotus' story of the Lydian king Kandaules and his wife (1.8f.). For a Greek, the Lydian setting of the story doubtless gave this passion an appropri-ately exotic tinge: "This Kandaules conceived a passion for his own wife, and inspired by this passion he thought her the most beautiful woman in the world. Persuaded thus, he raved about his wife's body to Gyges, son of Daskylos, who was his favorite guard and to whom he entrusted his most important business." In this passage, Kandaules is acting precisely as we might expect a smitten lover to behave, publicly proclaiming his feelings for a beloved. But for a husband to feel that way about his wife is extraordinary, and more extraordinary yet for him to talk about it. Such passion will lead (the story implies) to calamity.

---

4. Cf. also Archilochus' *First Cologne Epode* vv.22–24 and Semonides 7.110ff (West).

5. Odysseus, for example, comforts the Greeks at Troy (*Iliad* 2.292f. cited by Dover) by saying that their impatience is understandable: to be away from one's wife for even a month would make one impatient, and they have been away for nine years!—but the public expression of such desire, least of all in song, evidently did not fit the popular conception of what was proper in a marriage.

6. The wife as object of desire was safely relegated to comedy. There, of course, the playwright could exploit the idea of conjugal passion, as a fantasy, for humorous purposes. Thus in Aristophanes' *Lysistrata* the citizen wives of Greece go on a sex strike so as to force an end to the Peloponnesian War. Here, in the utopia of the play, the sexual avenues normally open to men outside of marriage (i.e. *hetairai*, prostitutes, and boys) have mysteriously vanished, and the males are driven wild with sexual passion for their wives.

For the Lydian king goes on to do what no lover would ever dream of: "After a little while, he said the following to Gyges. 'Gyges, I don't think you believe what I've told you about my wife's body (men trust their ears less than their eyes), so you've got to see her naked'." Though Gyges tries to refuse, the king insists. Hidden by Kandaules in the royal bedroom, Gyges sees the queen naked, but as he tries to slip away she notices him. The next day, filled with shame, the queen tells Gyges that he must either avenge this disgrace by killing Kandaules and marrying her—or be killed himself. Gyges, of course, chooses life, and so Kandaules' dynasty comes to an end.

Who, then, are those women referred to publicly, in song, as the objects of masculine desire? In antiquity there were easy sources available to a man to gratify his (hetero-) sexual urges, namely *hetairas* (i.e. "female companions") and prostitutes. These were certainly not citizens. They could, on the one hand, be foreigners, i.e. female professionals not bound by the constraints of citizenship, and (as far as adultery laws were concerned) fair game for the citizen male; or, since slavery was a regular part of ancient society, they were slaves. *Hetairas* were typically hired by just one man (or only a few) over the longer term, and a relationship with one is thought to have included the possibility of real affection and intellectual exchange. On the other hand, slaves were available for quick gratification, and to this end a man could use either his own slaves or go to a brothel where slaves were kept for this purpose. In addition, there were various female performers (likewise foreigners or slaves) who were hired to entertain at male drinking parties (*symposia*) and were apparently also available for sexual services.[7]

When, therefore, in Archaic and Classical Greek poetry, a man expresses sexual desire for a female, or addresses her with this subject in mind, chances are that she will be a *hetaira*, performer or slave. Consider, for instance, a poem by Anacreon (*PMG* 358):

> Once more Eros of the golden hair
> hits me with his purple ball,

---

7. On the various heterosexual outlets for men, cf. K.J. Dover, *Greek Popular Morality in the Time of Plato and Aristotle* (Berkeley 1974) 210.

calls me out to play with the girl
with the flashy slippers.
But she, since she comes from noble
Lesbos, scoffs at my hair,
since it's white, and gapes
for another girl.

First of all, the girl described in this poem is a foreigner (would it otherwise be necessary to point out that she comes from Lesbos?); secondly, she is left anonymous; finally, she is wearing exotic, strikingly unmodest slippers—all of which suggest that we are dealing here not with a female citizen, but with one of the categories of woman mentioned above.

The same holds true for Anacreon *PMG* 417:

Thracian filly, why do you eye me with mistrust
and stubbornly run away, and think that I'm unskilled?
Rest assured, I could fit you deftly with a bridle
and, holding the reins, could steer you past the end posts of
our course.
Now as it is, you graze the fields and frisk in childish play
since you lack a rider with a practiced hand at horsemanship.

As before, the girl is left anonymous and seems to be a foreigner. Thracians, moreover, were frequently used as slaves (the name "Thraissa" was a common slave name). The poem suggests that she is still a virgin—not what we might initially expect in a prostitute or *hetaira*. But perhaps we are to imagine the speaker propositioning a child-musician at a *symposium*; or the new girl in a brothel. One is reminded of the scene in Menander's comedy, *The Men at Arbitration* ("Epitrepontes"), where a *hetaira* recalls how only one year ago she was still a virgin (vv.476–479): "last year. . . . I played the harp for some young ladies and shared in their games myself. I didn't know then, not yet, what a man is."

As for adulterous relationships, it goes without saying that liaisons with "respectable" women occurred in daily life. But in the *poetry* of this era such women are the objects of male sexual attention only in invective, that is, in "iambic-," or blame-poetry (such as that of Archilochus or Hipponax). Here, the woman is typically *not* left anonymous: for her name is deliberately dragged through the mud.[8] The disgrace consists precisely in her being treated as though she were a foreigner or slave.

It will be clear that heterosexual passion, at least as publicly expressed in poetry, always involved a difference in status: the male always dominant; the female subordinate. Consequently, images of pursuit and flight are ubiquitous; the relationships predatory. At the same time, however, it was generally considered shameful to devote too much time and resources to the chase, since immoderate indulgence in sexual passion could encroach on one's responsibilities as a citizen and compromise one's ability to serve the state. Private matters thereby could, and often did, become public affairs. And a man stood the chance—if he didn't take care—of exposing himself to attack by his enemies. Paradoxically, therefore, even as images of masculine control and possession abound, we also find the notion that sexual desire is a madness, that it subdues and enslaves a man—as, for instance, in Ibycus *PMG* 287, where the image of the horse which we saw used of the girl in Anacreon, is here used of the male lover:

> Once more Eros, under darkened
>   lids, fixing me with his melting gaze,
> drives me with every kind of spell into the
>   tangling nets of Kypris.
> And yes, I tremble at his coming,
> as a horse who's borne the yoke and won the prize, but aging
>   now,
> when hitched to the speeding chariot, goes to the race against
>   his will.

---

8. Cf. Neoboule in Archilochus' *First Cologne Epode*. We assume that her sister was also named in the lost beginning of the poem; but she is in any case sufficiently identified as "daughter of Amphimedo" in v.7. Cf. also Arete in the poetry of Hipponax. Herotima in Anacreon *PMG* 346 may also belong in this category.

It was only in the Hellenistic period (323–30 B.C.) that status distinctions in heterosexual relationships in and outside of marriage began to break down. Because of the rapid expansion of the Greek world in the wake of Alexander the Great's conquests, the traditional family unit—and the restrictions it placed on female activity—could not always be maintained. The dislocation of parents from children, siblings from one another, husbands from wives, meant that women began to enjoy a certain independence.[9] A figure such as Simaitha, in the second idyll of Theocritus (1st half of the 3rd cent. B.C.), who is clearly not of servile status (she has her own servant), yet appears to be under no male supervision and is free to pursue a lover, is a figure of a new age. The same holds true of the girl in the Grenfell papyrus and numerous other examples.

From our discussion of the heterosexual realm, we turn now to the subject of homosexuality. Throughout antiquity homoerotic love was considered normal and appropriate. Nor did it preclude heterosexual activity (including marriage). The two were considered entirely compatible. The prevalence of homosexuality should, perhaps, not surprise us given the obstacles faced by a citizen male in initiating a relationship with a female of like status, and given the heterosexual outlets available to him—outlets in which he could never be sure if affection was real, or just paid for. Yet the many restrictions and inhibitions applying to homosexual love make it implausible that this kind of desire was fostered merely in response to the possibility of carnal relations with a social equal—here, as elsewhere, we are wrong if we think that the Greeks "lived in a rosy haze of uninhibited sexuality."[10] The reasons for ubiquitous homosexuality are different: Whereas people today commonly think of themselves as exclusively hetero- or homosexual, and consider the one or the other an integral part of their "identity" (for this exclusive distinction conforms to their experience and so they commonly suppose it natural and normal), the ancients considered bisexuality the norm—

---

9. On this phenomenon, cf. A. Cameron, "Asclepiades' Girlfriends" in H. Foley, ed., *Reflections of Women in Antiquity* (New York 1981) 275–302; S.B. Pomeroy, *Women in Hellenistic Egypt* (New York 1984) 72–82.

10. Cf. Dover (1974) 205.

though here also modern bisexuality is not a reliable guide, since ancient norms and restrictions were different.

Male homosexuality characteristically occurred between a mature man and a younger boy. And as in heterosexual relationships, the adult male plays the dominant role: he is the pursuer, designated by the active term *erastes* or "lover." The boy, by contrast, is pursued, and his passivity is reflected in the passive term *eromenos* or "beloved." One comes to appreciate the commanding role of the *erastes* when one realizes his nearly complete control of the poetic discourse. His is the voice we almost always hear. Look high and low for the voice of the *eromenos* in ancient Greek lyric—you will almost never find it.[11]

But this did not mean that the *erastes* could simply have his way with the *eromenos*. For the boy was a citizen. And as such, many of those same sexual taboos connected with citizen women applied to him too. In order for the boy to be able, eventually, to realize his function within the community, he must not be demeaned or made to play the role of a woman, foreigner or slave. "It was necessary," as Henderson has aptly said, "to distinguish a *pais* (citizen male child) from a *pais* (slave)."[12]

Accordingly, an elaborate etiquette was set up. It was, on the one hand, considered desirable for a boy to have the intimate companionship of an older male who could act as role-model, inculcating in him those qualities valued by the *polis*: loyalty to friends and state, valor in war, political responsibility, etc. One scholar has memorably called this "pedagogical pederasty."[13] And if an adult of good qualities showed interest in a boy, it was considered flattering—both to the boy and his family. But while an adult was, characteristically, smitten by the physical beauty of his beloved,[14] encouraged to press his suit as aggressively as possible, and admired for a conquest, it was considered dis-

---

11. The only clear-cut example we have found is Theognis 1097–1100, though one might also consider Anacreon Elegy 2 (West), cf. note *ad loc.*

12. Henderson (1988) 1260.

13. Thus B. Sergent, *Homosexuality in Greek Myth* (Boston 1986) 3.

14. The physical ideal—observable in vase-painting and sculpture—is summed up in Aristophanes' *Clouds* (vv. 1012–1014): "a smooth chest, shining skin, large shoulders, a small tongue, a big ass and a tiny cock."

graceful for a boy to be swayed by a suitor's good looks or wealth, or to yield too soon. He was expected, rather, to test his suitor's intentions over a period of time and when, finally, he allowed the *erastes* to achieve his sexual desire, he nevertheless did so chastely.

The evidence of vase-paintings makes clear just how modest the behavior of the *eromenos* was throughout: in scenes of courtship, we regularly see the *erastes* fondle a boy's genitals—yet the boy is never shown with an erection. Similarly, penetration of the *eromenos* is rarely depicted—for being penetrated, a clear sign of subordinate status, was thought proper only for women and slaves. Rather, it is the *erastes* who must stoop so as to have sex intercrurally, while the *eromenos* stands modestly upright and scarcely seems aware of his lover's feverish activity.[15] This picture of homosexual relations corresponds to the essential modesty of its depiction in poetry as well—though this also applies to heterosexual copulation. As a rule, the sex act is referred to with metaphor and euphemism.

The twin sites of the pederastic relationship were the *palaestra* or wrestling ground, where the boy and adult male engaged in physical exercise, could size each other up and initiate contact, and the *symposium* or male drinking party, where the boy would be integrated into the social group of companions to which his lover belonged, be educated as to its values, and initiated into the musical arts especially as regards the poetry of sexual desire. Also connected with the *symposium*—though not exclusively in homosexual affairs—is the subsequent (usually drunken) procession, known as the *komos*. Here, if the beloved had not been present at the *symposium*, the partier would go and try, by means of serenades, pleas, threats, force, etc., to gain admittance to his or her home. This pilgrimage to the beloved's house was an especially favored theme in the Hellenistic and Roman poets.[16]

---

15. For an excellent discussion of the evidence from vase-paintings, cf. the sections on "Courtship and Copulation" and "Dominant and Subordinate Roles" in Dover (1978) 91–109.

16. Cf. e.g. Theocritus 2.126, 3, 7.96–127; Asclepiades G-P 11 = AP 5.64, G-P 12 = AP 5.145, G-P 13 = AP 5.164; Callimachus 42 Pf. = G-P 8; Tibullus 1.8; Propertius 2.29a.

The *symposium* was the chief poetic locus of the male erotic discourse. And much of the poetry assembled in this anthology was composed for performance at the *symposium*.[17] Music was apparently the chief form of entertainment at such a gathering, and it was often performed in turn by the various participants in this intimate circle. The intimacy of the sympotic setting, combined with the very intimacy that was often the theme of such song, may help explain why erotic poetry is for the most part a solo genre (though much Greek poetry was sung by a choir) : that is, it is usually either 1) monody (solo song in a variety of lyric meters accompanied by the lyre, as in Sappho, Anacreon, Ibycus, etc.), 2) elegy (solo song in couplets consisting of a dactylic hexameter followed by a pentameter, and accompanied by flute, as in Mimnermos, Theognis, and most epigram), or 3) one of the spoken or chanted meters such as iambic trimeter (Archilochus, Hipponax, and Herodas) or dactylic hexameter (Theocritus).

Our discussion of the importance of the *symposium* for the expression of male sexual desire leads us finally to a consideration of its female counterpart, the *thiasos*, and with it to female homosexuality in the poetic tradition. Our evidence comes mainly from the Archaic period, in the poetry of Sappho and Alkman. Consequently, we can only construct a very fragmentary picture limited, probably, to that period and to the regions in which these poets were active (namely Lesbos and Sparta respectively). In these societies, as it seems, a young girl's training in preparation for marriage was accomplished within a formal group, consisting of many such girls, and known as a *thiasos*. A sisterhood of this kind was supervised by an older woman who presumably instructed the girls in domestic skills, religious observance, and musical arts. In the poetry of Alkman and Sappho we see that strong attachments—evidently sexual in nature—were formed among the girls, and

---

17. For the importance of the *symposium* as a Greek cultural institution, cf. O. Murray, "The Greek Symposion in History," in *Tria corda: scritti in onore di Arnaldo Momigliano*, ed. E. Gabba (Como 1983) 257–272; idem, *Early Greece* (Glasgow 1980) 197–203; idem (ed.), *Sympotica: The Papers of a Symposium on the* Symposion, *Oxford 1984* (Oxford 1990); M. Vetta, *Poesia e simposio nella Grecia antica* (Rome 1983); E.L. Bowie, "Early Greek Elegy, Symposium and Public Festival," *JHS* 106 (1986) 13–35; William J. Slater, ed., *Dining in a Classical Context* (Ann Arbor 1991).

between the girls and women leaders in the group.[18] In the poems (such as Alkman *PMG* 1, Sappho 94 and 96 L-P) there is often a tension between the girl's desire to stay within the group and so preserve the relationships she has formed there, and to yield to the necessity of marriage, likewise desirable, but which will bring to a close her homo-erotic bonds. For the assumption always seems to be that female homosexuality is essentially premarital. As in the male homosexual realm, the poetry here recurs with great poignancy to the necessary transience of the homoerotic relationship, since the girl is ultimately destined to marry, just as the boy—as soon as he sprouts a beard—will outgrow his status as *eromenos*.

Rome:[19]

Roman attitudes toward sexual behavior bear many strong resemblances to those in Greece, and this is especially so in the Latin poetry we have selected for this anthology. As in Greece, that poetry was generated almost exclusively by men and reflects upper-class values. It is, moreover, the product of a period (the late 1st cent. B.C.) when the

---

18. On these groups generally, and their homo-erotic activities in particular cf. C. Calame, *Les choeurs de jeunes filles en Grèce archaïque* (Rome 1977) 367–381, 427–436; B. Gentili, *Poetry and its Public in Ancient Greece* (Baltimore 1988) 72–89

19. In this section we are especially indebted to R.O.A.M. Lyne, *The Latin Love Poets* (Oxford 1980) esp. ch. 1: "Traditional Attitudes to Love. The Moral and Social Backround"; A. Richlin, "Approaches to the sources on adultery at Rome" in *Reflections of Women in Antiquity*, H. Foley, ed. (New York 1981) 379–404; *idem, The Garden of Priapus: Sexuality and Aggression in Roman Humor* (New Haven 1983); J.N. Adams, *The Latin Sexual Vocabulary* (Baltimore 1982); J.P. Hallett, "The Role of Women in Roman Elegy: Counter-cultural Feminism," in *Women in the Ancient World: The Arethusa Papers*, J. Peradotto and J.P. Sullivan, eds. (Albany 1984) 241–262; T.P. Wiseman, *Catullus and His World* (Cambridge 1985) esp. 10–14: "Sexual Mores"; E. Cantarella, *Pandora's Daughters: The Role and Status of Women in Greek and Roman Antiquity* (Baltimore 1987); A. Rousselle, *Porneia. On Desire and the Body in Antiquity* (Blackwell 1988); J.P. Hallett, "Roman Attitudes toward Sex," in *Civilization of the Ancient Mediterranean*, eds. M. Grant and R. Kitzinger (New York 1988) vol. 3 pp. 1265–1278; S.K. Dickison, "Women in Rome," *ibid.* pp. 1319–1332; S. Treggiari, "Roman Marriage," *ibid.* pp. 1343–1354.

"life of luxury" had been thoroughly Hellenized—i.e. the final years of the Roman republic and, following Octavian's accession to sole power after he had defeated Antony at the Battle of Actium in 31 B.C., the early years of the empire.[20] It was felt that these Hellenizing ways, with their sexual permissiveness, their *symposia*, *eromenoi* and *hetairas*, had begun infiltrating the more traditionally austere Roman lifestyle already in the 2nd cent. B.C.[21] There were periodic attempts to revive that more puritanical morality. But even when the emperor Augustus (formerly Octavian) supported such attempts with laws severely punishing adultery and bolstering family values, there remained a strong inclination towards these "Greek" pleasures that belied efforts to legislate them out of existence. Indeed, scholars have argued that the amorous life portrayed in Tibullus, Propertius, and Ovid may be read as an overt act of (political) defiance against Augustus' legislation.[22]

In this society, marriage, once again, is not the normal locus of sexual desire. For while Roman women were, in theory, on an equal footing with men as regards marriage (and could even retain property rights independent of their husbands), and though their consent was indispensible for the legality of the union, the practical reality did not often conform to legal theory. For women married young[23]—the legal minimum was twelve years old—and they would still be under the sway

---

20. Cf. the chapter entitled "Augustan Poetry and the Life of Luxury," in J. Griffin, *Latin Poets and Roman Life* (London 1985) 1–31.

21. Cf. R.O.A.M. Lyne, *The Latin Love Poets* (Oxford 1980) 8ff.

22. Thus J.P. Hallett, "The Role of Women in Roman Elegy," in *Women in the Ancient World: The Arethusa Papers*, J. Peradotto and J.P. Sullivan, eds. (Albany 1984) 241–262, cf. p.246: "the 'new, monied' aristocracy, the equestrian rank, opposed Augustus' marriage and moral legislation. We have, in addition, a far more eloquent and extensive protest against the sanctimonious moral assumptions and abusive social conventions of the late Republic and early Empire. . . . I refer to Latin love elegy, a form of self-revelation and indirect social criticism created and developed by members of the dissident equestrian class." Or cf. R.O.A.M. Lyne, *op. cit.* , "The Life of Love" pp.64–81.

23. Cf. K. Hopkins, "The Age of Roman Girls at Marriage," *Population Studies* 8 (1965) ; S. Treggiari, "Roman Marriage," in *Civilization of the Ancient Mediterranean*, eds. M. Grant and R. Kitzinger (New York 1988) vol.3 pp.1343–1354.

of their parents, who arranged marriages for reasons of political or economic expediency—not for love. Sexual fulfillment was thus sought outside of marriage.

As in Greece, it was socially acceptable for men to turn to slaves and common prostitutes. Catullus refers any number of times to the latter type of liaison,[24] as apparently in his poem number 41:[25]

> Ameana, a fucked out girl,
> has asked me for ten fucking thousand—
> that one with the slimy little nose,
> the girlfriend of the bankrupt Formian.
> You relatives who care for the girl,   5
> call her doctors and her friends,
> the girl's insane, she must not be checking
> the mirror to see how she looks.

Is the speaker saying this *before* he has had Ameana, or after? The poem does not allow us to say for sure. But if we assume it is afterwards, there is the additional, very cutting point that Ameana may already have been "fucked out"—by the speaker!—before the haggling even began. The joke, in other words, is on her. She may be a pro, but she doesn't have much of a head for business.

Other poets also regularly complain about the high price of love, but instead of referring to vulgar cash transactions, they speak of precious gifts they must give the object of their desire. For the speaker in Tibullus 2.4.21ff., for instance, things have gone so far that he feels driven to a life of crime simply so that he can come up with sufficient loot for a girl:

---

24. Cf. also Catullus 110. For discussion of price on the Greek side, one might compare Hipponax fr.34 Degani = 21 West: "she demands eight obols to give him a peck on his prick."

25. The woman referred to in this poem may also be spoken of "as if" she were a prostitute, and the whole thing could be construed as an insult directed at the Formian (v.4), who has been identified as Mamurra, a Roman knight from Formiae. For this Mamurra, cf. our note on v.4 of this poem.

I've got to come up with some gifts—even by killing, by
                              crime,
  so I won't have to lie in tears at her bolted door.
Or, I could steal precious objects hung in holy shrines.
  But it's Venus above all, that I should violate.
She talks me into crime, gives me a money-grabbing   25
  girl: she should feel my sacrilegious hands.
Death to whoever gathers green emeralds,
  and tinges snowy wool with Tyrian purple!
And Coan cloth's another source of greed in girls
  and sleek pearls from the Red Sea.   30
These things made girls bad. . . .

In this poem, Tibullus may be referring to a liaison with a more
sophisticated professional than Catullus' Ameana, in the mould of a
Greek *hetaira*. And doubtless, if this were an Archaic or Classical Greek
poem we would be sure that he could only be referring to a professional:
a prostitute, *hetaira,* or female performer. The Latin equivalent of *hetaira*
is *meretrix*, usually rendered in English as "courtesan."[26] As in Greece,
a Roman man could turn to one of these as a sexual outlet somewhat
more glamorous than a slave or common prostitute. And there are
plenty of examples in Roman literature of men who lavish gifts on such
women—one thinks particularly of the many presents that lovers bring
courtesans in Roman comedy.[27]

    Yet there is a crucial difference between Romans and Greeks that
creates doubt as to the woman's status in Tibullus' poem—particularly
in the absence of explicit mention of payment for her affection—and it
is to this difference that we must now turn. It is this: Upper-class
Roman women enjoyed a far greater public freedom than did their
counterparts in Archaic and Classical Greece. A passage from the 1st

---

26. *Meretrix* could, however, also be used of common prostitutes.
    27. e.g. the robe, about which much of the action of Plautus' *Menaechmi* revolves,
stolen by Menaechmus from his wife as a gift for the courtesan Erotium. Cf. also
Asinaria Act 1 scene 2, vv. 127ff.

cent. B.C. author, Cornelius Nepos, throws the distinction into sharp relief:

> Many customs which seem proper to us, are considered shameful by the Greeks. For what Roman would hesitate to bring his wife to a party? Whose wife wouldn't occupy the main room at home or mingle with a crowd outdoors? The situation is very different in Greece. For a wife is not taken to a party unless it is a party of relatives, and she is confined to the inner part of the house known as the women's quarters, where no male can go unless he is a close relation. (*De viris illustribus* pref.6–7)

Upper-class Roman wives (*matronae*) were visible in public to an extent that Greek women simply were not, and their freedom of association was incomparably greater. The opportunity for amorous encounters was consequently much increased, and with it, potentially, a woman's sexual choices. The possibilities become clear in a poem such as Propertius 2.22a (vv.3–10), where the speaker says that "every public place" is a promising pick-up spot:

> Every public place I go, it never fails,   3
>   and the theater, O god, was born to be my
>   downfall:
> Whether some dancer stretches his arms in a supple
>   gesture,   5
>   or plays varying melodies with his mouth,
> all the while my eyes are seeking to wound themselves,
>   in case a dazzler's sitting down with her breast
>   exposed,
> or her floating hair wanders across her perfect brow,
>   slipped out from the pearl clasp atop her head.

Ovid, too, in his *Ars Amatoria* (1.67ff.) provides a long list of prime places for pursuing women, including various colonnades and shrines, lawcourts, the theater, and circuses.

We know from a variety of ancient sources that Roman wives took lovers.[28] The very establishment by Augustus of harsh laws against adultery bespeaks how commonplace it had become. Nor did these laws eliminate adultery. For while statesmen of this period regularly paid lip-service to that strict morality which, they alleged, reflected the way of their ancestors (the *mos maiorum*) before it had become infected with foreign license, there is in fact plenty of evidence that these politicians did not practice what they preached, that hypocrisy, in other words, was common. In Roman poetry it is not unusual, then, to find what is almost completely absent on the Greek side,[29] namely the blunt portrayal of erotic situations that are adulterous. In Catullus 83, for example, the poem's bite depends on Lesbia being married:

> Lesbia badmouths me a lot—with her man [i.e. husband]
> right there,
>   and this, to that fool, is utterly delightful.
> Ass, don't you get it? If she'd forgotten me, and said
> nothing,
>   she'd be cured. Now since she rails and snarls,
> she not only remembers, but—a far more poignant
> matter—   5
> she's furious. That is, she's burning, so she talks.

In a poem by Ovid (2.19), the speaker even complains that his adulterous affair lacks spice because it is too easy. The woman's husband does nothing to prevent it, even when the affair is thrust in his face. The adulterer comically exhorts the apathetic husband to guard his wife more energetically—otherwise, he says, he will lose interest:

> Steal sand from the shore when no one's there: 45
>   that's what it is to love the wife of a fool.

---

28. Cf. A. Richlin, "Approaches to the sources on adultery at Rome" in *Reflections of Women in Antiquity*, H. Foley, ed. (New York 1981) 379–404.

29. One Greek example might be the anonymous "Locrian Song," *PMG* 853, included in our section "Miscellaneous Lyric and Inscriptions.".

I'm telling you now: if you don't begin to guard your
                                                    girl
    she'll begin not being mine.
I've long put up with a lot, often I hoped that maybe,
    if you'd guard her, I could fool you good.   50
You're slow, you take things no man [i.e. husband]
                                        should take.
    I've just about had it with love that's handed over.
Alas, shall I never be kept from going to her?
    Will the night be mine forever—unavenged?
Shall I have nothing to fear? Dream without sighs?   55
    Won't you give me one reason to wish you dead?
What do I want with an easy—a pimp of a—husband!
    Your quirk is wrecking our joy.

At this point it may be appropriate to recall the tradition alleging
that Roman poets habitually referred to their beloveds with a pseudonym. Given the expanded possibility of adulterous relationships, it is
understandable that a poet would want to protect a *matrona* (especially
"his" *matrona*) from the scandal and possible legal consequences that
could follow upon the disclosure of her identity. Our source for this
practice is the 2nd cent. A.D. orator and author, Apuleius. But though
our evidence comes more than 150 years after the fact, it is nonetheless
plausible. Apuleius (*Apology* 10) reports that Catullus used the name
"Lesbia" for a woman called Clodia, Propertius used "Cynthia" for
Hostia, and Tibullus "Delia" for Plania. We might add to these Ovid's
"Corinna." There has been much speculation about the identity of these
women.[30] But that is not the critical point. What is interesting from

---

30. It is generally thought that "Lesbia" was Clodia Metelli, the woman Cicero
attacks in his speech on behalf of Caelius. This identification gets some support in what
seems to be an allusion to her brother in Catullus 79: This poem refers to one "Lesbius"
(the masculine form of "Lesbia") who is *pulcher* ("handsome"). The name of Clodia's
brother was her name's masculine equivalent, Clodius; their family name, Pulcher.
Propertius' "Cynthia" was Hostia, possibly a descendant of the distinguished 2nd cent.
B.C. epic poet Hostius (cf. Prop. 3.20.8). About Tibullus' "Delia," scil. Plania, nothing
further is known.

our perspective is that it was sufficiently common for *matronae* to have extramarital affairs that the use of a pseudonym is a credible possibility, if not in each case a certainty.

All these names, we should note, are Greek. What is more, they all have poetic associations: "Lesbia" is probably a nod to the sensual verse of Sappho of Lesbos (for whom Catullus' interest is well attested, cf. poem 51), and to the proverbial beauty and refinement of its women. "Cynthia" recalls Mt. Cynthus on Delos, the birthplace of the song-god Apollo. The same is true of Tibullus' "Delia." "Corinna" was the name of a famous Greek poetess. These, then, are not names that merely suggest permissive "Greek" sexuality; nor do they refer to "foreigners" and thus to socially acceptable sex objects (that, we recall, was the Archaic and Classical Greek attitude towards foreign women, e.g. Anacreon's "Thracian filly" or his "girl with the flashy slippers," who comes "from Lesbos," see above). On the contrary, these names must be taken in a positive sense, as a poet's "graceful compliment."[31]

Horace, in this respect, is somewhat exceptional—at least in his *Odes*. His use of Greek women's names does indeed point to the association of Greeks with the life of luxury in Rome, especially with the *symposium*. Typically, he does not portray the intense, long-lasting relationships we find in Catullus, etc. His are rather the transient pleasures afforded by *hetairai* or sympotic entertainers. And the names of his numerous loves are characteristic names of *hetairai*: e.g. Pyrrha, Chloe, Lalage. As noted above, Rome had become permeated with Greek culture in the course of the first two centuries B.C. By the time of the poets included in this anthology, it was an integral part of life among the well-to-do.

This brings us to the subject of homosexuality. In Rome, homoerotic desire was considered just as normal (and as compatible with heterosexual love) as it was in Greece—though it never developed that status as an essential cultural institution, in which the young were educated and integrated into the political and social fabric, that it had enjoyed in the Hellenic world. Indeed, that feature that had ensured homosexuality's central importance in Greece was frowned on in Rome, namely the cultivation of relationships between adult males and boys who, apart

---

31. Thus T.P. Wiseman on Catullus' Lesbia, *op. cit.* (n.19 above) 136.

from their age, were social equals. For while it was entirely acceptable for a free-born man to seek gratification with foreign youths, with slaves, or freedmen (as long, that is, as he played the "active" role and not the pathic), a certain stigma—and even legal interdiction—attached to his doing so with a free-born boy.[32] This is not to say that such relationships didn't happen. They were evidently quite common. And there is no indication that when, for example, Catullus describes his love for the noble youth Iuventius (poems 48 and 99),[33] he is seriously afraid of legal repercussions. Still, homosexuality between social equals never achieved the general acceptance it had in Greece.

Finally, a word about female homosexuality. There was in Rome no equivalent to the Greek *thiasos* where girls were encouraged to explore their sexual feelings for each other prior to getting married. Perhaps if we had any female testimony about the matter our view would be different. But our only references come from men, and these are very few. Those that do exist suggest that men disapproved, that "such behavior was considered 'masculine' and 'unnatural'."[34]

Reading an Ancient Erotic Poem:

We turn now from a consideration of the general historical and social context of ancient sexual activity to the texts themselves, the utterances of the ancient erotic poets.

Every human utterance—at least every one that is intelligible—has a specific context, a time and a place, a speaker and a receiver, and presupposes a common language. It refers to a situation, is part of a person's life, and can only be understood by knowing something about the circumstances, the culture, the relationship existing between speaker and addressee, etc.

---

32. Cf. Richlin's appendix on "The Circumstances of Male Homosexuality in Roman Society of the Late Republic and Early Empire" in *The Garden of Priapus: Sexuality and Aggression in Roman Humor* (New Haven 1983) 220–226.

33. On the high standing of Iuventius' family cf. Cicero, *Pro Plancio* 19.

34. Thus J.P. Hallett, "Roman Attitudes toward Sex," in *Civilization of the Ancient Mediterranean*, eds. M. Grant and R. Kitzinger (New York 1988) vol.3 p.1266.

Each utterance in ancient erotic poetry represents one or more kinds of speech-action (or alludes to them).[35] We believe that action—praxis—is the soul of this poetry,[36] and consequently we shall direct our attention to this aspect of the problem. And to this end, we would like to make the following preliminary observations and suggestions:

1. These texts represent the actions and utterances of lovers.

2. The utterance may be part of an action, represent an action, narrate or refer to an action, etc., but every utterance is only comprehensible in the context of an (unfolding) action.

3. The linguistic and social competence of the audience enables it to recognize kinds of action and utterance—and thus also to gauge (roughly) changes, variations, innovations, inversions, and so on. Advised of cultural information they may lack, our readers should—by virtue of their own knowledge of erotic activities and utterances—be able to play this game like their ancient counterparts.

4. A primary responsibility in studying classical erotic poetry is to describe those fundamental speech-actions which are the nuclei, or kernels, of erotic activity in its verbal expression.

5. The relation of the poem to a kind of speech-action may be direct (direct imitation of speech: "I love you") or indirect (narration: "she loves her"; metaphoric representation: "there's fire beneath the ash"; declaration presupposing an action: "So you're back . . .") or may make use of a combination of direct and indirect means.

---

35. By speech-action we do not mean Austin's "speech acts" but something closer to Wittgenstein's *Sprachspiele*. Cf. J.L. Austin, *How to Do Things With Words* (Oxford 1962) and L. Wittgenstein, *Philosophische Untersuchungen* (Oxford 1953).

36. In this belief, we are applying what Aristotle said about praxis with regard to tragedy, *Poetics* 1450a.

6. One kind of speech-action may be articulated by means of another (in Callimachus 45, thanking Hermes to celebrate the beloved's return). In this case we may say that one kernel serves as a vehicle for another.

7. One utterance may be framed by another—at one or both ends. In that case we may refer to a framed utterance and a framing utterance. The relationship between them may be complex.

8. A poem may contain the utterances of several speakers, and each utterance may contain one or more speech-actions. In the most complicated cases (e.g. Virgil's *Eclogue* 10), not only is the relationship between frame and framed complex, the assessment of a fundamental intention or kind of speech-action may also be difficult for both the framed and the framing speech.

To illustrate these preliminary observations, let us look for kinds of utterance among the elegies in the "Second Book" of Theognis (with occasional reference to the "First"). We have chosen this corpus because it is the first sizeable group of archaic Greek love poems that has come down to us, and because the poems, most of them two, four or six verses long, lend themselves well to analysis.

In trying to describe the kinds of utterance in the "Second Book" of Theognis, we may begin with two kinds of utterance that embody a basic opposition: "wooing" and "renunciation." Of the 45 erotic elegies in the "Second Book", 7 belong to the first category, and 6 to the latter. The remaining poems may be grouped in some relation to them (e.g. poems of wooing containing praise but no request; poems dealing with the infidelity of the beloved where we find reproach but no renunciation). But before looking at less easily delimitable categories, let us examine the two clearest.

In the first group, which we have labeled 'wooing,' the speaker explicitly asks the beloved at least for attention and at most for sexual gratification. We could also call them, 'boy, be nice' speeches. Each contains a vocative ('boy' or a variation) and an imperative ('listen,' 'stay,' 'give,' etc.).[37] The seven poems are: 1235–1238, 1295–1298, 1299–1304, 1305–1310, 1319–1322, 1327–1334, 1365–1366.

At the other end of the affair, we find speeches of renunciation or merely (final or provisional) rejection. They refer to 'leaving love,' or 'not being in love any more' and take basic forms such as "It's over" or "I don't love you." This kernel—corresponding to the request for amorous favors in poems of wooing—is variously expressed: I no longer love you (1337–1338); I'm free (1339–1340); looking at you no one (including me) would love a boy (1317–1318); I slipped out of the storm (1271–1274); I gained by losing you (1377–1380); you've lost my love (1361–1362). The way the speaker says the affair is over thus varies quite a bit. We note that he states it directly and non-metaphorically only once (1337–1338). In three cases the expression is metaphorical (1271–1274, 1361–1362, 1339–1340). In another case the renunciation is implicit (1317–1318). Still, these six texts all belong to a recognizable kind of utterance whose location in the trajectory of the love affair is generally clear: it comes at the 'end' (ends may be false, but that's another matter).[38]

In between wooing and rejecting there are a number of texts that belong generally to the wooing phase but which are not direct requests, such as a broad hint to Kyrnos (1353–1356), an indirect appeal by means of a mythic exemplum (1283–1294), a declaration of love in which the beloved is referred to in the third person (1341–1344, 1345–1350), affirmations of fidelity and constancy (1363–1364, 1279–1282), and advice to a boy not to go out 'reveling,' which probably implies 'stay and talk to me instead' (1351–1352).

Near the other end of the spectrum, but lacking explicit rejection or renunciation, we find poems warning the beloved not to be led astray (i.e. seduced–1238a-b, 1278a-b) or accusing the boy of capriciousness, infidelity or promiscuity (1257–1258, 1259–1262, 1311–1316,

---

37. Of the 45 texts in the "Second Book" of Theognis, 24 have vocatives, 14 have imperatives, and only 11 have both; yet 7 of those 11 figure in our group.

38. Cf. Ovid, *Amores* 3.11ab for a quick turnaround from renunciation to renewed courtship.

1373–1374), a complaint of ingratitude that seems to refer to the affair as over (1263–1266), a declaration of incompatiblity (1245–1246), and a threat of revenge (1247–1248). Beyond rupture, an ironic greeting to an unfaithful boy apparently serves as a response to an offer to renew the affair (1249–1252).[39]

We mentioned above (in the fifth of our general observations) that the relation between the utterance in a poem and the kind of speech-action represented may be direct or indirect (or a combination). Indirectness varies as to type and degree. Whereas the hint (to Kyrnos) 'if you don't get what you want, it's very painful . . .' is quite broad, the utterance in 1283–1294, though it contains the vocative and imperative combination that we have seen to be characteristic of explicit wooing discourses, is a bit trickier:

> Boy, don't wrong me—I still want to
>   please you—listen graciously to this:
> you won't outstrip me, cheat me with your tricks.
>   Right now you've won and have the upper hand,
> but I'll wound you while you flee, as they say
>   the virgin daughter of Iasios,
> though ripe, rejected wedlock with a man
>   and fled; girding herself, she acted pointlessly,
> abandoning her father's house, blond Atalanta.
>   She went off to the soaring mountain peaks,
> fleeing the lure of wedlock, golden Aphrodite's
>   gift. But she learned the point she'd so rejected.

---

39. In addition, there are three poems in which no beloved and no specific situations figure, but in which Eros or Aphrodite (Kypris) is addressed (1231–1234, 1323–1326, 1386–1389). In one of these (1323–1326) Kypris is asked to help the speaker renounce and act sensibly. In the other two there is no request. In yet two other poems Eros (1275–1278) or Kypris (1381–1385) is described. Also: four poems asserting that an individual in given circumstances is fortunate (1253–1254, 1255–1256, 1335–1336, 1375–1376) and three general descriptions of amorous delights (1367–1368) and problems (1267–1270, 1357–1360) or both (1369–1372).

Here we come upon our first extended mythic exemplum.[40] The question, as always, is: what is the logic of the exemplum and how does it function in context? The story of Atalanta in this version is more or less this: she was ripe for marriage, but fled with her virginity intact, hid out in the hills, but finally gave in and learned what the gifts of Aphrodite are. If the boy is like Atalanta, then, he is fleeing (resisting) but will eventually give in, 'wounded' by the speaker.[41] The myth, then, makes explicit the situation of the *erastes* and *eromenos*, which is otherwise not directly stated.

Another kind of indirectness appears in 1341–1344. Up till now we have looked at requests or wooing speeches spoken directly to the beloved,[42] but here we find the speaker talking *about* the boy: "I love a smooth skinned boy. . . ." The boy has revealed to friends that he and the speaker are involved, and the speaker, though insisting that he's annoyed by this, says he'll put up with it, since the boy is "not unworthy." Such a confession of love to a third party (apparently spoken to a peer or peers in a sympotic setting, though the audience is not specified) is itself a distinct kind of utterance. And the very next poem in the corpus, 1345–1350, is another example of this kind of utterance. Like 1283–1294 (see above), it contains a mythic exemplum, but here the exemplum is preceded by a brief gnome and followed by a reference to a personal situation: The speaker says, more or less: "Boy-love is fun. Zeus loved Ganymede. So don't be surprised, Simonides, if I, too, love a boy."

The line between an indirect speech-action and a different, but related, kind of speech-action may be difficult to draw. We have tentatively grouped 1363–1364 and 1279–1282 with the wooing poems, but they are rather murkier than any of the others in this category. Let us look first at 1363–1364:

---

40. Something we shall see often in Propertius and Ovid, but which we find from the beginning, e.g. in Sappho fr. 16.5–11.

41. Vetta, *ad loc.*, thinks that this discourse is spoken after an infidelity. If this is correct, we would have a wooing discourse taking place during the 'problem' phase of the affair: "you've cheated on me, but I'm still going to make you mine, boy."

42. After all, how can "I" woo "you" by talking to a third party? But see Tib. 1.8.

> I'll never hurt you, even when I'm gone; and no one
>   will talk me out of loving you.

The speaker seems to pledge good will ("I won't hurt you") and fidelity ("no one will dissuade me from your love"), but we may wonder why and under what circumstances, in what dramatic context, a lover would tell a beloved, "I won't hurt you even when I'm away." Does that mean that he's going away? Or merely that his love is constant even when he's not in the beloved's presence? And why say "No one will persuade me not to love you" instead of (e.g.) "I'll always love you"? Are they semantically equivalent? Can we offer an explanation of this utterance by supposing an imminent journey and thus an attempt to allay the beloved's possible jealousy? Or might the explanation be another, namely that the addressee has hurt his lover by being unfaithful, and the speaker, instead of threatening revenge (cf. 1247–1248), implies, "*I*, at least, won't hurt *you*, no one will seduce *me*"?[43] These are the sorts of questions that need to be asked in dealing with any ancient erotic poem. To understand the utterance, and so enjoy the poem, we must always try to imagine the circumstances in which it might be uttered, the intent of the speaker in relation to an unfolding action.

As an exercise, let's look at the context of similar statements in (much) longer poems of Propertius. At 2.9.43–46 we hear a lover say:

> There's nothing in my life more welcome than you,
>   and there won't be now either, no matter how nasty you
>   are.
> No mistress will ever leave tracks on my bed.
>   I'll be alone, since I'm not allowed to be yours.

---

43. This argument would be much easier to make, were there an expressed first person singular pronoun functioning as subject of the first clause in the Greek text, but there is not (the "I" is contained in the form of the verb). Nevertheless, in each of the two verses of the poem we do find (in Greek) both "me" and "you" in the objective case, in a chiastic order (. . you . . . me . . / . . me . . you.), so that the opposition suggested may be articulated by the artful arrangement of first and second person (object case) pronouns, even without the emphatic subject pronoun that we might have expected.

The speaker has been displaced by a rival, but asserts his own fidelity. Similarly, in Propertius 3.20, where he wants to get back with a girl who has just been dumped by his rival, he says: "Your home would be happy, if only you had a faithful friend./ I'll be faithful, girl, come running to my bed!" There the pledge of fidelity explicitly contrasted to the faithlessness of both the rival and the girl, is immediately followed by a request.[44] Another Propertian example is even more suggestive:

> Won't you come back?! So help me, no other flimsy girl
>   has placed her pretty feet on my doorstep.
> (Though this pain in here owes you lots of bitterness,
>   still, my anger will never be so savage
> that I'd cause you to rage forever at me rightly, and your eyes
>   to grow unpretty from spilling tears.) (1.18.11–16)

The logic in this passage ("Come back. I, at least, have been faithful. Though you richly deserve it, I will never make you sad by cheating on you") bears certain similarities to the the utterance in Theognis 1363–1364. And one might be tempted to see in the Theognis a compressed and elusive example of the same kind of utterance. Such an association may be fraught with dangers, however, since it could also be argued that what we find spelled out in the Propertian passages is precisely what is not there in Theognis. Nevertheless, it is only by comparing and contrasting texts that we can begin to get a feel for the kinds of utterances in ancient erotic poetry and the kinds of contexts which they may imply or presuppose.

Theognis 1279–1282 reads like a slightly expanded version of the kernel we've been looking at. We may paraphrase: "I won't mistreat you, even [if you deserve it]; I won't condemn petty errors, they're forgivable." In this case, though, we have a clear reference to the boy's "errors" or infidelities, a vocative (O pretty boy) which apparently

---

44. The request, it may be noted in passing, takes the form "run, girl"—imperative and vocative.

signals wooing, and an act of forgiveness, expressed as "I don't sit in judgment." A delicious Latin version of this kind of utterance is to be found in the last love poem of Ovid's *Amores* (3.14), where we need only look at the first verse (Since you're beautiful I don't ask you not to cheat) and the last (You'll be forgiven since the judge is yours) to see the kernel. She's pretty, so he won't judge harshly. Theognis 1279–1282, then, might be a speech of "forgiveness," presupposing a prior request for forgiveness on the part of the boy, or at least a situation in which the speaker must forgive if he is to continue with the relationship.

In 1247–1248 the judge is harsher, and we herewith move toward that phase in the erotic scenario in which the relationship is falling apart, i.e. towards renunciation. "Think about my hatred and the crime. I'll get you back." The situation is undefined beyond "anger," "crime," "wrong" and the threat of revenge, but we surely can say that this utterance presupposes renunciation. (If I say to a lover who has betrayed me, "I'll get you back" I may not mean "I don't love you any more," but in fact some rupture is probably presupposed.[45])

In renunciation as in wooing we encounter various kinds of indirectness. Theognis 1323–1326, for example, expresses the desire to renounce by means of a hymn or prayer to Aphrodite (and is to be distinguished from the other elegies addressed to Eros 1231–1234 and Aphrodite 1386–1389 which begin and end the Second Book of Theognis, since neither of those includes a hymnal request). Here we may say a word about prayers invoking the aid of a deity. Such speeches, inasmuch as they express a wish for a given end to be realized, are themselves carriers: they serve as vehicles for another kind of utterance

---

45. Cf. Prop. 2.5, a renunciation which includes a threat of revenge ("You'll pay, liar . . ." v.3). Later in the same poem (21ff.) after having said that he will fight back, he adds that he will not tear the clothes from her perjured body, etc., but will merely write some erotic invective (*scribam* 27). Similar is the threat at Catullus 37.10, carried out in the poem itself. A distinctly less literary kind of revenge is called for by Ariadne in Catullus 64.190–201 (*iustam a divis exposcam prodita multam*). That speech (64.132–201), one of the most influential erotic discourses in Latin, is not included in this anthology since we have avoided excerpts.

expressed in the wish. For instance, Anacreon *PMG* 357 "Dionysus, get Kleoboulos to receive my love" would count as a wooing poem. One might be tempted to group these poems according to the carrier, assuming that the primary situation is that existing between the speaker and the deity invoked. In erotic poetry, however, the request to the deity always reveals an intention within the sphere of amorous activity, so we would always treat the prayer as a carrier and the kind of utterance revealed in the request as the governing speech-action. The prayer typically conforms to the following simple pattern: 1) A deity is named; 2) attributes and/or powers of the deity are described, by means of adjectives and/or relative clauses; 3) the speaker makes a request. In addition, one often finds a reference to a prior relationship between the deity and the speaker—expressed through an "if-clause" (e.g. "if ever you helped me before"). In Theognis 1323–1326 we find what might be described as a "streamlined" form: name + imperatives (five of them): "Cyprian, end . . . scatter . . . turn . . . end . . . give." In some respects this poem is similar to Sappho 1.[46] But we should note two important differences. First, in Theognis the speaker asks Aphrodite to release him from amorous suffering and allow him to act wisely, since he is no longer young; whereas Sappho asks the goddess to help her win (back?) her beloved. Second, in Theognis the speech-action is transparent, whereas in Sappho it is so subtly elaborated that it could easily be missed. There, the optional "if ever you've helped me before" section describes how Aphrodite helped her in the past and quotes what she said to Sappho when she arrived, and it is from that speech of Aphrodite (whose kernel is: "Tell me about your love life"[47]) that we learn what Sappho presumably wants this time: Aphrodite should "lead [someone] back to her love."[48] At any rate, in both cases the prayer indirectly expresses the speakers' intent

---

46. Cf. Vetta, *ad loc.*

47. This kind of utterance, in which a speaker asks someone to tell about their current flame, is also represented, rather amusingly, in Catullus 6 and 55. Cf. Callimachus Epigram 30 Pf.; Tibullus 1.8.1–26.

48. But there is a textual problem in this line, cf. Page, *Sappho and Alcaeus, ad loc.*

within a given amorous situation, and in Theognis what the speaker wants is to renounce love.

So much for indirect renunciations. Further into the generic murk we encounter Theognis 1263–1266.

> Boy you paid back a bad exchange for kindness,
> no thanks from you for favors.
> You've never given me pleasure. And though I've often
> been kind to you, I never won your respect.

What is going on here? We might compare Catullus 76.1–16, with its complaint of a "thankless love" (v.6) and unreciprocated favors:

> Because whatever men can say or do in kindness
> towards anyone, you've said and done.
> And all of it has been wasted, entrusted to a thankless mind.
>
> (7–9)

But there a second section (vv. 17–26) contains a prayer to the gods with the form: "O gods, if you can feel pity (19) . . . look at me (19) . . . rip out this plague from me (20) . . . give me this for what I've done right (26)." This prayer to be able to renounce the beloved reveals the kind of utterance in Catullus 76, where the first section (1–16) is so like Theognis 1263–1266. But in the Theognis we have no implicit renunciation, no desire to renounce, just the complaint.[49] Why then can't we read 1263–1266 as mere reproach, and moreover in the service of a request for "*kharis*" ("thanks"= amorous favors)? Or does "You never gave me pleasure" sound perhaps as though the speaker considers the relationship over?

To pursue this question, let's turn for a moment to an elegy of two verses from the "First Book" of Theognis (957–958):

---

49. Catullus 73, not included in this book, is more like Theognis 1263–1266 in that there is a complaint on the futility of treating anyone well, since there is no gratitude. It is arguably non-erotic, but there is no evidence either way.

> If, after being so well treated by me, you're ungrateful,[50]
>   I hope you come back longing to my door.[51]

The rebuke is expressed more succinctly here than at 1263–1266 and serves as a kind of springboard for a threat. The logic is, "If you're going to be ungrateful, just wait till you come back to me in a moment of need: I'll throw you out and get you back that way." To "come back" may itself be shorthand for "come back to an ex-lover to renew the affair."[52] The addressee is imagined as "longing" (*khreizon*) to do just that. Thus 957–958 belong to a moment of possible rupture, and threaten revenge if certain conditions are not met. By so threatening, they anticipate yet another moment—when the rejected ex-beloved returns and asks to be reinstated.

This latter moment can be made out, we believe, in 1249–1252, as well as in two elegies from "Book One" of Theognis, 371–372 and 599–602. Here we shall linger a while.

> Boy, you're like a horse. Just now sated with seed,
>   you've come back to my stable,
> yearning for a good rider, fine meadow,
>   an icy spring, shady groves. (1249–1252)

In these verses we can see that the boy is back, and he is greeted in metaphoric but unmistakable terms:[53] "Boy, you've come back,

---

50. Literally, "If, having received [undergone] a great good from me, you do not know *kharis* [=gratitude, reciprocal bestowal of (sexual?) favors] . . ."

51. It could be argued that this poem is not erotic (indeed, the same could be said for several of the elegies from "Book 2"), but even if it merely referred to a friendship, the kind of utterance would remain essentially the same. In other words, the accusation of ingratitude and the threat of revenge ("just wait 'till you come back in need") could be expressed in the same way, whether the relation were erotic or not.

52. Cf. Callimachus' *palin oikhetai* in Epig. 41.3 (Pf.).

53. The metaphoric system used in 1249–1252 is also employed at 1267–1270, though without any explicit reference to the speaker's (or anyone else's) personal situation:
> Boy and horse: a similar brain: the horse
> doesn't cry when its rider lies in the dust.

yearning. . . ." This, presumably is the moment when the speaker can take revenge, if he so chooses; but there is no explicit rejection. If we strip this utterance of its metaphors, it says merely, "you've come back, yearning."[54] Yet this may be an unfair procedure since the whole metaphoric system seems, by its irony, to suggest that the answer to the returning beloved's request is "no." The absence of a clear rejection in 1249–1252 may be read as characterizing a certain reluctance with respect to a coming "yes" [=I'll take you back]—or as gloating over an imminent "no"[=I won't take you back].

At 599–602 there is no reluctance in rebuffing the returning lover.

> No you didn't fool me—wandering down the road
>> where you used to ride, defrauding our love.
> Get out! The gods hate you, men can't trust you.
>> That snake in your lap turned out to be shifty and cold.

Comparing this elegy with 1249–1252, we may observe that the one says, "Slut, get out!" (but not, "You're back"), and the other, "Slut, you're back," (but not, "Get out!").

Let's look now at one final poem of Theognis, a puzzling couplet (371–372) which neatly illustrates the great variety of considerations a reader must sometimes bring to bear on a text in attempting to elucidate it. The poem represents the utterance of a lover rejecting a boy (beloved) who is trying to stir things up. The question is, is the boy trying to stir things up for the first time, i.e. to *begin* an affair, or is he not rather trying to *renew* it, i.e. to stir things up *again*?

> No, it takes on the next man, once it's sated with seed.
>> Same with a boy: whoever's there he loves.

In this poem, we learn that being "sated with seed" is associated with the acquisition of a new rider (1269) and the dumping off of the former rider in the dust (1268). A boy loves the one that's there (1270).

54. This is what the Speaker says in Catullus 107.4–6 (you've come back to me . . . you've returned to me). Neither does Catullus unleash there the abuse of which he is fully capable (cf. Cat. 11, 37, 58).

Don't drive me to the wagon, pricking hard—I won't go,
　　Kyrnos, though you drag me all too deeply into your
　　　　　　　　　　　　　　　　　　　　　　　　love.

The wagon, or cart, is one of a number of common metaphors for love or an amorous relationship. Variants include the yoke and the plow. To be led or driven or pushed to the yoke (or wagon) is to be seduced, involved in a relationship (cf. Tibullus 1.4.16: "Little by little, he'll put his neck in the yoke"—that is, will yield). To leave the yoke, then, would be to get out of an affair, renounce (cf. Propertius 2.5.14: "Take your neck out of that cruel yoke"). In Horace *Odes* 3.9 the speaker offers a reconciliation by saying:

What if the old love returns,
and though we broke up, drives us back to the yoke of bronze,
if blond Chloe gets kicked out
and the door swings open for Lydia left behind? (17–20)

There, much is clear; here, in Theognis 371–372, things are much more opaque. In the Horace we know, for example, that Lydia, the old girlfriend, has been rejected (20), in other words, that she and the speaker have broken up (*diductos* 18). We also know that to be led (by Venus) "to the yoke of bronze" means to kick out Chloe (19) and open the door to Lydia (20). So that when we translate *cogit* by "drive (lead, push, force) back" this "back" is amply justified by the lexical evidence of the text. Not so in Theognis 371–372, where thirteen words constitute our only evidence and there is no explicit statement about the situation, such as we find in the ode of Horace. Can we, then, understand the Theognis as meaning "Don't drive me [*back*] to the wagon"?

In Anacreon *PMG* 417 (cf. above), the filly is unbroken and the rider wants to put on the bridle and work the young horse in. In Horace *Odes* 2.5 the girl has not yet (*nondum* 1) borne the yoke, isn't even ready. These poems are both explicit: the bridle (Anacreon) or yoke (Horace) has never been applied. In Ibycus *PMG* 287, by contrast, we are equally sure that it *isn't* the first time. "Once more Eros . . ." We are told that the horse has borne the yoke, he's even a former prize winner. And knowing the races, and feeling old, he is unwilling (*aekon*—the third word in Theognis 371) to go back.[55] And so he trembles (v.5). But in Ibycus there is no evidence that the speaker is being drawn back into a former relationship, just back into love. Sappho fr. 15 (L-P), however, arguably contains a reference to the (deprecated) return of her brother to Doricha, the woman he has left. We paraphrase: "Kypris, please [if he tries to go back to her] be especially bitter [=make sure it doesn't work out at all]. I don't want her to be able to [lure him back in and then] boast that he came a second time to the woman he desired." Sappho imagines a scene and a speech in which (and this is what she doesn't want) Doricha can rub her hands and say, "Hah! I told you! He's come back!"[56]

We could try to cut through the problem by saying that Theognis, whose habitual addressee is Kyrnos, would not likely be referring to a first time.[57] But "would not likely" is different from "could not possibly"—and one cannot absolutely rule out the possibility that Theognis *is* referring to a first time. Or we could appeal to logical presupposition, that is: if, in "don't push me to the cart" cart means affair, the affair must already exist. But is the cart an affair when there's no animal beneath the yoke? Here we call on Callimachus (44 Pf.) for a little light.

> There is, oh yes by Pan, though hidden, there is,
>   oh yes by Dionysus, some fire beneath the ash.
> I'm afraid. Don't put your arms around me. Often, unseen,
>   a tranquil river undermines a wall.

---

55. Cf. also AP 12.79 (anon.) There *akon* (v.3) appears in a context where the situation is fully explicit: "Twice I fell, *against my will*, in the same flame."

56. Exactly what the speaker does say in Callimachus 45.3–4 Pf. There, however, even though it's clear that the beloved has returned, it is not certain that a relationship had already begun; that is, the runaway may merely have been unwilling to begin an affair.

57. Yet some scholars have misread Catullus 109, where the speaker seems to respond naively to an offer, as belonging to an early phase of the affair—they have missed the irony, and some have even suggested emending the text to cut the offending words. W. Kroll, *Catull* (6th ed., Stuttgart 1980) 280: Das Gedicht gehört ziemlich an den Anfang seiner Beziehungen zu ihr."

> So now again I'm afraid, Menexenus, that this......
>   will slip into me and hurl me into love.

In the first couplet of this epigram, the speaker asserts, in metaphoric terms, that a relationship may be about to flare up again (cf. AP 12.79). This assertion is backed up with a double oath—by Pan and by Dionysus. Then the utterance focuses on the dramatic moment. The logical relation of "I'm afraid" to "don't embrace me" is parallel to that between "I'm unwilling" and "don't push me" in Theognis 371–372.[58] In both cases the logic is: "I'm not up for it, so don't insist," thus presupposing a request and constituting a refusal. The pressure being exerted on the speaker and his corresponding sense of being drawn in is expressed in Theognis partly in 371 ("by pricking forcibly") and partly in 372, "drawing me all too strongly . . . into your love." Does the adverb *lien*, ('exceedingly,' 'greatly,' 'too greatly,' 'too much') suggest that the speaker resents the pressure? Or is he beginning to cave in? In Callimachus the addressee's insistence is reflected in the speaker's fear (vv. 3–5) and suggested by the logic of the gnome: "Often, unseen, a quiet river eats away at a wall."[59] Finally, in both texts the vocative comes in the center of the section expressing the speaker's sense that he is being drawn too much by the addressee (literally "drawn" in Theognis 372; in Callimachus, infiltrated).[60]

In the epigram of Callimachus, we know from the metaphor in the first two verses that we are dealing with the possible renewal of a love affair. And, given its similarity to the Theognidean couplet,

---

58. In Callimachus' poem we have parataxis, in Theognis the participle *aekonta* modifying the object of the verb (me) expresses the additional statement: "I'm not willing" which we have rendered as "I won't go".

59. The same gnome is used by Ovid at *Remedia Amoris* 682–683, specifically referring to the renewal of an affair: "The mind of lovers is besieged by innumerable strategems, like a rock beaten on every side by waves of water."

60. In Callimachus, the speaker literally says he fears that something (lost in the crux in v. 6) may "slip into" him and so "hurl" him (back) into love. This expression, despite the textual problem, seems sexually suggestive. In Theognis, "pushing" in 371 and "pulling" in 372 seem, taken individually, quite innocuous; yet given the "forceful spurring/pricking" in 371, and the erotic context, one wonders if these expressions might not also carry sexual overtones.

Callimachus' epigram certainly makes a similar interpretation of Theognis' poem very plausible. Still, in Theognis our problem is that we have no hard and fast lexical evidence that Kyrnos is trying to *come back*, and it could be argued that he is in fact *coming on* (for the first time). Is there any other evidence which could help us towards resolving this question?

Perhaps the general cultural etiquette regarding homosexual relationships can shed some light on the problem. As we noted in the first part of this introduction, it was not considered proper for the boy (*eromenos*) to initiate a relationship with a man (*erastes*). There is, of course, the example in Plato's *Symposium* where Alcibiades—though the younger, and by all rights the one who should have been wooed—takes it on himself to court Socrates. But this example only proves the rule. For Alcibiades is himself aware of the peculiarity of his action and how it inverts the normal procedure, causing him to woo the much older Socrates as though he (Socrates) were the *paidika* (217b, literally "boy-things," though used to denote the beloved). There is doubtless a deliberate and comic incongruity between Alcibiades' previous characterization of Socrates as a Silenos (a hoary old satyr, 216d) and that here as a "boy-thing."[61]

Given the various arguments which we have enumerated—i.e. the fact that Kyrnos is Theognis' *habitual* addressee, that the *eromenos* was *not* normally the pursuer at the start of a relationship, the suggestive parallels from other poems and the lack of a corresponding kind of utterance representing the rejection of a boy's first come-on—we are inclined to see in Theognis 371–372 the response to an attempted renewal of an affair rather than its beginning, and we have rendered the couplet accordingly in the body of our translations: "Don't drive me back to the wagon. . . ." In any case, by playing out the various possibilities, we hope that we have illustrated some of the questions our readers might ask in order to locate a given utterance within the amorous scenario and so provide a frame for interpretation.

---

61. Even here, however, one could argue that Kyrnos in the couplet in Theognis is going against the standard sexual etiquette, just as Alcibiades does, and that the adverb lien ("all too deeply" v.372) suggests precisely such a breach.

We have tried, by looking at the elegies in Theognis, to sketch out some of the kinds of speech-actions that classical poets played with. Now we shall take seven particularly difficult texts and suggest how they may be read. For whereas many, if not all of the erotic poems of Theognis represent speech-actions rather clearly, and therefore can be easily understood, other ancient poets seem to have taken a certain delight in constructing complex, highly indirect representations of speech-actions. We have purposely chosen some of the most challenging texts, and hope that our readers will first read the poems in question carefully, trying to figure out what's going on, and then use our suggestions in rereading them.

Catullus 11:

The situation is apparently this: two persons known to the speaker have been sent to him bearing a message from Lesbia. They have reassured him of their own friendly devotion to him, and in response to his presumed impulse to flee (go into a renunciatory exile), they have made exaggerated oaths of their reliability and determination to help. But they have come not to accompany him to the distant points that he mentions (India, Egypt, Britain, etc.) but to carry her offer of reconciliation. The speaker responds as follows: "Friends, you say you're ready to go anywhere with me, but you needn't; just take back this unpretty message to her":

let her live and be well with her fuckers,	17
whom she clasps three hundred at a time,	
loving none truly, but over and over busting	
the balls on them all;	20
let her not look, as before, to my love,	
for thanks to her it has fallen like a flower	
at the meadow's edge, after it's been nicked	
by a passing plow.	24

The formal rejection occupies verse 17, whose last word launches an insult about her promiscuity which runs to the end of v. 20. At v. 21 he says explicitly "She cannot look to my love again [*respectet*] as she has been able to before [*ut ante*]; it is gone, fallen like a flower merely nicked by the passing plow." She is a plow, she plows the whole field; his love was a delicate flower at the edge of the meadow, but it's been cut down.

The rejection of an offer of reconciliation is here framed by an elaborate address to the "friends." We are expected to see their elaborate pledges of friendship reflected in the speaker's reference to their readiness to accompany him anywhere in the world (*omnia haec . . . temptare simul parati* 13–14) should he wish to go. And why might he wish to go? Because, as we know from many classical sources, exile was a regular and recommended way of getting over a failed love affair.[62] There is no explicit reference to their having delivered a message from Lesbia (nor is she even mentioned by name), but when the speaker says, "just announce to my girl a few / unpretty words," we begin to suspect that they are acting as go-betweens. Since it is characteristic of the best poets to imply certain fundamental aspects of the situation in a given poem, we can only suggest what the *Sprachspiel* being played here is. But we ask the reader to compare poems like Theocritus 6 where a friend of Polyphemus points out to him that Galatea is obviously interested in renewing their courtship and Polyphemus rejects the implied offer, or Propertius 3.8, where Lygdamus is carrying messages of reconciliation back and forth between Cynthia and the Speaker.

Virgil, Eclogue 10:

This is arguably one of the most difficult and complex poems in this book, along with Theocritus 1 and 7 and Alkman's first Partheneion.

---

62. Ovid *Remedia Amoris* 213–238 provides the recommendation "*i procul, et longas carpere perge vias,*" etc., but the practice is mirrored in many passages, for instance: Prop. 1.1.29 "*ferte per extremas gentis et ferte per undas,/qua non ulla meum femina norit iter,*" 2.30. and 3.21; Plautus *Asin.* 156ff., *Merc.* 644ff.

It should be noted well, by those who do not know, that it is heavily dependent on Theocritus 1. In that poem the song which is its center is a lament for Daphnis, who is dying. He is apparently in love with a girl who is in love with him, but he won't go to her. In his tenth Eclogue, Virgil asks the Muses to give him a song for Gallus (himself a well-known elegist) that Lycoris (Gallus' ex-girlfriend, as we learn in the poem) can read. This is the frame at the beginning (vv. 1–8), which is closed at the end of the poem (vv. 70–77). In the middle, in the framed utterance, Gallus is treated somewhat like the dying Daphnis of Theocritus 1. All come to mourn him, Apollo and Pan address him: Apollo basically tells him he's crazy to keep loving if the girl has gone off with someone else; and Pan assures him there's nothing he can do to mollify "cruel love." Both gods, that is, insist that his situation is hopeless and that he should just forget about it. Then he speaks (31–69). First he addresses the Arcadians (31ff.), saying he wishes he had been one of them. But soon, lost in an amorous phantasy about the lovers he could have had among the Arcadians, he turns suddenly and addresses Lycoris, whom we know is Virgil's secondary and Gallus' primary addressee ("ones that Lycoris herself could read," *quae legat ipsa Lycoris*, v. 2). Just at the moment when Gallus has been imagining himself with one or more lovers among the Arcadians, he blurts out (vv. 42–43): "Here there are *cold springs*, Lycoris, here there are *soft fields,/* there's *a grove* here. Here I could have squandered an age with you." (*hic gelidi fontes, hic mollia prata, Lycoris,/ hic nemus; hic ipso tecum consumerer aevo*).

The imagery in this passage is remarkably like that in Theognis 1249–1252, where a speaker metaphorically designates the comforts of a former relationship to which his ex-beloved wishes to return: "Boy, you're like a horse. Just now sated with seed, you've come back to my stable, yearning for a good rider, *fine meadow, an icy spring, shady groves.*" Although in another context these terms need not belong to an offer of reconciliation, in both the poem of Theognis and our passage in Virgil they do. Thus, for a moment, Gallus breaks down and invites Lycoris (against the advice of Apollo and Pan) to come into the world where he has apparently taken refuge in an attempt to get over her. He proceeds to sympathize with her (he hopes she won't get frostbite as she follows another man through ice and snow (46–49; cf. 22–23). Then, at v.50, he begins to realize that she's not coming, that it's a dream, alters nothing. Thus he will engage in activities which (a generation later) Ovid recommends to renouncers (hunting, traveling), but he finally admits that these won't work either (v.60: "as if this could cure my frenzy," *tamquam haec sit nostri medicina furoris*). Now he no longer takes pleasure in nymphs or songs.[63] Love doesn't care, and he must yield. And so the curtain falls on Gallus' song and thus on the framed discourse to which it belongs. Thereupon the first speaker (who asked the Muses to give him a song for Gallus that Lycoris could read) returns, telling the Muses "that's enough," and begins to tell of *his love for Gallus*, which grows on him hour by hour. Finally he dismisses the pastoral scenery and tells his goats it's time to go.

The frame, with its explicitly erotic references at vv.75–76 make the framed speech a love gift from the speaker to Gallus. Gallus, except for his sudden plea ("Here there are cold springs," etc.), is trying to get over Lycoris. His speech belongs to the renunciatory phase: Lycoris has dumped him and he should just give up, Apollo tells him. Meanwhile, the speaker (Virgil, for short) loves him, and gives him this gift. In this sense, the frame is hardly perfunctory. As token of his love, and hence apparently as an act of "wooing," Virgil gives Gallus a song whereby he can renounce Lycoris, and which itself contains a number of other kinds of speeches, including those of Apollo and Pan. We leave it to the reader to wrestle with the details.

Horace Odes 1.5:

The dramatic situation of this poem is revealed in the last four lines of the poem (13–16), where we can recognize the metaphor "I've escaped

---

63. Quite similar is Horace *Odes* 4.1.29–32 where Horace claims he had given up love (1ff.) but is still dreaming of Ligurinus, and, implicitly, asks him not to be cruel (38–40).

from the storm" as a declaration that the speaker is no longer in love.[64]
A person afraid of drowning at sea may pray to Neptune (or any god he
chooses) to save him, and promise to put a votive offering in the god's
temple as a token of gratitude. Our speaker, then, says that the offering
on the temple wall shows that he's escaped and been able to hang up
his sopping clothes in fulfillment of his vow. And this is the bitter lens
through which he pictures a scene of love-making between the girl he
says he's renounced and a new lover. "Who is it you're tricking today?,"
he asks (1–5), "he'll be sorry" (5–11) to find out how treacherous the
wind is, though now he thinks it'll be clear sailing. The speaker mocks
those who feel attracted to her because they haven't tried her (12–13),
and then declares that he has been saved. Thus his memories of his own
days of wooing are expressed by images of a hypothetical new lover who
now occupies his old position at the girl's side (Cf. Catullus 8.16ff.).
Wooing, infidelity, and renunciation are bound together, but in such
a way as to privilege that bitter lens of the speaker. "How often he'll
weep . . . who now enjoys you" (*Quotiens flebit . . . qui . . . fruitur*).
For in the syntax of vv. 5–12, the subject (*qui . . .*) is identified within
the framework of "how often will he weep over your betrayal," so that
before we get to the boy's present enjoyment (*fruitur* 9) we already know
that it is going to be engulfed by his weeping (*flebit* 6), and the black
storm winds (7) put the boy's naive vision of the inviting breeze (11)
into context. Still, a legitimate doubt may remain whether the poem
is self-consciously ironic—whether the speaker is not in fact still in
love.[65]

---

64. Cf. Theognis 1271–1274, Prop. 3.24.14 (*portum tetigere carinae*); Ovid, *Amores*.
2.11.29–30. Sappho fr. 15.7 apparently used the same metaphor, *limenos* = harbor,
speaking of her brother who has escaped from a love affair (though cf. L-P's caution
about the reading in the app. crit.). Similarly Anacreon *PMG* 346, fr. 4.1–5, where
the speaker apparently says he's just come to the surface of the waves.
65. In the *Remedia Amoris* Ovid warns would-be renouncers: "I'd rather you kept
quiet than that you said you're out of love; whoever keeps telling everyone 'I'm not in
love' is in love" (647–649: *et malim taceas quam te desisse loquaris: / qui nimium multis 'non
amo' dicit, amat*).

Tibullus 1.8:

The situation, as it can be inferred from the evidence of the text, appears to be this: The speaker, whom we shall call Tibullus (at 1.9.83—in a poem not included in our anthology—when referring to the same amorous triangle, he names himself), is in love with a boy, Marathus (as revealed at 1.4.81–84). Marathus, on the other hand, cruel to Tibullus (cf. 1.8.81), is in love with Pholoe. So Tibullus goes with Marathus, as a kind of spokesman, to persuade Pholoe to receive the boy. In vv.1–26 he addresses Marathus ("You can't fool me, I know you're in love").[66] From vv.27–66 he woos Pholoe on behalf of Marathus (in vv.55–66 he allegedly quotes what Marathus says about her in her absence). In vv.67–68 he addresses Marathus, suggesting that they give up the attempt to persuade her ("Let's give up. She's not going to yield, and look, you're crying"). Then he turns back to the girl (69–78), but in admonishing her he reveals what we take to be his real design: to seduce Marathus. "Don't be so proud," he says to Pholoe, "because it will boomerang. Just look at Marathus here, who used to be so cruel [to me] and now realizes his mistake [don't you, Marathus?!]." This poem, then, contains at least four different speeches: "Admit it, you're in love" (1–26); "Girl, make love to the boy" (27–66, 69–78); "Girl, don't be cruel" (55–66: Marathus' lament, quoted by Tibullus); and, "Boy, make love with me!" (expressed by means of the whole speech to Pholoe (27–78). We believe that the larger context of Tibullus' cycle for Marathus (including also 1.4 and 1.9) suggests that the seduction of Marathus is the speaker's primary intent.

---

66. It could be argued (and was suggested orally to us by Alva Bennett) that in 1–26 Tibullus is addressing *himself*. We do not exclude this possibility, and have tried to leave the translation as ambiguous in this regard as the original.

Propertius 3.6:

The speaker is talking with Lygdamus, who is either his slave or his girlfriend Cynthia's. Lygdamus has apparently just come from seeing Cynthia, and is being used as an intermediary to negotiate a peace (vv. 36, 41–42). As the poem begins, the speaker is asking to hear again what he has just heard (cf. Prop. 2.22.49 [=2.22b.7] "and pesters his messenger to repeat what he's already heard," *et rursus puerum quaerendo audita fatigat*). He wants the straight truth, no exaggerations (3–4) and implicitly threatens Lygdamus with some form of punishment if he is not completely accurate in his account. We do not, however, hear from Lygdamus directly. After asking him to begin from the top (7–8) and promising to listen attentively, the speaker begins to echo Lygdamus' alleged assertions (from the account he has apparently just given? or are they supposed to be interjected comments?—"so you saw . . ." 9–18). Then, at v. 19, after the speaker says, "and she told you about our fight in a mournful voice," we hear what are supposed to be Cynthia's words. She complains of the speaker's unfaithfulness (19–20), calls the girl she thinks he's keeping at home a whore ("I won't say what she is" v. 22), and says that this disreputable woman has bewitched him with the aid of magic (25–30). All in all, Cynthia comes across as hurt, jealous, and sad ("I melt away here on this lonely bed" 23), and eager for him to come back to her. She has apparently dreamt that he will return, and the image of him groveling at her feet and asking to be taken back is an obvious source of pleasure to her.[67] Finally she prays that our speaker and his alleged lover have no fun (33–34). Clearly Cynthia wants him back: and this news is everything the speaker could hope for.[68]

Like the speaker (2, 11, 42) Cynthia addresses Lygdamus in the vocative (19, 24, 31). Yet her speech is evidently aimed at Propertius. Like-

---

67. Cf. Theognis 957–958: "I hope you come back longing to my door!"

68. A kind of dream, one might say. In Prop. 2.26a he does dream that Cynthia offers him a reconciliation. He sees her shipwrecked (=madly in love with him) stretching out her arms and calling to him, confessing her lies. But he wakes up just as he's about to dive in: it's been a dream, there is no offer.

wise, what he says to Lygdamus after the latter's tale has been told is directed to Cynthia. "Go back, tell her: (1) I may have been angry but I did not deceive her; (2) I am twisting in the same fire." And he adds, apparently to Lygdamus, that he will swear he has been "untouched" (faithful) during the twelve days of their separation. In short, he sends back a message of reconciliation. Is it an offer? A response to an offer? Offer and response seem to blend, since we may read Cynthia's speech either as an implicit offer or merely as information that emboldens Propertius to make an offer of his own.

Finally, back in the outer frame, Propertius offers Lygdamus freedom if he can pull off these negotiations for peace (*pax*). Looking carefully at the poem, then, we can distinguish at least five sections: Propertius speaks to Lygdamus (1–8); then, in effect, gets answers from him (9–18); these answers include Cynthia's discourse, directed to Propertius through Lygdamus (19–34): thereupon Propertius tells Lygdamus the message he wants to send back (35–40); finally he offers the slave freedom if he can help conclude the peace (41–42).

Ovid, *Amores* 3.7:

One measure of indirection is the difficulty of identifying the speech-action which is the basis of the utterance, and so the relation of that action to the "syntax of actions" (Aristotle, *Poetics*) in which it is imbedded. Though this poem contains 84 verses, one reaches the precise dramatic context of the discourse only at vv.77–80. Here's the story: the speaker had wooed a certain girl (2); he had the opportunity to make love with her but wasn't up to it (*passim*); she tried everything to arouse him (7–12, 55–56), but it didn't work (13–16, 57–60, 65–66). In the present moment of the discourse, the speaker is addressing his penis.[69]

---

69. As, apparently, the speaker does in Catullus 2. Though controversy has been raging over Catullus' *passer* since the Renaissance (and the bibliography grows year by year), we feel the case is rather clear, especially in view of vv.11–13, which most modern editors senselessly detach from the poem and consider a fragment. Catullus 3, then, in which the *passer* (= penis) has "died" and its "passing" is mourned by the speaker, may be read as a problem of male sexual exhaustion. The girl reacts by

Now, he says, it has sprung to life again (67–68), and he addresses it directly at vv.69ff. But then, when the dramatic situation seems clear (he's dressing down his penis for its slump) we learn just what the girl said to him when she realized that he was utterly incapable of making love to her:

> "Why are you toying with me?" she said. "Who told you
>   to come, you nut,
>   if you didn't want to, and dump your balls on my
>   bed?
> Either a poisoner from Aeaea[70] has bewitched you with
>   binding
>   threads, or you've come to me slack from another
>   love."   80

She says basically: "either: (a) you've been bewitched; or (b) you've just been with someone else and have spent all your strength there." The speaker asks if he might not be bewitched (27–30) and explains that chants and magic herbs have powerful properties and effects (31–34). This passage very closely resembles Tibullus 1.8.17–26, where the speaker says to Marathus in effect: maybe magic is responsible; after all, magic is powerful (Tib. 1.8.17–22). But after following Tibullus nearly beat for beat, Ovid omits Tibullus' conclusion:

> Why should I wail that chanting has hurt you, or herbs?
>   Beauty needs no magic aids.
> What hurts is to have touched the body, to have given long
>   kisses, to have tangled thigh with thigh. (Tib. 1.8.23–26)

Instead he insists (vv.35–36), "Who says magic spells aren't causing

---

crying, and Catullus denounces the *passer* for causing her tears (which would be rather inappropriate, were the *passer* really Lesbia's pet sparrow—or other kind of bird—that had died). In any event, in this poem of Ovid, there can be no question (see vv.65–72). Cf. AP 12.216 (Strato).

70. Cf. note on 2.15.10.

this slump in my powers? Maybe that's why my crotch feels nothing." In other words, whereas Tibullus ascribes Marathus' condition *not* to magic but to prior erotic activity, Ovid follows his Tibullan model to the abyss of confession, and then calls out plaintively, "Who says magic's not the reason I was temporarily impotent?!" Who says? The girl says! ("you've come to me slack from another love," *aut alio lassus amore venis* v.80). The speaker passes quickly on to his sense of shame (37–38), the girl's beauty (39–40), and so on. The question he never addresses, which is curious if he's really alone with his penis, is whether he had in fact been "elsewhere" before the embarrassing encounter with the girl in question. He says rather pointedly that he had Chlide (23) twice, Pitho (23) and Libas (24) thrice each, and Corinna nine times in a brief night (25–26). So what's wrong? Knowing Ovid, we suspect a ruse.[71] He has been accused of arriving exhausted from another lover. And whereas that accusation is one of two possibilities the girl has suggested (aut . . . aut 79–80), and, indeed, pointedly the second and harder hitting of the two, it is not even mentioned in his response (like a press conference in which the answer bears little relation to the question).

In a word, *Amores* 3.7 may be read as a defense, logically directed by the speaker to the girl, explaining to her that he has merely had a bad day, may be getting old, and at any rate has probably, as she (ironically) suggested, been bewitched. It's full of praise for the girl, and maybe we should see a reference to the real thrust of the discourse when, after praising her ("What a girl! yet I was merely looking and touching," *at qualem vidi tantum tetigique puellam*, v.39), he asks, "What line can I think up now to win her again?" (*quas nunc concipiam per nova vota preces*, v.45). Perhaps by trying to hide the real cause of his failure and distract her from the charge that he has come sexually exhausted (*aut alio lassus amore venis* 80) he means to recover from the embarrassing situation in which he's been caught and proceed with his suit. One final clue may

---

71. In *Amores* 2.7 he indignantly asks Corinna, "How could you suspect me of having an affair with the girl who does your hair?!" In the next poem, 2.8, he addresses that very girl: "Ok, how did Corinna find out about us?" Such humor is typically Ovidian.

be gleaned from the last couplet (83–84): after his awkward non-performance, the girl jumped up, ran off, and douched herself with a bit of water so that her attendants wouldn't know that nothing had happened. Her attempt then to cover up reality may be mirrored by his own now. She tried to fool her serving girls. Who is he trying to fool?

Archilochus, P. Colon. 7511:

Subtlety in the use of kinds of utterance, carriers, and frames is hardly a late invention. In fact, the oldest large fragment of Greek erotic poetry that we have is one of the most subtle in this respect. Let's have a look at this controversial text.[72]

As the fragment begins, a woman is speaking (a framed discourse). We can tell very little from the actual text of the first two verses of her speech, but can infer from the first ten of the man's response that he has been trying to seduce her, and that she has responded by modestly imposing certain limits on any prospective love-making between them. This presumably is the context of "holding back," *aposkhomenos* (v. 1). In vv. 2–5 the woman suggests to the speaker that if he's "in a hurry" he should think about another woman "in our home" (whom, curiously, she doesn't name—the speaker, however, knows exactly who she's talking about, so she might have mentioned the name earlier, or it might merely have been unnecessary). According to the woman, this other woman (whom we shall hereinafter call Neoboule cf. v. 18) is eager (3), beautiful and slender (4), and utterly blameless (5)—in short, impeccable and irreproachable. Four of the five verses that remain (in the fragmentary text, that is) of her discourse are used to refer to this woman, to describe her, praise her, and suggest that the man make her his beloved. This suggestion (5) concludes her discourse, and is thus emphatic. He senses its importance, as we shall see.

Verse 6 is a narrative transition ("that's what she said, and I an-

---

72. First published by R. Merkelbach and M.L. West, "Ein Archilochos-Papyrus", *ZPE* 14 (1974) 97–113.

swered") and vv. 7–28 represent the man's response. Clearly he is out to have her, and he does, as the concluding narrative section (29–36) indicates. So we know, at least in part, what his motive is; and, indeed, typical elements of a wooing speech are present:

1) vocative [plus praise of deceased mother][73] (7–8)
2) praise of amorous activities (9–10)
3) willingness to be ruled by her (10–13)
4) request [metaphorically stated, and including an impera-
   tive] (14–16)

Yet of the 27vv. occupied by the two speeches (5vv. and 22vv., respectively), 16 are about Neoboule (5 of hers, 11 of his), and as soon as the speaker has made his amorous request (14–16) he turns to the subject of Neoboule, with which the woman concluded her speech. His verbal attack against Neoboule occupies the rest of his speech, except for a brief bit of praise of the woman at 24–25, and even this praise ("You I like a lot; you're not faithless or double dealing. She, on the other hand . . .") seems merely to pivot back to his attack on Neoboule (He doesn't say, "She's a slut; you I like." Rather: "You I like; she, on the other hand, is a slut . . ." and goes off in that direction.). He must, then, have perceived the suggestion, "Take *her*" as an important element in what the woman has said. His attack on Neoboule is full of elements usual in rejections and renunciations:

1) another can have her [= I don't want her] (17–18)[74]
2) she's not beautiful (18–20)[75]
3) she's promiscuous (26)[76]

---

73. We wonder whether, by naming the mother and not the father, the speaker may be impugning the child's paternity. This insult would have been aimed at Ly-kambes, who according to the tradition was the target of Archilochus' abuse (cf. introduction to Archilochus).

74. Cf., e.g., Ovid, *Amores* 3.11a.28.

75. Cf., e.g., Prop. 3.24.1–8.

76. Cf., e.g., Cat. 11.16–20; 37.14–15; 58.1–5.

4) I'd be a laughing-stock [if I took her] (22–24)[77]

5) she's faithless, two-timing [by implication] (26–28)

This attack on Neoboule runs from just before the center of his speech
until its end. If imperatives and their equivalent (independent optatives)
are any measure of his energy level, we may note *gnothi* (17), *ekheto* (18),
apekhe (22), *me tout' ephoit'* . . . (22). But why this energy (clearly there,
if not measurable by verbal mood)? Why would he be so vehement in
his rejection of Neoboule if they had not been lovers? Is he just trying
to persuade the woman all the more by heightening the contrast between
his desire for her and his revulsion at the thought of Neoboule? Or does
he mean to imply that, since reconciliation between Neoboule and
himself is impossible, the woman should not hesitate (out of deference
to Neoboule's claims on the man) to step in and take advantage of the
opportunity at hand?

Let's backtrack for a moment. Why has the woman been so insistent
in trying to push Neoboule on the man? Is she just being sarcastic,
since she knows that he has 'had' Neoboule and that she is generally
available? Or has she come in complicity with Neoboule, empowered
or even charged by her to make an offer to the man on her behalf?[78]
(We might compare Catullus 11, where such an offer, apparently
delivered by third parties, is rejected by the Speaker.) The weight
given in both speeches to Neoboule and to the possibility of a renewed
relation between her and the man suggests to us that the interchange
may be read as, in part, an offer of reconciliation and a rejection of
that offer. This offer/response and the seduction seem to operate
simultaneously, and with a complex relation between them. Indeed,
they are so tightly interwoven that it is difficult to determine which,
if either, might be considered a vehicle for the articulation of the other.

The beginning of the poem is missing, of course, but it seems logical
to suppose that, if the woman did have a message from Neoboule to

---

77. Cf., e.g., Prop. 3.25.1–2.

78. It may of course be argued that she is speaking in all innocence, knowing
nothing of a prior relationship. Or then again, she might know nothing of a prior
relationship and still be the unwitting agent of an offer from Neoboule.

the speaker, she had not delivered it before 2ff., since she seems to be bringing up the subject there ("But if. . . ., there is in our house," *ei d' . . .lestin en hemeterou . . .*). We must suppose that at the beginning of (what remains of) her speech (vv. 1–2) she was responding to a come-on, since she imposes conditions which the man then responds to. Thus, if we are on the right track, the woman has come with an offer of reconciliation, and the man has tried to seduce her before she can deliver it. As an exercise, we might try to imagine the most rapid way to begin such a scene, either by direct speech, by narrative, or by a combination (the form is purely speculative, but the substance is based on inference supported by evidence from the text):

> I knew what she'd come for, but I headed her off.
> "You're a beautiful girl," I told her, and began to move in.
> "Not so fast," she said, excited. "I'm not like that,
> you'd better slow down . . ."

A frame containing more or less this information would not be inconsistent with anything in the text. We must, at a minimum presuppose a prior attempt at seduction, and some reason why the woman is so insistent in suggesting Neoboule and why the speaker responds at such length and with such vehemence. Plausibly: (1) she is fulfilling a mission, although she may herself feel drawn to the man; (2) he sees her plan, senses that she might hesitate if she thinks that he and Neoboule could get back together, and so bitterly rejects the offer; (3) whether by persuasion or by force, he gets his way with her.

Thus, emphatically rejecting the message is an important part of the seduction. The man senses he must put the woman at ease on this score if he is to have his way with her. In any event he moves from speech to action and gets what he wants.

We have seen that some of the speech-actions represented in relatively simple form in Theognis have been worked by poets from all periods into rather complex configurations, making use of various techniques which are themselves difficult to describe in general terms. We have spoken of framing and framed utterances, of utterances including several speech-actions and of poems that overlay or interweave different speech- actions within a single utterance. If we are correct, these poems are not unlike puzzles or riddles. That is, they should be read for enjoyment as an aesthetic game. The designer of each game has left the audience clues with which to reconstruct a more or less elaborated dramatic situation, identify the speaker(s) and the addressee(s), over-hearer(s), etc., and try to gauge the intent of the actors and the nature of the action which their utterances are part of, perform, or represent. This is one of many pleasures these poems were meant to offer, and by no means the fullest one. But it is a fundamental aspect of the game, which must be handled well for the rest to make sense. To take an analogy from music, the speech-action, like the bass line, tends to reveal the harmonic structure of the melody it supports. One ought, as Brahms said of the bass line, to look for it first. But it is not to be mistaken for the full pleasure of the music. Sometimes we have enough information to form a relatively clear idea of the intended scene and action; sometimes the words seem to suggest more than we can logically infer. But our inference must be guided in part by a familiarity with amorous practice, both word and deed.[79]

79. Cf. S.C. Levinson, "Activity types and language," *Linguistics* 17 (1979) 365–399.

GREECE

ARCHILOCHUS

A contemporary of king Gyges of Lydia (ca.687–652 B.C.), Archilochus came from the island of Paros. He went as a soldier to the Parian colony of Thasos, and died back in Paros some time after 648 (fr. 122 West mentions a total solar eclipse probably dateable to April 6 of that year) in a battle against the Naxians. In antiquity Archilochus was considered the foremost representative of "iambos," or blame-poetry. Such poetry was especially connected with iambic trimeter—though there was enough blame to go around to other meters too. Archilochus' invective was most famously associated with the story of Lykambes and his daughters. Lykambes was said to have promised his daughter Neoboule to Archilochus in marriage, but to have gone back on his word. Archilochus avenged this insult by attacking the family in poems so vitriolic that it drove them all to hang themselves. In this story (as in those surrounding the later blame-poet, Hipponax), however, we must reckon with the possibility that these figures were "stock characters in a traditional entertainment."[1] In support of this theory, it has been noted that the names of both Lykambes and Neoboule may be significant, the former possibly meaning "Wolf-walker," the latter "she who always has a new plan," i.e. who is fickle. It is characteristic for Greek and Roman poetry as a whole that we find in such invective the coarsest, most explicit sexual language and descriptions. Blunt sexuality, then as now, was a favored mode of derogation and attack.

---

1. Thus West, *Studies* p.27. On the controversy unleashed by this suggestion, cf. R. Rosen, "Hipponax, Boupalos and the Conventions of the Psogos," *TAPhA* 118 (1988) 29–41.

The First Cologne Epode, P. Colon.7511 = SLG 478[2]

"......[3]

    holding back completely; and you've got to do the same.
But if you're in a hurry and passion urges you on,
    there is someone in our house who really wants to now[,
a lovely, tender girl. I think
    her looks are flawless. Make her your [...."   5
So much she said, and I answered
    "Daughter of Amphimedo, that good and [
lady whom the mouldy earth holds,[4]
    there are many pleasures of the goddess for young men
besides the divine thing;[5] one of those will suffice.   10
    But those things you and I shall consider
at our ease, with help from heaven, when......darkens.
    I'll do what you tell me.......me a lot.

---

2. This poem, which comes from a papyrus in Cologne, was first published in 1974. It is the longest fragment of Archilochus to date. We call it an "epode" because it consists of a couplet, one verse of which is in a given meter, and the next (the so-called "epodos stichos" or "verse sung after") in an independent meter.

3. The speaker at the beginning of the fragment (vv. 1–5) is a girl, who rebuffs the sexual advances of a male addressee, proposing another girl in her house as a substitute. She does not mention the other girl's name, and her description implies that she thinks that the girl is not known to the addressee (though perhaps she ironically feigns ignorance). Verse 6 reveals that the fragment as a whole is narrated by the male addressee, who then recounts his reply to the girl (vv. 7–29). In verse 17ff. we find out that far from not knowing the proposed substitute, he knows her all too well, and from personal experience: she is Neoboule. The female speaker at the beginning of the fragment is thus probably Neoboule's sister, the younger daughter of Lykambes known from the tradition.

4. The fact that the girl's mother is dead means that the traditional guardian of her maidenhood is absent.

5. Probably a euphemism for sexual intercourse.

But under the coping-stone and the gates,[6]
   don't grudge me, darling [15
for I will land in the grassy meadows.[7]
   But there's something I want you to know right now: some
                                  other man can
have Neoboule. Oh god! she's overripe; twice as old as you;
   her maiden blossom's fallen away,
and the grace that once was hers; for she can't get enough[.   20
   That rabid woman has shown the lengths she'll go to.
She can go to hell. I hope I never get stuck
   with a woman like that and become
the laughing-stock of the neighborhood. You're the one I
                         really want.

   You I can trust, you're no double-dealer.   25
She, though, is cunning, and makes many men [
   I'm afraid that, in my hurry, I gave birth
like the bitch in the proverb to blind pups, born too soon."[8]
   This much I said. I took the girl and laid her down
among blooming flowers, and covering her with my soft   30
   cloak, cradling her nape in my elbow,
....]just like a fawn[.
   With my hands I gently clasped her [;

---

6. Almost certainly sexual metaphors. The coping is the top course of stones on a wall, here perhaps referring to the top of the vulva. Gates are a common metaphor for an opening, vaginal or anal, cf. J. Henderson, *The Maculate Muse* (New Haven 1975) 137.

7. The metaphor probably refers to the *mons Veneris*, i.e. the speaker promises to ejaculate outside the vagina.

8. In this context, the proverb "the hasty bitch bears blind pups," may refer to an unhappy past involvement between the speaker and Neoboule (if we equate the speaker with Archilochus, we may think of the story of his intended marriage to Neoboule, cf. intro. above), i.e. by being overhasty in his previous dealings with her, the speaker was hurt.

her fresh skin showed, the magic of her youth.

    And handling her beautiful body,   35

I spent my . . . . force, touching her blond hair.[9]

Iambic Fragment 23 (West)

                  ]I replied to her:

"Woman, don't be at all afraid of what men

say. I'll take care of . . . .

So soften your heart.

Did you think I'd sunk to such a state

of wretchedness—did I seem to you so cowardly?

That's not the kind of man I am, nor was my family.

I know how to love where I am loved

and hate the hateful and . . . . .

An ant . . . . . .

This city [   ]you're roaming over

men have never sacked; but you've

taken it at spear-point and won great fame.

Rule it now, be tyrant of the place;

you'll be the envy of many men.[10]

---

9. While this passage evidently refers to orgasm, it is unclear how the speaker achieves it and whether he keeps his promise to make do with lesser pleasures. This uncertainty—as Slings (in J.M. Bremer, A. Maria van Erp Taalman Kip and S.R. Slings, *Some Recently Found Greek Poems,* Mnemosyne Suppl.99 [Leiden 1987] 51) has proposed—may be deliberate. We may ask what is the intention of a poem in which the male narrator proposes sex other than full intercourse, fails to tell whether he keeps to this proposition, and includes a lengthy section of abuse aimed at Neoboule. Is the younger daughter merely the instrument of his revenge against Neoboule and Lykambes?

10. We agree with West, *Studies* p.119f. and Burnett, *Three Archaic Poets* (London 1983) pp.70–76, that the city is an erotic metaphor, as at Theognis 949–954. A woman has succeeded in her sexual conquest of the speaker where previously men had failed. Against this interpretation cf. Slings (*op. cit.* p.6).

Iambic fragment 30–32 (West)

she took pleasure in holding a sprig of myrtle
and the lovely blossom of the rose, and her hair
shaded her shoulders and back.

Iambic fragment 41 (West)

(the girl, like a) halcyon
perched upon the jutting stone, flapping.

Iambic fragment 42 (West)

As on a straw a Thracian man or Phrygian
sucks his brew, forward she stooped, working away.

Iambic fragment 43 (West)

His cock, like that
of a crop-gobbling donkey from Priene, overflowed.

Iambic fragment 46 (West)

out of the pipe and into the pail

Tetrameter fragment 119 (West)

and to go at a hard-working bag and thrust
belly on belly, thigh on thigh.

Epode fragment 184 (West)

She's cunning, in one hand she
carries water, in the other, fire.

2nd Cologne Epode = P. Colon.7511 = SLG 478b (188 West)[11]

No longer does your soft flesh bloom, the swath
is sere........of horrid age is overtaking you.
The sweet lure of your alluring face has dissolved
......Yes, many gusts
of winter wind have blasted you.

Epode fragment 189 (West)

Many's the blind eel you've taken in

Epode fragment 191 (West)

Such desire for love, coiled at my heart,
shed a thick mist over my eyes,
stealing the tender senses from my breast.

Epode fragment 193 (West)

Wracked with desire I lie,
lifeless, pierced through the bone
by the crushing pains of the gods.

---

11. Both subject matter and meter of this fragment are consistent with those of 189
and 191, and may be from the same poem.

Epode fragment 196 (West)

but desire unhinges me, my friend, it masters me

fragment 331 (West)

fig tree on the crag, feeding hordes of crows,
friendly to all comers, Pasiphile the welcomer.[12]

---

12. In Greek, "Pasiphile" means "a woman loved by all."

ALKMAN

Alkman lived in the mid-7th century B.C. and is the earliest composer of choral lyric of whose work we can form a detailed picture. Though he may originally have come from Lydia, he worked in Sparta and his songs, unlike most choral lyric which is written in a literary Doric dialect, are composed in the Laconian vernacular. More than other choral lyric, moreover, his insistently refers to personages and rites of purely local significance. It is consequently particularly hard to interpret his poems. His "Partheneia", or "Maiden Songs," were evidently sung by a chorus of young girls (see the preface to Sappho), but in what context is difficult to tell.

In the first of these songs, the Louvre Partheneion (so-called because it comes from a papyrus in the Louvre), the chorus of girls sings of Agido and also of Hagesichora, whose name means "chorus leader," presumably a reference to her function in the group. Between vv.70–77, we hear of various girls (Nanno, Areta, Thylakis, Kleesithera) who are unable to ward off an unspecified event, and of an unnamed feminine addressee in 2nd person singular (vv.74–78) who will no longer come to Ainesimbrota's house and say "if only Astaphis were mine, or Philylla would look my way, or Demareta, or lovely Vianthemis—but Hagesichora wears me out with desire." Ten names occur in the course of eight lines, plus the unnamed 2nd person addressee. Conspicuously *un*named here is Agido. Since the chorus says at vv.98–99 that it now consists of ten members instead of eleven, perhaps we may interpret that feminine 2nd person singular at vv.74ff. as Agido, who would then be leaving the circle of girls. Perhaps it is her departure that the other girls cannot prevent—a departure which, given the erotic nature of what the girl is leaving, is most plausibly connected with marriage.

The Louvre Partheneion = PMG 1

.... Polydeukes[1]
I do not number Lykaisos among the dead
(but) of Enarsphoros and swift footed Sebros
.... and the brutish...
.... and the helmeted warrior...   5
and Euteiches and Lord Areios
and.... who stood out among demigods

.... the leader
.... great, and Eurotos
.... the tumult of the miserable...   10
.... and the bravest...
.... we (won't) leave out.
.... Aisa
and Poros], the eldest
of the divinities.[2] No man's impatient power   15
should try to soar to heaven,

---

1. Polydeukes, one of the Dioskouroi, and brother of Helen. The mythical narrative
which follows probably referred to the vengeance of the Dioskouroi on the sons of
Hippokoon (named in v.3ff.), one of whom—Enarsphoros—tried to rape Helen (cf.
Plutarch, *Life of Theseus* 31.1). This leads up to the maxim in v.13ff., which warns of
the dangers of an improper coupling, and is appropriate to the theme of marriage,
which we take to be central to this poem.

2. Aisa means "binding limitation"; Poros, "open possibility." H. Fränkel, *Early
Greek Poetry and Philosophy* (New York 1973), explains the general sense of the passage
thus:

> "Whereas Aisa imposes a compulsion from which we cannot
> withdraw, Poros offers open possibilities to the inventive or favorably
> situated man. When Aisa and Poros are called .... eldest of the
> gods, the implication is that absolute compulsion and relative freedom
> are the basic principles of the world. Alcman illustrates Aisa as well as
> Poros in the following. Aisa establishes our human limitations firmly
> and places us far below the gods .... Defiant struggle cannot win
> for man the utopia of the divine and the perfect, it does not open the
> heights of heaven to him or the depths of the sea—'but the Graces
> with lovely eyelashes come to the house of Zeus'—No contentious
> violence but Charis ('charm, amiability, complaisance, grace' and the

or wed Aphrodite
.... Queen, nor any ....
.... nor the daughter of Porkos:[3]
but the Graces, whose eyes look love,   20
(come) to the home of Zeus

.... the most
.... divinity
....
.... gave a gift   25
....
.... destroyed his youth
....
....
.... went; one of them hit by an arrow   30
(another) by a marble millstone
.... to Hades ...
....
Their plans were evil,
their suffering unforgettable.   35

Somehow the gods get you back.
Happy is he, who wisely
weaves the day to its end
without tears.
But I sing   40
the light of Agido. I see
her like the sun, which
Agido asks to shine
as our witness. But I can't praise

---

like) leads man to the house and throne of god, which he must
approach as a guest, not as a presumptious claimant."
3. Porkos is another name for Nereus. His daughter is the sea-nymph Thetis, whose
marriage to a mere mortal (Peleus) produced an unhappy son: Achilles.

or blame her. Our glorious leader   45
won't let us, who clearly stands out
herself, as if you put
among the herds a racehorse,
sturdy, thundering, a champion
from soaring dreams.   50

Don't you see?—That's a
Venetic steed. But the tresses
of my cousin
Hagesichora blossom
like pure gold;   55
and her silvery face—
why do I say what's obvious?
There's Hagesichora herself.
But the girl who's next to Agido in beauty
shall race but as a Kolaxeian horse behind an Ibenian: 60
for while we bear the torch to the dawn
the Pleiades, rising like the dog-star
through the ambrosial night,
strive against us.

For all the purple dye we have   65
won't help at all,
nor a dazzling serpent
all of gold,[4] nor Lydian
cap, the pride
of tender-glancing girls,   70
nor even the locks of Nanno,
nor god-like Areta,
nor Thylakis, nor Kleesithera,
and no longer coming to Ainesimbrota's house will you say:
"if only Astaphis were mine,   75
or Philylla would look my way,

---

4. This refers to a bracelet in the shape of a serpent.

or Demareta, or lovely Vianthemis—
but Hagesichora wears me out with desire."

For Hagesichora of the lovely
ankles is not here: 80
she waits with Agido,
applauding our festival.
Hear their prayers,
you gods; to gods belong the outcome
and the end. My chorus leader,   85
maiden as I am, I say
I have only shrilled in vain from the rafter
like an owl; yet I too wish to please
the Dawn; she's the one who
cures us of our labors.   90
And thanks to Hagesichora, maidens
find their way to lovely peace.

For you have to heed
the trace horse and
whoever's at the helm.   95
We (can't) sing better
than the Sirens—
they are goddesses, and we're just a bunch
of children—ten, in place of eleven—singing,
our tone like a swan's on Xanthos'   100
streams. But she, with her gorgeous golden hair
. . . .
. . . .
. . . .
. . . .   105

Second Partheneion = PMG 3

Muses of] Olympus, around my senses
      ] of song
      ] and to hear
      ]the voice
      ]of girls singing the lovely song   5
      ].....
will scatter sweet sleep from the lids
    while] it leads me towards the dancing-meet
where I'll really toss my yellow hair,
                ]and my soft feet   10
(shall dance?)
    50 verses missing

and with desire that loosens limbs, but more meltingly   61
than sleep and death she looks me over;
and not in vain she.... sweet;

But Astymeloisa doesn't answer me;
but holding a garland,[5]   65
like a star
in flight through the blazing sky,
or a golden branch, or soft feather
      ]
      ]she passed on slender feet;   70
and on the tresses of the girls hangs
the dew of Kinyras,[6] gracing their lovely hair.

Astymeloisa (moves) through the band,
the city's darling,[7]

---

5. According to Athenaeus 15.678a, this word referred to a garland offered to Hera. This may place the action of the poem in a ritual of this goddess.

6. A Cyprian perfume or hair-oil. Kinyras was a Cyprian king.

7. A play on the name Astymeloisa, which means "she who is a care to the city."

```
                      ]I take                                  75
                      ]and say
. . . . . . . . . . . . . . . . . . . . . . . . . . . . . . . . . . . . . . . . . . . . . . . . . . . . . . . . . . .
. . . . . . . . . . . . . . . . . . . . . . . . . . . . . . . . . . . . . . . . . . . . . . . . . . . . . . . . . . .
If she drew near
and took me by my tender hand                                  80
I'd instantly kneel down before her.


But now....a girl (heavy?) hearted
with a girl.[          ]keeping me
                       ] the girl
                       ] grace;                                85
5 verses missing
```

Alkman P. Oxy. 2443 fr.1 + 3213.9ff. (cf. M.L. West, *ZPE* 26 [1977] 38)

```
]...[....]no one .[
] I was thinking alone[
] . of Poseidon[
 ] ...
.. coming to the lovely grove of the white goddesses[8]
from Trygeai; and they were holding
two sweet pomegranates.
And when, by the lovely streams of the river,
they prayed[9] to reach the wedlock they desired,
and feel the utmost things that men and women
feel, and gain the marriage bed[
```

---

8. Nereids.
9. The subject of the sentence is feminine.

MIMNERMOS

Mimnermos lived in the second half of the 7th cent. B.C. and came either from Smyrna or Colophon on the coast of Asia Minor. He was a poet of elegy, and is known to have written a long poem called the *Smyrneis* on the history of Smyrna and its successful battle (in the 660s B.C.) against the the Lydian king Gyges. Pasquali (*SIFC* 3 [1923] 293ff. = *Pagine meno stravaganti* [Florence 1935] 113ff.) ingeniously suggested that the poet may have been named in honor of the crucial role played in this conflict by the river Hermos: for Mimnermos can be construed as meaning "the one who commemorates the Hermos." If this suggestion is correct, it is natural to suppose that the battle took place shortly before Mimnermos' birth. Mimnermos was best known in antiquity for his love poetry. He is said to have written a long elegiac work called *Nanno*, after a flute-girl he loved. The two passages presented here may come from that work.

1 (West)

What is life, what is joy, without golden Aphrodite?
    May I die when these things no longer move me,
a secret love, soothing gifts, the bed,
    those tempting flowers of youth there to be plucked
by men and women. But when agonizing age sets in,   5
    making repulsive even a handsome man,
then constant anxious cares afflict his mind,
    he takes no joy in seeing the shafts of the sun,
but is loathsome to boys, despised by women.
    What a pain the god made age.   10

5 (West)

Suddenly an immense sweat streams down my skin,
   and I tremble, seeing the blossom of youth,
its beauty and joy. If only it lasted longer,
   but it is shortlived like a dream,
youth which I adore. Heavy, formless   5
   age suddenly hangs overhead,
loathsome and despised, making a man unrecognizable,
   and, poured about his eyes and brain, it mangles them.

SAPPHO

Sappho was born ca.630 B.C. on the island of Lesbos, where she lived until exiled to Sicily between 604/3 and 596/5. A composer of "monody," i.e. solo song sung to the accompaniment of the lyre, Sappho seems to have been part of—maybe the head of—a female circle, whose members were young girls being educated in musical and other skills before marriage. Perhaps this was a circle comparable to that which we can glimpse in Alkman's "Partheneia" or "Maiden Songs." The poems speak of the relationships between Sappho and the various girls, and also of the strong sexual feelings they have for each other.

1 (L-P)

Sparkling-wreathed,[1] O deathless Aphrodite,
daughter of Zeus with your web of cunning, I beg you,
please don't crush my heart with longing,
lady, or anguish   4

no, come to this place, if ever before
you heard my voice singing from afar
and listened and, leaving your father's house,
came on the golden   8

yoked chariot, and lovely speeding
sparrows, wings whirring, brought you

---

1. *poikilothron* is usually translated as "on a richly-worked throne," but perhaps Sappho was playing on the unique Homeric "throna" (woven flowers) at *Iliad* 22.441 and its collocation with "poikila": *en de throna poikil' epasse*.

over the black earth, down from heaven
through the midst of the air,   12

and quickly landed.² But you, O blest,
a smile on your immortal face,
asked what was wrong this time, why
was I calling this time,   16

what did I most want to happen to me
in my raging heart. "Whom shall I sweet talk this time
and lead back to your love? Who, Sappho,
is doing you wrong?   20

For if she runs, she'll soon be chasing;
if she won't take gifts, well, she'll give them;
and if she doesn't love, soon she will love—
even unwilling." ³   24

Come to me now once more, and free me from jagged
sorrow, and make what my heart is
longing for, happen. You yourself
fight alongside me.   28

------

2. Sparrows were especially associated with Aphrodite because of their proverbial
wantonness, and their eggs were eaten as aphrodisiacs, cf. D. Page, *Sappho and Alcaeus*
(Oxford 1955) ad v. 10. "Sparrow," moreover, was slang for the penis, cf. J. Henderson,
Aristophanes' Lysistrata (Oxford 1987) ad vv.722–723. On the possibility that the
sparrow of Catullus 2 and 3 stands for the penis, see n. *ad loc.*

3. In Aphrodite's words we observe a facet of female homosexuality in Greece that
distinguishes it from its male counterpart, and from most heterosexual love in the
Archaic and Classical periods: namely the expectation that either partner can be the
pursuer *or* the pursued in a relationship, and that desire will be reciprocal. Male
homosexuality, as one may observe it e.g. in the elegies of Theognis, adheres to a strict
hierarchy in which the older male (the *erastes*) is always the pursuer, a youth (the
eromenos) always the pursued. And while the youth inspires passion in the older male,
the reverse is not the case—nor was it considered proper, since for the youth to allow
himself to feel such desires was considered womanly.

2 (L-P)

out of the heavens (?). 1a

here to me from Crete, to this sacred
temple, where you have a pretty grove
of apple trees, and altars smoking
with incense,   4

here icy water echoes through the apple
boughs, shadows of roses cover
the ground, from shimmering leaves
a heavy sleep descends;   8

here horses graze in a field aflower
with springtime blossoms [4] and breezes
gently glide [
[   ]   12

Then, Kypris, take this garland,
and into our golden cups
pour nectar mingled lusciously
with merriment.   16

---

4. The meadow where horses graze has strong erotic connotations, cf. Anacreon
PMG 346 fr. 1, Alkman P. Oxy. 2443 fr. 1 + 3213.9ff. and generally J.M. Bremmer,
"The meadow of love and two passages in Euripides' *Hippolytus*," *Mnem.* 28 (1975) 268–
280. One may contrast the untouched garden of the maidens in Ibycus *PMG* 286 and
the address of Hippolytus to the virgin goddess Artemis at v.73ff. of Euripides'
Hippolytus: "This woven wreath which I have fashioned / I bring you, lady, from an
unmown meadow / where neither herdsman dares to feed his flock / nor scythe has ever
come, but the bee / in Spring darts across the unmown meadow, / and Reverence tends
it with droplets from the river. / Only those who, not by learning but by nature, / are
ever chaste in all things, / only these may reap the harvest—the wicked are forbidden."

15 (L-P)[5]

Kypris, and may he[6] find you bitter as can be,
and Doricha not boast, telling the tale
of how he came a second time
to the love he longed for.

16 (L-P)

Some say a squadron of horse, some, infantry,
some, ships, are the loveliest thing
on the black earth. But I say
it's what you desire.   4

And it's easy enough to get everyone
to grasp this. For the woman who far surpassed
all women in beauty, Helen, left behind
the very best   8

of husbands, sailed to Troy,
and gave no thought at all to child
or loving parents, but.... led her astray
.   12

. . . .
. . . . lightly . . . . .

---

5. This fragment apparently refers to the relationship between Sappho's brother, Charaxus, and the *hetaira* Doricha. According to Herodotus (2.135), Sappho roundly abused her brother, on his return from Egypt (where Doricha had taken up residence), for his affair with her, evidently because he had been cheated by her out of a large sum of money. Athenaeus (13.596ab) says that Sappho reviled Doricha in her poetry. In any event, here the poetess asks Aphrodite to make sure the pair doesn't get back together.

6. We assume that this refers to Sappho's brother, Charaxus. The gender, however, cannot be determined in the Greek.

reminded me now of Anaktoria
who is elsewhere.   16

I'd rather see her comely step,
the shining luster of her face
than the Lydians' chariots and infantry
in armor.[7]   20

31 (L-P)[8]

He seems to me the equal of the gods,
that man, who sits with you
face to face and, near you, listens closely
to your lilting voice,   4

your tempting laugh, which sets
my heart a-flutter in my breast.
For when I see you even a moment, I can't
speak any longer,   8

but my tongue goes mute...., a sudden, slender
flame invades my flesh,
my eyes go dark, my ears
are roaring,   12

cold sweat covers me, a trembling
seizes all my body, paler than grass
am I, and little short of dead
I seem to myself   16

but I must bear it all, since....even a poor man
....

---

7. Lydia was a kingdom on the western coast of Asia Minor.
8. This poem was adapted by Catullus (poem 51).

36 (L-P)

I yearn and go searching

47 (L-P)

Eros shakes up my heart
like a mountain wind smashing into oaks

48 (L-P)

you came, and I was looking for you
and you cooled my breast aflame with lust.

94 (L-P)

. . . .
and I frankly wish I were dead.
She left me sobbing   2

streams and told me this:
"God, what awful things we've been through,
Sappho. Really, I'm leaving you against my will."   5

And I answered her like this:
"Go, goodbye and remember
me; for you know how we looked after you.   8

If not, then I want
to make you remember[. . . (.)] . [. . (.)] . . . .
. . [   ] and we've been through beautiful things   11

..[   ]you put on so many wreaths
of violets and of roses
and of....by my side,   14

and many woven garlands
made.... of blossoms
around your supple neck   17

and ...with exquisite
myrrh................
that a queen could use, you anointed......   20

and on plush beds
the supple ....
you'd satisfy your longing for   23

and there was no..... nor any
shrine ....
where we didn't go,   26

no sacred grove.[....]no dance
                    ]rattling
                    ]........   29

96 (L-P)

........Sardis[9]...
.....often here in her thoughts   2

as though......we........
she (honored?) you like a goddess
plain to see and took the greatest pleasure in your song. 5

---

9. Sardis was a city in central Lydia, a kingdom in western Asia Minor.

But now she stands out among the Lydian women
just as, at sun-
set, the rosy fingered moon   8

surpasses all the stars; it casts its light
alike on the salt sea,
the blossoming fields,   11

and the dew is scattered in beauty and
the roses bloom and the delicate
chervil and flowery melilote.   14

But wandering back and forth, she often
remembers gentle Atthis, and her fragile heart
is consumed with blanching desire.   17

To go there we.... this not
to our minds............... much
sings.............. in the middle   20

It isn't easy for us to match
the comely form of
goddesses....but you would have....   23

....
....
and............. Aphrodite   26

..........poured nectar from
a golden.................
...........in her hands Persuasion   29

102 (L-P)

Sweet mother, I just can't weave the web.
I'm mastered by longing for a boy[10] because of slender Aphrodite.

105a (L-P)

As the sweet-apple reddens on the top-most branch,
the very tip of the top-most, and the apple pickers had forgotten it;
no, not forgotten; they couldn't reach it.[11]

111 (L-P)

Up with the roof—
Hymenaios!—
carpenters, heave it high—
Hymenaios!—
the groom is coming in, the equal of Ares,
more massive than a massive man.[12]

---

10. The Greek is of indeterminate gender and could mean "girl."

11. According to an ancient source, it is a girl who is here compared to an apple. And the meter—dactylic hexameter—suggests that the fragment belonged to Sappho's book of *Epithalamia*, or wedding songs (cf. Page, *op. cit.* pp.72–73, 119–122). Winkler explains "why apples were a prominent symbol in courtship and marriage rites. *Melon* signifies various 'clitoral' objects: the seed vessel of the rose, the tonsil or uvula, a bulge or sty on the lower eyelid, and a swelling on the cornea. The sensitivity of these objects to pressure is one of the bases for the analogy . . . . . The vocabulary and phrasing of this fragment reveal much more than a sexual metaphor, however; they contain a delicate and reverential attitude to the elusive presence-and-absence of women in the world of men" ("Gardens of Nymphs: Public and private in Sappho's lyrics" in *Reflections of Women in Antiquity*, ed. H. Foley [New York 1981] 79).

12. As the invocation of the wedding god, Hymenaios, indicates, this fragment comes from a wedding song, and as was customary on such occasions, the bride and groom were subjected to ribald mockery. Here, a chorus pokes fun at the groom's aroused anticipation.

114 (L-P)

Bride: Virginity, virginity, you've left me, where have you
                                           gone?
Virginity: I'll come to you no more, I'll come no more.

121 (L-P)

But since you are my friend,
take the bed of someone younger.
For I couldn't bear to live
with you if I were the elder.

130–131 (L-P)

Eros, that slackener of limbs, twirls me again—
bittersweet, untamable, crawling thing.

But you, Atthis, hate the thought of me,
and go flying off to Andromeda

134 (L-P)

in a dream I spoke with you, Kyprogeneia [13]

146 (L-P)

for me, neither the honey nor the bee [14]

---

13. A cult-epithet of Aphrodite meaning "born on Cyprus."
14. The sense seems to be that the speaker wants neither love's sweetness nor its bitter sting.

80   SAPPHO

168 B (Voigt = Adespota PMG 976)

The moon has set
and the Pleiades, it's mid-
night, the hours go by.
I sleep alone.

IBYCUS

Born at Rhegium in southern Italy, Ibycus worked in the second half of the 6th cent. B.C. We know little about his life except that, like his contemporary Anacreon, he went to Samos to work at the court of the tyrant Polykrates, who ruled 533–522 B.C. It is unclear whether Ibycus' poems are choral or monodic. His association with Anacreon on Samos may suggest that the latter is the case in at least some of his poems.

PMG 282 + SLG 151[1]

and they crushed Dardanian Priam's
city, great, far-famed, and prosperous,
starting out from Argos
urged by the will of mighty Zeus,   4

for the sake of fair-haired Helen's beauty
engaging in the oft-sung struggle
of a tearful war.
And ruin scaled long-suffering Pergamon,
because of golden haired Kypris.   9

---

1. While this lengthy fragment consists mostly of a catalogue of martial themes from the Trojan war, the speaker insists that he does *not* really want to deal with these (v. 10ff.). They function rather as foil to the central point, which comes only at the poem's culmination: praise for the good looks of a certain Polykrates (perhaps the tyrant), whose physical beauty is put on a par with the most beautiful heroes at Troy, including Troilos. Triadic in structure (i.e. consisting of strophe, antistrophe, and epode), the fragment begins in an antistrophe—we are thus missing at least one strophe (4 verses), if not more. Perhaps the erotic theme was also prominent in the opening of the poem, now lost to us.

But now it's not Paris, who tricked his host,
nor Cassandra with her slender ankles
that I desire to sing,
or Priam's other children   13

or the unspeakable day when
Troy with its towering gates was taken; nor even
the haughty excellence of the heroes
whom the tightly fitted   17

hollow ships carried,
Troy's demise, those noble heroes
whom lord Agamemnon
ruled, the Pleisthenid king,[2] leader of men,
child sprung from noble Atreus.   22

These are things the expert Muses,
Heliconians, could easily take on,
but no man who lives and dies
could tell one by one   26

of all the ships that came
from Aulis, crossing the Aegean sea from Argos
on to Troy
teeming with horses, the men   30

with bronze shields, sons of the Achaeans,
among whom the greatest man with a spear
was swift-footed Achilleus
and Telamonian Aias, huge and valiant
.   35

---

2. Pleisthenes seems to have been a son of Pelops, and thus an ancestor of Agamemnon.

84   IBYCUS

.......the most beautiful]from Argos

........Kyanippos]to Ilium

..............]

..............].[.].   39

...Zeuxippos whom] Hyllis
with her golden sash gave birth to.[3] Troilos seemed
as much like him
to the Trojans and Danaans   43

as thrice-cleaned gold's like brass—
so alluring was his form.
And along with them, from now on you,
Polycrates, shall have the imperishable fame for beauty
proper to song and to my fame.   48

PMG 286

In Spring Cydonian
quince trees flower, watered by the sluice
of streams, where the Maidens'
untrimmed garden stands,[4] and vineshoots
rise and bloom beneath the shading branches
of the vine. But for me desire
knows no season of rest:
ablaze with lightning—
a Thracian north wind—
        swooping from Kypris with
            searing frenzies, black, unabashed
he brutally wrenches my heart
at the root.

---

3. Zeuxippos may have been king of Sikyon during the Trojan war.
4. See note on Sappho fr.2 (L-P) verse 10.

PMG 287

Once more Eros, under darkened
    lids, fixing me with his melting gaze,
drives me with every kind of spell into the
    tangling nets of Kypris.
And yes, I tremble at his coming,
as a horse who's borne the yoke and won the prize, but aging now,
when hitched to the speeding chariot, goes to the race against his
                                           will.

PMG 288

Euryalus, sprung from the blue eyed Graces,
darling of those with the dazzling tresses,
Kypris and gentle-eyed Persuasion
nursed you among the blossoms of the rose.

ANACREON

Anacreon (ca.570–485 B.C.), the great poet of solo lyric or "monody" for the *symposium*, came from the Ionian city of Teos in Asia Minor. He fled together with his countrymen before the advancing Persians (ca.545), and settled with them in their newly founded colony of Abdera in Thrace. Thereafter, he worked in Samos at the court of the tyrant Polykrates (who ruled ca.533–522). When Polykrates was swept from power, Hipparchus, the son of the Athenian tyrant Peisistratus, sent a ship to fetch Anacreon to Athens, and there he joined such other musical luminaries as Simonides and Lasus of Hermione, who had likewise been invited by Hipparchus. Together with these, he probably contributed to the literary flowering in Athens that culminated in the development of tragedy, cf. J. Herington, *Poetry into Drama* (Berkeley 1985) 92–95, 110–111.

Elegy 2 (West)

I don't kiss the guy[1] who guzzles wine beside the brimming bowl
    and talks battles and tearful war,
but the one who mingles dazzling gifts of the Muses and Aphrodite
    singing of lusty play.

PMG 346 fr.1

. . . .
but your heart trembles before another man,
O pretty child.   3

---

1. These words are usually rendered in a more neutral way: "I have no love for the man who. . . ." (Fränkel), "I have no liking for one who. . . ." (Gentili), or the like. We feel, however, that the Greek, *ou phileo, hos*. . . ., can sustain the more erotic

87

...........thinks
she is raising you among the lilies
as a sensible girl, but you......have slipped off   6

to the fields of hyacinth
where Kypris has unharnessed
her horses and hitched them on a rope.   9)

And you have burst.......into the middle
........exciting the hearts
of many citizens,   12

Herotima, whom all men ride.

fr.4

....I was fighting with a tough.....
....now I see....and raise my head.....
...deeply thankful
that I got away from love...
...completely, ...from stubborn bonds....
.....by Aphrodite.....
....bring wine.....
....bring water....
.....call ....

PMG 347

and of the hair that
shaded your delicate neck.

---

translation we have given it. If we are correct, this may be one of the rare instances in
which we hear the voice of the *eromenos* (cf. n. on Theognis 1097–1100).

But now your hair is cropped.
It fell into rude hands
and tumbled into the black dust
in a heap

patiently abiding the slash
of the knife. But I am worn away
with distress. For what can one do....

PMG 357

O lord, with whom Eros the subduer
and the dark-eyed nymphs
and glistening Aphrodite
join in play, you who roam
the high crests of the mountains,
I kneel and beg you, come to me
kindly, hear my prayer,
and may it please you:
Give wise counsel
to Kleoboulos, get him,
Dionysus, to accept my love.[2]

PMG 358

Once more Eros of the golden hair
hits me with his purple ball,
calls me out to play with the girl

---

2. The prayer to Dionysus may indicate a sympotic setting, and the underlying assumption may be that if Kleoboulos gets sufficiently drunk (i.e. accepts Dionysus' counsel) he will yield to the speaker. The speaker's request receives an added twist with a play on the name Kleoboulos ("famed for counsel"). Anacreon thus humorously appropriates the dignified, formal language of prayer to voice his hopes for a drunken seduction.

with the flashy slippers.
But she, since she comes from noble
Lesbos, scoffs at my hair,
since it's white, and gapes
for another girl.[3]

PMG 359

For Kleoboulos I yearn,
of Kleoboulos I rave,
at Kleoboulos I gaze.

PMG 360

Boy with the girlish glance
I pursue you, but you won't listen,
you don't know that you hold the reins
of my soul.

PMG 376

Flung once more from the cliffs of
Leukas, I plunge into the foaming wave, drunk on love.

---

3. The interpretation of the girl's rejection of the speaker is much disputed. Our translation reflects what we consider the most probable solution, i.e. that the girl is attracted to another female. This is, however, in no way connected with the fact that she is from Lesbos. As Dover points out, " 'Lesbian' did not, in his (sc. Anacreon's) time or at any other time in antiquity, have a primary connotation of homosexuality" (*Greek Homosexuality* [New York 1978] 183); it connoted sexual aggressivity and shamelessness, and the verb *lesbiazein* could mean to "fellate." Another possibility is that the (feminine) "other" that the girl gapes at can, in the Greek, take the (feminine) noun "hair" as its antecedent. In this case, the girl would reject the speaker's white hair for "another" (scil. younger man's) head of hair; or, if the poet is playing on the

PMG 389

Girl, since you're sweet to strangers, give a thirsty fellow a drink.

PMG 396

Bring water, bring wine, boy, bring us blossoming
garlands, bring them, so I can box with Eros.

PMG 398

The dice that Eros plays with
are raving madness and battle din.

PMG 400

Running away from love,
I slipped back to Pythomandros—again.

PMG 413

Once more, like a blacksmith, Eros battered me with his huge
axe, and doused me in an icy torrent.

PMG 414

But you cut the flawless blossom of your delicate hair.

Lesbian reputation for fellation, the girl might prefer the dark (pubic) hair of another,
younger man.

PMG 417

Thracian filly, why do you eye me with mistrust
and stubbornly run away, and think that I'm unskilled?
Rest assured, I could fit you deftly with a bridle
and, holding the reins, could steer you past the end posts of our
course.
Now as it is, you graze the fields and frisk in childish play
since you lack a rider with a practiced hand at horsemanship.

PMG 428

I love again, and do not love;
I am insane, and still I'm sane.

THEOGNIS
THE "SECOND BOOK"

These elegies, all of them pederastic in content, have come down to us as the "2nd Book" of Theognis of Megara, a poet of the mid-6th cent. B.C. According to the Suda, a late antique encyclopedia, they were originally interspersed in the rest of Theognis' works. When they were segregated, however, is a matter of dispute—perhaps it was done by a moralistic Byzantine scholar, perhaps somewhat earlier. Apart from introductory and closing elegies on the power of Eros and Aphrodite respectively, the poems are unified by little more than the persistent address to the "boy." A memorable poem on the power of song, in the "1st Book" of Theognis (v. 237ff.), suggests that they were sung at *symposia* (i.e. "drinking parties") to the accompaniment of a simple flute melody, and that they circulated at such occasions throughout Greece: "I have given you wings with which you can fly over the boundless sea and all the earth, borne up effortlessly. You will be present at all feasts and revels, will be on the lips of many; and to the tune of clear-sounding pipes handsome youths will sing you sweet and clear in unison. . . . the radiant gifts of the violet-wreathed Muses will propel you. You'll belong to all who love song, both now and in the future, as long as the earth and sun exist—still, I don't get the slightest respect from you, but you trick me with words as if I were a little boy." The relationship between (male) lover and (male) beloved—*erastes* and *eromenos* in Greek—is likewise entirely in keeping with the pedagogical ideals of the Greek aristocracy as embodied in the *symposium*: only the elder male speaks (persuading, warning, instructing, cajoling, reprimanding, etc. in short, controlling the discourse); the "boy"—the addressee in most of these poems—is left (almost) voiceless.[1]

Following the poems of the "2nd Book," we add some remaining erotic elegies of Theognis which have been transmitted within the body of the "1st Book." (See Introduction, pp. 21–36.)

------

1. Cf. vv. 1097–1100.

1231–1234

Merciless Eros, the Frenzies cradled you and gave you suck,
    because of you Troy's citadel was crushed,
Theseus, great son of Aigeus, was crushed, and Aias crushed,
    the noble son of Oileus, by your recklessness.[2]

1235–1238

Boy, my passion's master, listen. I'll tell no tale
    that's unpersuasive or unpleasant to your heart.
Just try to grasp my words with your mind. There is no need
    for you to do what's not to your liking.

1238a–1240

Don't leave the friend you have to find another,
    yielding to the words of vulgar men.
You know, they'll often lie to me about you,
    to you about me. Don't listen to them.

1241–1242

You'll take pleasure in this love that's gone,
    and that one will elude your mastery.

---

2. Significantly, Eros is seen as a dangerous, socially disruptive force. Paris' abduction of Helen, the cause of the Trojan war, violated the norms of guest-friendship and marriage; Theseus tried, together with Perithoos, to rape the queen of the underworld, Persephone, thereby overstepping the line between mortal and immortal, living and dead, as well as the sanctity of marriage; Aias raped Apollo's priestess, Cassandra, thus incurring the god's wrath. Cf. J.M. Lewis, "Eros and the Polis in Theognis Book II," in T.J. Figueira and G. Nagy, eds., *Theognis of Megara* (Baltimore 1985) 210–211.

1243–1244

Let's love long. Then go be with others.
    You are a trickster, fidelity's antitype.

1245–1246

Water and fire will never mix. And we shall never be
    true to each other and kind.

1247–1248

Think about my hatred, and the crime. Know in your gut
    that I will pay you for this wrong as I am able.

1249–1252

Boy, you're like a horse. Just now sated with seed,
    you've come back to my stable,
yearning for a good rider, fine meadow,
    an icy spring, shady groves.

1253–1254

Happy the man who's got boys for loving and single-foot horses,
    hunting dogs and friends in foreign lands.

1255–1256

The man who doesn't love boys and single-foot horses
    and dogs, his heart will never know pleasure.

1257–1258

Boy, you're like those adrift in risks,
   your mood now friendly to some, now others.

1259–1262

Boy, you were born good-looking, but your head
   is crowned with stupidity.
In your brain is lodged the character of a kite, always veering,
   bending to the words of other men.

1263–1266

Boy, you paid back a bad exchange for kindness.
   No thanks from you for favors.
You've never given me pleasure. And though I've often
   been kind to you, I never won your respect.

1267–1270

Boy and horse, a similar brain: the horse
   doesn't cry when its rider lies in the dust;
no, it takes on the next man, once it's sated with seed.
   Same with a boy: whoever's there he loves.

1271–1274

Boy, your slutting around has wrecked my affection,
   you've become a disgrace to our friends.
You dried my hull for a while. But I've slipped out of the squall
   and found a port as night came on.

1275–1278

Eros, too, rises in season, when the earth
    swells and blooms with Spring flowers.
Then Eros leaves Cyprus, that lovely island,
    and goes among men, scattering seed on the ground.

1278a-b

Whoever offered you advice about me, also urged you
    to leave behind our love and go your way.

1279–1282

I won't mistreat you, even if the deathless gods
    would treat me better, pretty boy.
And I don't sit in judgment on petty errors.
    Pretty boys get away with doing wrong.

1283–1294

Boy, don't wrong me—I still want to
    please you—listen graciously to this:
you won't outstrip me, cheat me with your tricks.
    Right now you've won and have the upper hand,
but I'll wound you while you flee,[3] as they say
    the virgin daughter of Iasios,
though ripe, rejected wedlock with a man
    and fled; girding herself, she acted pointlessly,
abandoning her father's house, blond Atalanta.
    She went off to the soaring mountain peaks,

---

3. West translates: "yet I will prick you from behind" (*Studies* p. 166).

fleeing the lure of wedlock, golden Aphrodite's
   gift. But she learned the point she'd so rejected.[4]

1295–1298

Boy, don't stir my heart with rotten anguish,
   don't let your love whisk me off
to Persephone's halls. Beware the anger of the gods
   and men's talk. Think gentle thoughts.

1299–1304

Boy, how long will you be on the run? I'm following,
   tracking you down. I only wish I'd reach the end
of your anger. But you, lusting and headstrong,
   run off reckless as a kite.
Stop now, do me a favor. You won't
   hang on to the gift of Kypris, violet-wreathed, much longer.

1305–1310

Knowing in your heart that boyhood's bloom, for all its loveliness,
   is quicker than a sprint around the track, seeing this,

---

4. These verses seem to conflate two versions of the Atalanta story: v. 1286 seems to allude to the story in Hyginus (*Fab.* 185) according to which Atalanta, spurning marriage, competed with her suitors in a footrace in which she chased them with a spear and killed all who were not as swift as she. Ultimately she was bested in the race by Milanion, who scattered golden apples of the Hesperides in her path, which she could not resist stopping to pick up. On this interpretation, our speaker appears initially to adopt the role of Atalanta, wielding her spear in pursuit ("I'll wound you while you flee"). The remainder of the passage, however, tells of how Atalanta tried to escape marriage by fleeing into the mountains, thus equating the *eromenos* with Atalanta.

undo these bonds. You may be bound someday, wild boy,
   when you get to the harder parts of love,
like me now with you. So be careful
   or you could be undone by a bad boy.

1311–1316

You haven't fooled me, boy—I'm on your trail—
   you've stolen off to your new fast friends,
and thrown my love away in scorn.
   But you were no friend of theirs before.
No, out of them all, I thought it was you I'd made a trusted
   mate. And now you hold another love.

1317–1318

I, who served you well, am laid low. Looking at you
   no one on earth would want to love a boy.

1319–1322

Boy, since the goddess Kypris gave you a lusty
   grace, and your beauty's every boy's concern,
listen to these words and for my sake take them to heart—
   knowing how hard it is for a man to bear desire.

1323–1326

Cyprian, end these pains, scatter the cares
   that eat my soul, turn me back to merriment.
End this awful anxiety, be merciful,
   and let me act wisely now that my youth is gone.

1327–1334

Boy, as long as your cheek is smooth, I'll never
   stop praising you, not even if I have to die.
For you to give still is fine, for me there's no shame in asking,
   since I'm in love. At your knees...I beg,
respect me, boy, give pleasure, if you're ever
   to have the gift of Kypris with her wreath of violets,
when it's you who's wanting and approach another. May the goddess
   grant that you get exactly the same response.

1335–1336

Happy the lover who has a work-out when he gets home
   sleeping all day with a beautiful boy.

1337–1338

I no longer love the boy, I've kicked away terrible pains
   and fled in joy from crushing sorrows.

1339–1340

I've been freed from desire by Kythereia of the lovely wreath.
   Boy, you hold no charm for me at all.

1341–1344

Ah me, I love a smooth-skinned boy, who flaunts me—
   though I'm unwilling—to every friend.

I'll put up with not hiding—much is forced on my will.
   I'm revealed, tamed by a boy not unworthy.

1345–1350

It's a thrill to love a boy: even Kronos' son,
   king of immortals, once longed for Ganymede,
snatched him, brought him to Olympos and made him
   a god with the lovely bloom of boyhood.
So, Simonides, don't be amazed if I too
   am revealed, tamed by love for a gorgeous boy.

1351–1352

Boy, don't go reveling, heed an old man
   reveling's not good for a young man.

1353–1356

It's bitter and sweet, alluring and tough,
   the yen for youths, Kyrnos—until you get what you want.
'cause if you get, it gets sweet; but if you pursue
   and don't get, it's the painfullest thing of all. [5]

1357–1360

Always, for lovers of boys, the yoke on the neck lies
   none too light, a chafing mark of welcome;

---

5. An early reference to "blue balls"?

for as you labor at the boy, you've got to coax him into love
  as you would a hand into a fire of vine-twigs.[6]

1361–1362

A ship, you struck a rock and missed my love's haven,
  boy, laid hold of a rotten hawser.

1363–1364

I'll never hurt you, even when I'm gone; and no one
  will talk me out of loving you.

1365–1366

Prettiest, most desirable of boys—
  stick around and listen to me a bit.

1367–1368

There's beauty in a boy. But to a woman, no one's a true
  mate. She always loves the one that's there.

1369–1372

Boy-love's fine to have, fine to get rid of;
  much easier to find than to satisfy.

------

6. The final couplet may also be rendered thus: "for you know, you must, if you labor at a boy for his love, / more or less put your hand into a fire of vine-leaves."

A thousand ills depend on it, a thousand goods,
   but even in this there's a certain charm.

1373–1374

You've never waited for my sake, no, you always
   chase eagerly after every message.

1375–1376

Happy the lover of boys who doesn't know the sea
   and worry, there on the waves, about the coming night.

1377–1380

Being good-looking and loving vice, you hang out with worthless
   men, and for this you get ugly reproaches,
boy. But though I lost your love against my will,
   I've won, can act like a free man.

1381–1385

Men thought you came with the gift of the golden
   Cyprian.[7] Yet the gift of the violet wreathed
can be the hardest load men have
   if the Cyprian doesn't give hardship some relief.

---

7. Many editors indicate a lacuna at this point due, perhaps, to the harshness of
the asyndeton and their difficulty in making sense of the poem as it stands. While
acknowledging the problem of the asyndeton, we feel that our rendering is by no means
impossible.

1386–1389

Cyprian Kythereia with your web of cunning, Zeus did you honor
    by giving you this transcendant gift:
you master men's clever minds, and there is none
    so strong and skilled that he can flee.

EROTIC ELEGIES FROM THE
"FIRST BOOK" OF THEOGNIS

87–90

Don't caress me with words, your heart and mind in another place,
    if you love me and your heart is true.
Love me with a pure heart or renounce me,
    start a fight, hate me openly.

257–260[8]

I'm a lovely mare, a racer, but I carry
    the worst man, and this really pains me.
Yes, I've often thought of breaking the bridle
    and running away, flinging that bad rider down.

263–266

In this girl's home, I guess, her dear folks drink cold water,
    'cause she often goes to draw it, moaning for me as she takes it.
Then and there I grab the girl's middle, kiss
    her neck, and a faint cry sounds on her lips.

---

8. This is one of the few instances in the Theognidea where the speaker is female (the others are 579ff. and 861–864—the latter not included in our selection; outside of this anthology see also Alcaeus 10 L-P, and Anacreon *PMG* 385). The words "I've often thought of breaking the bridle..." suggest that the relationship is long-term, i.e. that this is the complaint of a *hetaira*. For the conception of the female as horse, cf. Anacreon *PMG* 417. For the male *eromenos* as horse cf. 1249–1252 and 1267–1270.

371–372

Don't drive me back⁹ to the wagon, pricking hard—I won't go,
  Kyrnos, though you drag me all too deeply into your love.

457–460

A young woman isn't right for an old man,
  she won't respond to the rudder like a boat,
anchors won't hold her, she'll often break
  the ropes, find another harbor in the night.

579–584¹⁰

I hate a cheating man, yet still I've come—veiled,
  lightheaded as a little bird.
I hate a wandering woman, or a greedy man
  who wants to plow another's field.
But what is past can't possibly be
  undone; we must look to what will come.

599–602

No you didn't fool me—wandering down the road
  where you used to ride, defrauding our love.

---

9. The word "back" is not present in the text, but we consider it likely that this poem refers to a boy's attempt to get his lover back. On the interpretation of these lines cf. Introduction, pp. 31–35.

10. Despite the objections of West, *Studies* p.156, we think it likely that these verses are a dialogue (cf. Horace 3.9). The first couplet is spoken by a woman who, though she knows better (her shame is revealed by her wearing a veil), has decided to return to a man who betrayed her. In the second couplet the man's replies, accusing

Get out! The gods hate you, men can't trust you.
   That snake in your lap turned out to be shifty and cold.

695–696

I can't give you everything you want, heart,
   be patient. You're not the only lover of pretty boys.

949–954

I grabbed a fawn from a deer, as a lion sure of his power
   runs one down; but I didn't drink its blood.
I scaled the tops of the walls, but didn't sack the town;
   yoked the horses, but did not mount the chariot;
I did it, but didn't do it; got there, but didn't get;
   I acted, yet didn't act; made it, and didn't make it.

959–962

While I alone was drinking from that deepwater spring
   the water seemed to me sweet and fine.
But now it's muddied, the water's mingled with water—
   I'll drink from another spring, or stream.

---

her of infidelity in turn (though one might take his comment about the "greedy man"
as an admission of his own fault rather than a hit at the woman's lover). The third
couplet may be spoken once again by the woman, since after all it was she who made
the gesture of returning. But one might also take it as a continuation of the man's
speech, or even as spoken by both characters.

1045–1046

Yes, by Zeus, even if any of them is under the covers asleep,
    he'll readily receive our reveling.[11]

1063–1070

In youth you can sleep the night through with a friend,
    unloading the desire for lusty action,
and you can go wooing and sing to a flute-girl's tune—
    no other thing is more thrilling than these
for men and women. What are wealth and honor to me?
    Pleasure conquers all—and merrily.
Mindless men and fools weep for the dying
    instead of the blossom of youth that's falling.

1070a–b

Take your pleasure, heart. Soon other men will
    be; and I, dead, shall be dark earth.

1091–1094

My heart's in pain because of my love of you,
    for I can't either hate or love,
knowing it's hard when a man's your friend
    to hate him, and hard to love him if he doesn't want.

---

11. The word *komos*, which we render here as "reveling" can elsewhere indicate a
wooing song (cf. v. 1065).

1097–1100[12]

Already I've risen up on wings like a bird
    from a great marsh, leaving a rotten man behind,
breaking the bond. And you, who've lost my love,
    will know one day how wise I was.

_____

12. This is the only poem we have been able to find in which it is fairly certain that the *eromenos* addresses the *erastes*. One might, however, also consider Anacreon Elegy 2 (West).

HIPPONAX

After Archilochus, Hipponax was the most famous exponent of "iambic" or "blame" poetry in the Archaic period. He worked in the latter part of the 6th century B.C. and is known for his use of the "choliambic" or "limping" iamb, which varies the traditional iamb by having each line drag to a close usually with three long syllables (x-ᵕ- x-ᵕ- x- - -): a "deliberate metrical ribaldry, in keeping with these iambographers' studied vulgarity" (West, *Greek Metre* [Oxford 1982] 41). Hipponax' special targets of abuse were a woman called Arete, and two brothers, the sculptors Boupalos and Athenis. The story goes that these sculptors made a statue of Hipponax which brutally emphasized his ugliness. Hipponax consequently retaliated by subjecting them to such scathing abuse in his poems that he drove them to hang themselves.

18 (Degani) = 15 (West)

Why have you shacked up with that wretched Boupalos?

20 (Degani) = 12 (West)

tricking the children of the Erythraians that way,
Boupalos, that mother-fucker, with Arete
....about to pull back his ill-famed foreskin [1]

---

1. We read <d>arton at the end of v.3 with Masson.

23 (Degani) = 16 (West)

But with a bird of good omen
I came at dusk and bivouacked with Arete

24 (Degani) = 17 (West)

for Arete stooped over me by lamplight and

34 (Degani) = 21 (West)

she demands eight obols to give him a peck on his prick

69 (Degani) = 70.1–10 (West)

. . . .

this enemy of the gods, who plunders   7
his mother's pussy while she sleeps

86 (Degani) = 84 (West)

and came
. . . . .
of pennyroyal
a]nd he told me[
].....[5
].....[
. . . . .
. . . . .
(spitting) on the ground[
stripping[10
we bit and we ki[ssed

peering through the doors
so he wouldn't catch us
naked
and she was eager   15
and I began fucking[   ]and[
drawing it out to the tip, as one dries a sausage,
saying Boupalos should go hang
and suddenly she unstrung (?) me and I overflowed (?)
but we really kept at our work   20
I like a shriveled sail . . [
to slit open . . . . [. . . . . . .]

95 (Degani) = 92 (West)[2]

and speaking in Lydian, she said "Bring . . . . here," [3]
in Arsish, "the ass [,"
and pulling (?) my balls [
she thrashed them with a branch, like a scapegoat's
. . . .] by a two-pronged stick   5
and so (I was racked?) with a double torment,
and the branch scraped (?) me from the other side [
she fell on me from above, which made [my ass hole
drip with turds [

---

2. As K. Latte ("Hipponacteum," *Hermes* 64 [1929] 385–388 = Kl. Schr. [Munich 1968] 464–467) was the first to see, this fragment seems to depict a magic rite to cure impotence, similar to that portrayed in Petronius' *Satyrikon* ch. 138. There, the priestess Oenothea treats Encolpius, the narrator, for his impotence by shoving into his anus a leather dildo dipped in oil, peppers, and crushed nettles, then scourging his nether parts with nettles. In Hipponax, it is likewise a woman who administers the treatment, though the scourging apparently comes first, and the inserted branch causes the narrator to become incontinent.

3. The woman's words in this line are Lydian perhaps because "foreign words are appropriate to spells," as M.L. West suggests, *Studies* p. 144.

and the outhouse reeked; and whirring dung-beetles   10
zoomed in towards the stench, more than fifty;
some attacked [my
and knocked me down; others tore at [my balls (?)
and others rattled (?) the doors in attack

PINDAR

The Boeotian poet, Pindar (ca. 522–ca. 438 B.C.), is known today almost exclusively for his victory odes on aristocratic competitors in the great panhellenic games. Only these poems have come down to us intact. But the two fragmentary encomia included here make one wish more survived on other topics. In the first we find an amusing incongruity between Pindar's customarily elevated style and a subject that tests the resources of a praise-poet: for Pindar must celebrate the dedication by Xenophon of Corinth of a hundred new temple-prostitutes at the shrine of Aphrodite in Corinth—an aspect of the goddess' cult probably taken over from that of the Near Eastern goddess Ishtar, and by no means universal in Greek worship of Aphrodite, cf. W. Burkert, *Griechische Religion der archaischen und klassischen Epoche* (Stuttgart 1977) 239 n.9. Xenophon had promised this lavish dedication—essentially a gift of 100 female slaves—if victorious in the Olympic games of 468 B.C. He won both the footrace and pentathlon, victories commemorated by Pindar in his *Olympian Ode* 13.

122 (Snell-Maehler): Encomium for Xenophon of Corinth

All-welcoming girls, handmaids
of Persuasion in opulent Corinth,
who burn the yellow tears of pale
frankincense, flitting frequently in your thoughts
to heavenly Aphrodite,
mother of the Loves,

you, O daughters, may reap
the harvest of soft youth

115

blamelessly upon alluring beds.
All is fair in constraint......

* * *

But I wonder what the masters of the Isthmus
will say of me for finding such a prologue to my honied song
that opens with women who open to all.

We prove gold on a pure touchstone

* * *

O lady of Cyprus, here into your grove
Xenophon, cheered by answered prayers, has driven
a hundred-head herd of grazing girls.

123 (Snell-Maehler): Encomium for Theoxenos of Tenedos

You must harvest desires at just the right moment, heart, at
        just the right age.
But any man who has seen
the dazzling rays
of Theoxenos' eyes and does not swell with longing
has a black heart forged of adamant or iron

in an icy flame. Disgraced by Aphrodite of the roving gaze,
either he struggles for money with all his might,
or, a slave to female arrogance,

is towed down every path. But me,
I melt at her urging[1] like wax

of sacred bees stung by sunlight, whenever I see
the fresh young limbs of boys. Yes, on Tenedos too
Persuasion and Charm are at home
in the son of Hagesilas.[2]

---

1. i.e. at Aphrodite's urging.
2. i.e. Theoxenos.

BACCHYLIDES

A nephew of the poet Simonides, Bacchylides was born ca. 510 B.C. on the island of Keos and died ca. 450. He was Pindar's contemporary and rival (we possess odes which the two composed for the tyrant Hieron of Syracuse in celebration of the same Olympic victory: Bacchylides 5 and Pindar *Olympian* 1). Little was known of Bacchylides work until the spectacular recovery *en bloc* of substantial fragments of fourteen victory odes and six dithyrambs in a single papyrus published in 1897. The encomium printed below appeared somewhat later in Oxyrhynchus papyri (11, 1361 and 17, 2081). It is for Alexander, king of Macedonia from 498–454, and known as "philhellene" because he was the first Macedonian ruler to promote Greek literature and arts actively in his country. We know that he competed in the Olympic games (Hdt. 5.23) and invited Greek poets such as Simonides, Pindar, and Bacchylides to his court.

20B (Snell-Maehler): Encomium for Alexander, son of Amyntas

Lyre, dangle no longer from the peg
stifling the clear song of the seven chords;
come here to my hands. I long to send some
golden wing of the Muses to Alexander

and his drinking mates, some glory for the time
when the sweet compulsion of the
rippling cups heats up the tender heart of the young
and expectations of Love send shivers through the mind

mingled with Dionysiac gifts;
it makes a man's thoughts soar to the heights:

at a stroke he razes the ramparts of cities,
imagines himself monarch of humanity;

his houses glitter with gold and ivory,
wheat-bearing ships on the shimmering sea
deliver endless wealth from Egypt;
such are the stirrings of the drinker's heart.

O son of mighty[   ]Amyntas
. . . .
. . . . .for what greater gain is there
for men than indulging the heart in beautiful things. . . . .

MISCELLANEOUS LYRIC AND INSCRIPTIONS

CEG 454: The Ischia Cup (ca.730–720 B.C.)

Nestor's cup was quite a swill.
Whoever drinks from *this* one will at once be seized
by the need for Aphrodite of the lovely wreath.[1]

PMG 853: Anonymous (Locrian Song)

What's wrong with you? Don't give us away, I beg you;
before he comes, get up
so he doesn't beat you to a pulp
and me, too—poor me.
It's already day. The light
through the door, don't you see it?

PMG 872: Anonymous

Throw out age, throw it out
O gorgeous Aphrodite.

---

1. This, one of the earliest Greek metrical inscriptions, already presumes some familiarity with the Homeric tradition: In book 11 of the *Iliad* (v.631–636) we learn that Nestor had a huge, four-handled cup adorned with doves, which a normal man could barely lift when it was full, but which Nestor—even at his advanced age— handled with ease. In the Ischia cup we may, perhaps, already have an implicit rejection of martial epic in favor of love-themes such as we see in Sappho 16, Anacreon El.2 (West), Ibycus *PMG* 282, Stesichorus *PMG* 210, Xenophanes B1 (West), etc. (the latter two not in this book).

PMG 873: Anonymous

Boys, you have charm and noble fathers,
don't refuse to give good men a share of your youth.
For limb-melting Love blossoms with manliness
in the town of the Chalcideans.

PMG 900: Anonymous[2]

I wish I were a lovely ivory harp
and lovely boys would wear me to the Dionysian dance.

PMG 901: Anonymous

I wish I were a hunk of unsmelted gold[3]
and a lovely woman would wear me next to her pure heart.

PMG 904: Anonymous

The pussy longs to lap the cream, whichever she's got on hand;
and I to lap the pretty girl, whichever I've got on hand.[4]

---

2. This couplet and the next may be an example of the sympotic custom whereby one participant responded to or countered a theme raised by the preceding one, cf. Vetta pp.28–31.

3. i.e. unpurified gold.

4. The couplet is almost untranslatable. It may be rendered literally as "the sow longs to take the acorn, whichever one it's got; and I long to take the pretty girl, whichever one I've got." But "sow" is slang for the female genitals, and "acorn" for the *glans penis* or head of the penis ("glans" is Latin for acorn). The verb "to take" is often used in a sexual sense. In order to catch the force of the original's double-entendre, we have had to substitute one of *our* culture's sexual metaphors for one of theirs. We have done so, however, at a price: for the speaker's desire to "lap the pretty girl," while catching the sound of the Greek verb *labein*, introduces a reference to cunnilingus—an activity which, on the whole, the Greeks considered taboo.

PMG 905: Anonymous

Whore and bath-man, two of a kind:
in a single sink they soak both good and bad.

CEG 400: Inscription on phallus-shaped stone in Antipolis
(ca.450–425?)

I'm thrilled to be the staff[5] of the goddess, holy Aphrodite;
may Kypris return the favor to those who erected me.

CEG 441: Inscription in Attica (480–450?)

It's lovely to look at Antinoos, a thrill to talk with him.

---

5. Literally "the servant."

HERMESIANAX

A poet and scholar from Colophon, Hermesianax can be situated early in the Hellenistic era, around 300 B.C. since he was reputed to have been a friend and student of the scholar-poet Philitas of Kos. The long fragment which follows comes from the 3rd book of his *Leontion*, an elegy addressed to his beloved of that name. In its fanciful enumeration of the loves of great poets and philosophers from the past, the work is influenced by the catalogue poetry of Hesiod. It also reveals the new Hellenistic interest in the biography of poets as a poetic theme.

7 (Powell pp.98–100)

Like the girl that Oiagros' beloved son,[1] armed with a lyre,
    brought back from Hades, Thracian Argiope.
And he sailed to that harsh, unyielding land
    where Charon[2] pulls into his public skiff
the souls of the dead, and calls out loudly on the lake   5
    whose waters well through the high reeds.
Yet walking alone beside that wave Orpheus dared to play
    the lyre, and swayed gods of every form,
even wicked Kokytos,[3] who smiled beneath his brows.
    And he even withstood the sight of that most repulsive   10
                                  dog,[4]
its voice honed with fire, with fire the stone
    gaze wielding terror from three heads.

---

1. The mythical poet Orpheus.
2. The ferryman who brings the dead across the rivers of the Underworld and into Hades.
3. One of the rivers of the Underworld: literally "the river of wailing."
4. The three-headed hell-hound Cerberus.

Then with his song he persuaded those great lords
    to let Argiope draw the fragile breath of life again.

Nor did the son of the Moon, Mousaios,[5]   15
    the Graces' master, leave Antiope without honor,
who called out many a secret oracular cry
    to initiates on Eleusis' shore,
as she escorted the priest through the Rharian plain
    in Demeter's honor. She is famous even in Hades.   20

I claim that even Boeotian Hesiod,[6]
    master of every legend, left his home,
and came, for love, to the village of the Askraians,
    and courted the Askraian girl, Ehoie,
and weathered many pangs, and wrote down all his Catalogues   25
                            on scrolls
    while he sang, always starting up again with the girl.[7]

And the singer whom Zeus' word has fixed
    as sweetest spirit of all the Muses' staff,
godlike Homer,[8] strung slender Ithaka
    with songs for the sake of shrewd Penelope.   30

---

5. A mythical poet, supposedly the student of Orpheus.

6. Hesiod of Askra, in Boeotia, lived ca.700 B.C. and was the author of such epics as the *Theogony*, the *Works and Days*, and the *Catalogue of Women* (the last of which is alluded to below).

7. This plays perversely on Hesiod's epic *Catalogue of Women*, known also as the *Ehoiai*. In this epic, each woman was introduced with the phrase *ehoie*, "or such a one as. . . .," i.e. "or a woman like. . . . ." Hermesianax turns this formula into a woman's name and makes her Hesiod's putative beloved, whom he invoked anew at the beginning of each section.

8. Hermesianax here perversely says that Homer, poet of the *Iliad* and *Odyssey*, enamored of his own Odyssean heroine, Penelope, took up residence on Ithaka where, according to the *Odyssey*, she awaited her long-suffering husband. He thus makes Homer one of the ill-fated suitors of Penelope (all but suggesting that it was due to this personal motive that the poet kept Odysseus wandering for so long).

Weathering many pangs for her, he settled in that small
island,
    leaving his spacious fatherland far behind.
And he celebrated the race of Ikarios, the people of Amyklos,
    and Sparta, grappling with his personal pains.

And Mimnermos[9] who, after all he suffered, invented the   35
sweet
    resonance and breath of the soft pentameter,
and burned for Nanno. Still, with his ancient flute
    strapped to his mouth, often he went reveling with
Examues
and berated Hermobios, annoying as always, and Pherekles
    his foe; he hated the kind of verses that man uttered.   40

And Antimachos,[10] struck with desire for Lydian Lyde,
    trekked up the stream of the river Paktolos,[11]
and ... (?) when she died, he buried her beneath the
parched earth
    weeping; and in his grief he left her there and went back
to steep Colophon, filled his sacred scrolls   45
    with lamentation, resting from all work.

You know how often Lesbian Alkaios[12] went reveling,
    harping on his lusty yen for Sappho.

---

9. Mimnermos of Colophon (second half of the 7th cent. B.C.) was a poet who wrote
a lengthy elegy called *Nanno*, after a flute-girl who was his beloved.
    10. Antimachos of Colophon was active in the late 5th and early 4th cent. B.C. He
was best known for his "Lyde," an elegiac poem in at least two books on his beloved
Lyde. He anticipates the Hellenistic poets in his learned predilection for rare old words.
    11. The Paktolos was a river in Lydia.
    12. The lyric poet Alkaios of Lesbos (the island off the coast of north-west Asia
Minor), who lived in the late 7th and early 6th cent. B.C., was a younger contemporary
and countryman of Sappho.

The singer loved the song-bird and, with his songs'
    eloquence, caused pain to the man of Teos.[13]   50

Yes, for honey-sweet Anacreon strove for her
    who marched in the throng of many Lesbian girls.
Sometimes he would leave Samos,[14] sometimes his own
    land, nestled against the vine-clad slope,
and come to Lesbos, rich in wine. And often he gazed on   55
                    Mysian Lekton[15]
across the Aeolian wave.

And you know how the Attic bee left hilly Kolonos[16]
    and in the tragic chorus sang
of Bakkhos and his love for Theoris[17] . . .
    . . . . whom] Zeus gave to Sophocles.   60

And I claim that even that ever-wary man,[18]
    whose jibes at women won him universal
loathing, was smitten by the crooked
    bow and couldn't quell the nighttime agonies.
He wandered every alleyway of Macedonia   65
    aimlessly, searching for the steward of Archelaos,[19]
till the god worked out Euripides' destruction
    when he met Arrhibios' killer dogs.

---

13. Anacreon of Teos, the poet of monody, was active well after Sappho (in the latter part of the 6th cent. B.C.). Perhaps Hermesianax was thinking of Anacreon's poem on the "girl from Lesbos," *PMG* 358, cf. above, pp. 4–5, 89–90.

14. Samos is an island off the south-west coast of Asia Minor.

15. Lekton was a point jutting out into the sea at the very southern tip of the Troad in north-west Asia Minor. Mysia is a region in north-west Asia Minor.

16. Kolonos, a suburb of Athens, was the home of the 5th cent. B.C. tragic playwright Sophocles, who is the subject of this section.

17. Theoris was a *hetaira* with whom Sophocles had a son.

18. Euripides, the late 5th cent. B.C. tragic poet, who was infamous in antiquity for being a misogynist.

19. As an old man, Euripides left Athens and went to the court of Archelaos in Macedonia.

And that man from Kythera,[20] whom the nurturing Muses
    raised and taught to be the trustiest keeper   70
of the Bacchic pipe, Philoxenos: you know how,
    all shook up, he went through this city on his way
to Ortygia; you've heard[21] how Galateia thought less of his mighty
    longing than even of her firstborn sheep.

And you know that singer[22] whom the Koan citizens   75
    of Eurypylos raised in bronze beneath the plane tree,
Philitas, singing of nimble Bittis, when he was weak
    with all the glosses, all the forms of speech.

Not even all those men who chose the harsh life
    of searching for obscure wisdom,[23]   80
whom shrewdness itself bound tight with arguments,
    and the awesome skill concerned with speech,
not even these could resist the terrifying onslaught of desire
    in its raging, and submitted to that grim charioteer.

Such was the rage for Theano that bound the Samian   85
    Pythagoras,[24] who discovered the subtleties of geometric
spirals, and modeled in a humble sphere
    all the orb that the ether surrounds.

---

20. Philoxenos of Kythera (436/4–380/79 B.C.) was a poet of Dithyramb, a Dionysiac genre, and was said to be the first to portray the cyclops Polyphemus as a lovelorn
shepherd wooing Galatea. Cf. Theocritus 6 and 11.

21. This word (a feminine participle) is our first indication that the poem's addressee
is a woman.

22. Philitas of Kos was an influential elegist of the early 3rd cent. B.C., who wrote
about a girl called Bittis. He was the tutor of king Ptolemy Philadelphus of Egypt and
was famous also for his scholarly work on rare Homeric words, the *Glosses*.

23. The remainder of the fragment now turns from the loves of poets to those of
philosophers.

24. The philosopher Pythagoras probably lived in the late 6th cent. B.C. Geometric
and arithmetical relations are said to have played an important part in his speculations.

And with what fiery power did Kypris in her anger
    heat up Socrates,[25] whom Apollo proclaimed   90
the wisest of men. In that deep
    soul he labored at lighter afflictions
while frequenting Aspasia's[26] house; and he couldn't find
    the way out, though he'd found the way through many
                          an argument.

And Cyrenaean Aristippos,[27] though he was razor sharp,   95
    was drawn by terrible longing to the Isthmus
when he fell in love with Lais of Apidane.[28]
    He renounced all conversation in his flight......

---

25. The philosopher Socrates lived ca.470–399 B.C.

26. Aspasia was a famous 5th cent. B.C. *hetaira* and mistress of the Athenian statesman Pericles.

27. Aristippos of Cyrene (ca.435–360 B.C.), a friend of Socrates, developed a philosophy of hedonism, which made pleasure the basis of human happiness.

28. Lais was a famous *hetaira* from Apia in the Peloponnese who plied her trade in Corinth (here referred to as the Isthmus).

ASCLEPIADES

Born ca. 330 B.C. on the island of Samos, Asclepiades belongs to the generation of Hellenistic poets before Callimachus and Theocritus. Though he was associated in antiquity with a meter that came to bear his name, i.e. the Asclepiad, only a single line of it by Asclepiades survives (*SH* 215). Otherwise we know him only through his epigrams. According to an ancient tradition his nickname was Sikelidas, and (if true) it may be an indication of his high repute when, in Theocritus 7.39–41, Simichidas says "to my mind, I still can't beat noble Sikelidas of Samos . . . . in singing, but strive like a frog against the locusts."

G-P 2 = AP 5.85

You spare your virginity. What's the use? When you're gone
    among the shades you won't find a lover, child.
The ecstasies of Kypris are for the living. Down in Acheron,
    girl, as bones and dust we shall repose.

G-P 4 = AP 5.158

Once I was playing with alluring[1] Hermione
    who had a gleaming girdle of flowers, O Paphian,
lettered in gold, reading "Love me wholly
    and don't be hurt if another has me."

---

1. This word could also be translated as "easily persuaded," "willing."

G-P 6 = AP 5.203

Kypris, to you Lysidike is giving her riding spur,
    the golden prick from her comely foot.
With this she worked out many a horse on its back,[2]
    and shook it so lightly, her thigh was never reddened,
for she'd race to the end unprodded. And so this tool
    of gold hangs here for you in the entry hall.

G-P 7 = AP 5.207

Bitto and Nannion, the Samian girls, don't like
    to rendezvous with Aphrodite by her rules.
They stray to other, unlovely things. Kypris, queen,
    hate those renegades from your bed.[3]

G-P 9 = AP 5.7

Lamp, when Herakleia was here she swore three times by you
    that she would come. She hasn't come. So lamp, if you're a
                         god,
get back at the cheater. When she's got a friend inside
    and is playing, go out, give no more light.

---

2. This sexual position, known as the "riding-horse," may have been inherently titillating and humorous because of "the adventuresome and somewhat naughty character which this mode of sexual congress seems to have possessed. It seems to be associated only with shameless housewives and professional sex partners" (Henderson p. 164). Even then, it was "a favour which a prostitute could charge extra for or withhold entirely" (*idem, Aristophanes Lysistrata* [Oxford 1987] ad v.59–60), cf. also Machon 17.26ff.

3. As Dover notes, "this hostility on the part of a poet who elsewhere declares the strength of his own homosexual desire, is striking; that he treats a woman who rejects male lovers as a 'deserter' and 'fugitive' and as disobedient to the rules of Aphrodite suggests the possibility that the complete silence of comedy on the subject of female homosexuality is a reflex of male anxiety," *Greek Homosexuality* (New York 1978) 172–173.

G-P 11 = AP 5.64

Snow, cast hail, shed darkness, blaze, thunder,
      shake all those fire-bearing clouds at the earth.
If you kill me, I'll stop. If you let me live,
      and hit me with worse than these, I'll keep on wooing.
For I'm dragged by a god even stronger than you—yielding to him,
      Zeus, you entered as gold in the chambers of bronze.[4]

G-P 12 = AP 5.145

Hung here by the double doors, my garlands,
      wait, and don't rustle too rashly your petals
that I drenched in tears (the eyes of lovers are a storm),
      but when the doors open and you see him,
pour my shower over his head, so at least
      his blond hair can drink my tears.

G-P 13 = AP 5.164

Night, for you and no other I call to witness how she scorns me—
      that Pythias, Niko's daughter, lover of treachery—:
Called, I came, not uninvited. I pray she suffers the same
      and stands at my door, railing at you.

G-P 16 = AP 12.50

Drink, Asclepiades. Why those tears? What's wrong?
      Are you the only one Kypris dragged off, was tough on?

---

4. The reference is to the myth in which Zeus, mastered by Love, won access to the bedroom of Danae by coming through a hole in her roof as a shower of gold.

Did bitter Love sharpen his arrows and his bows
      against you alone? Why sit in the ash if you're alive?
Let's drink the pure potion of Bacchus. The dawn is finger thin.
      Shall we wait to see the lulling lamp again?
We drink. There is no love. And it won't be long now,
      poor guy, until we rest through the vast night.

CALLIMACHUS

While Callimachus (ca. 310–235 B.C.) was a native of the Greek city of Cyrene in Libya, he emigrated to Alexandria in Egypt, drawn—as were many of the most talented poets and scholars of his time—by the ambitious program of the Ptolemies, the Greek rulers of Egypt, to make Alexandria the cultural hub of the Mediterranean. There he found favor at the royal court and was entrusted with the pioneering work of cataloguing the library of Alexandria. His scholarly activities had a profound effect on his poetry. He became the chief representative of a new aesthetic which eschewed the large-scale, popular genres of the past, such as epic and tragedy, which were performed on the civic stage, for an elegant and refined type of verse, favoring smaller forms such as elegy, hymns, and epigram, and aimed at a learned elite "who loved the clear voice of the cicada, not the noise of donkeys" (*Aetia* fr. 1.29–30). The "Callimachean" aesthetic influenced numerous contemporary poets, including Theocritus[1] and Aratus, and was also of overriding significance for the Roman poets of the Augustan era.

25 Pf. = G-P 11

Callignotus swore to Ionis that he'd never
    love a boy or a girl more than her.
He swore. But they're right, who say that lovers' oaths
    do not reach the ears of the gods.
For now he's flaming with homoerotic fire, while of poor
    Ionis there is, as of the Megarians, no account or reckoning.[2]

---

1. See Lycidas' words at Theocritus 7.45–48.
2. The reference is to an oracle given to the people of Megara: thinking that their city was the greatest of all, they asked "what people were greater?" The oracle replied

28 Pf. = G-P 2

I detest trite epic poems, I don't like
    a road that carries crowds this way and that.
I despise a roaming lover, don't drink
    from the fountain.[3] I loathe everything vulgar.
But you, Lysanias,—oh, brother!—you're handsome, handsome—
                                 but before the words
    are out, an echo says "Another has his hands on him."

29 Pf. = G-P 5

Fill 'em up and say again "to Diocles." Water
    doesn't mix with this sacred toast.
The boy is gorgeous, all too gorgeous, by the river god![4] And if
                                   anyone
    says no—then only I know gorgeousness.

30 Pf. = G-P 12

Cleonicus of Thessaly, poor poor fellow, by the scorching
    sun, I didn't know it was you. Poor guy, where have you been?
You're merely skin and bones. Did that demon
    of mine get you, have you suffered a hard fate?
I know—Euxitheus has snared you too, you too, poor suffering fool,
    got an eyeful—two eyesful—of his good looks.

---

with an embarrassingly lengthy list and ended by saying "You, O Megarians, are not
third or fourth or twelfth; you're of no account or reckoning" (*Schol. Theocr.* 14.48–49).

    3. These lines clearly echo and combine the images from two elegies of Theognis,
vv.579–584 and vv.959–962.

    4. The Greek specifies the river Acheloos.

31 Pf. = G-P 1

The hunter chases every hare, Epicydes, in the
    mountains, the track of every deer
in frost and snow. But if someone says
    "There, the beast is hit," he won't touch it.
Such too is my desire: expert in pursuit of fleeing
    prey, it flies from what lies right there.

32 Pf. = G-P 7

I know that my hands are empty of cash. But, Menippus,
    don't tell me what I know too well, by the Graces.
It pains me through and through, hearing this bitter word—
    from you, darling, the most unloverlike of all.

41 Pf. = G-P 4

Half of my soul's still breathing, but half I don't know
    whether Love or Death has grabbed it—only it's gone.
Did it go back to one of the boys? I often warned them
    "Boys, don't take in the runaway."
Go look for Theutimos! The lovelorn hoodlum's
    headed somewhere—I know it—in that direction.

42 Pf. = G-P 8

If I *meant* to sing at your door, Archinus, gripe all you want,
    but if I came unwilling, let me off for my rashness.
Straight wine and desire made me do it, the one
    dragging me, the other not letting me let my rashness go.
And when I came, did I clamor "Is anyone home?"; no, I kissed
    the door-post. If that's a sin, I've sinned.

43 Pf. = G-P 13

We didn't notice that the stranger has a wound. What a painful
   sigh he heaved (did you see?)
when he drank his third cup, and the roses, shedding their petals,
   fell from the man's garlands all onto the ground.
He's burned, and bad! I'm not just guessing,
   by the gods. A thief knows the tracks of a thief.

44 Pf. = G-P 9

There is, oh yes by Pan, though hidden, there is,
   oh yes by Dionysus, some fire beneath the ash.
I'm afraid. Don't put your arms around me. Often, unseen,
   a tranquil river undermines a wall.
So now again I'm afraid, Menexenus, that this......
   will slip into me and hurl me into love.

45 Pf. = G-P 10

"You'll be caught, just try and run, Menecrates," I said on the 20th
   of June, and on July the—what?—the 10th
the ox came willing to the plow. That's fine, my Hermes,
   that's quite quite fine! I can forgive a 20 days' delay.

46 Pf. = G-P 3

How potent the charm Polyphemus found
   for the lover. Yes by Earth, he's not unschooled, that Cyclops.[5]

------

5. Theocritus portrayed the cyclops Polyphemus as alleviating his love with song in
*Id.*11, and it may be that our present epigram alludes appreciatively to his poem. If
so, Callimachus also tops it by adding the motif of "hunger" as a cure for love.

The Muses, Philip, take down love's swelling;
   poetic skill, you know, is medicine for everything.
But hunger's potent too, I think,—though only for
   those pains. It cuts away the boy-loving disease.
So what we can say to relentless Love
   is this: "Get your wings clipped, boy.
We don't have a crumb of fear for you: right here at home
   are the charms for the grim wound—we have them both.

52 Pf. = G-P 6

If that sultry beauty Theocritus hates me,
   hate him four times as much. But if he loves me,
love him too. Yes, by fair haired Ganymede,[6] O Zeus of the skies,
   you too once loved—'nough said, I think.

---

6. For Zeus and Ganymede cf. Theognis 1345–1350.

THEOCRITUS

Theocritus, a native of Syracuse in Sicily, flourished in the first quarter of the 3rd century B.C. and is chiefly known as the inventor of pastoral poetry (of which poems 1, 3, 6, 7, and 11 are examples). His works are typical products of the Hellenistic era inasmuch as they mix previously discrete genres. For instance, while using the meter of heroic epic (the dactylic hexameter), Theocritus' content is anything but heroic. Indeed, one could say that Theocritus turns epic inside out by foregrounding the most unheroic part of the epic tradition, namely the rustic world of the Homeric simile with its shepherds and hunters, wildlife, vegetation, etc. And while his diction is in many ways traditionally epic, he often casts it in an untraditional dialect: Doric. Further, Theocritus' frequently sets his poems in dramatic form (cf. poems 1, 2, 3, and 6) revealing yet another un-epic influence—that of the Sicilian mime. Characteristically Hellenistic is also the interest in lives of ordinary people, such as the woman Simaitha in poem 2, or the shepherds in 1, 3, 6, and 7; as also the deheroization of epic figures such as the cyclops Polyphemus in poems 6 and 11.

1

Thyrsis

That's some sweet song that pinetree's whispering, goatherd,
there by the springs, and just as sweet
your piping. You'd take second prize after Pan.[1]
If he chose the horned billy-goat, you'd take the she-goat,

---

1. The rural god, Pan, combined human and goat characteristics, and was the special patron of herdsmen. He was especially known for his pipe-playing on the syrinx or, as it is known after him, the pan-pipes.

but if he took the she-goat, you'd get   5
the kid. A kid's meat is tasty, at least till you milk her.

Goatherd

Your song, shepherd, is sweeter than the echoing
water that gushes down from the heights of that rock.
If the Muses took the ewe for their gift,
you'd make your prize the stall-fed lamb, but if they   10
preferred the lamb, you'd get the ewe as second prize.

Thyrsis

Wouldn't you, goatherd, wouldn't you like—by the Nymphs—to
                                                                                                      sit
over there by that sloping hill and the tamarisks,
and pipe? I'll mind the goats in the meantime.

Goatherd

Shepherd, it wouldn't be right at mid-day, it wouldn't be   15
                                                                                         right
to pipe. I'm scared of Pan. Since that's when he's tired
and rests from the hunt. His temper is short
and bitter anger is always perched on his nose.
But, Thyrsis, since you can sing the sorrows of Daphnis[2]
and have reached the heights in bucolic song,   20
let's sit beneath the elm across from Priapos[3]

---

2. For the cowherd Daphnis see the note on v.66.
3. The god, Priapos, was guardian of crops, fruits, and gardens. In art he is typically
represented with an enormous erect phallus. For more about Priapos, see Tibullus 1.4
where the god is addressed and speaks at length.

and the springs where that rustic
bench is, and the oaks. And if you sing
as you sang that time in the contest with Chromis of Libya,[4]
I'll let you milk a goat three times, a mother of twins   25
who, though she feeds two kids, is good for two pails besides.
And I'll give you an ivy bowl, coated with fragrant wax,
two handled, new-made, the smell of the knife still upon it.
Around the lip, on top, curls ivy,
ivy sprinkled with golden buds, and the tendril   30
winds along it, exulting in its yellow bloom.
And inside, a woman—some artwork of gods—has been
                                                    carved,
wearing a robe and headband. By her, one on either side,
two men with fine floating hair take turns, each trying to best
the other at words. But her heart's untouched.   35
Sometimes she looks with a smile on one,
sometimes she wafts her thought towards the other. They,
their eyes long hollowed by desire, struggle on uselessly.
Next to these are depicted an aging fisherman and jagged
rock. Here the old man strains to haul a huge net   40
for a cast, like a man engaged in a massive struggle.
You'd say he was fishing with all the strength of his limbs,
the sinews pop so from every part of his neck,
gray though he is—but his strength is like a youth.
Not far away from this old and sea-torn man   45
a vineyard is loaded thick with dusky clusters,
guarded by a little boy who's perched on a
rocky wall. But on either side are two foxes: one of them
                                                    ranges
the vine rows, raiding the riper grapes, the other
works every wile on his wallet, determined not to give up   50
till she's sat down to breakfast on his bread.
But the boy is weaving a pretty grasshopper cage, plaiting

---

4. Libya was renowned for its flocks and is thus a suitable place for a singer of
pastoral poetry to come from.

asphodel and rush. He's not the least aware of his wallet
or the vines—so great is his pleasure in weaving.
This way and that around the cup spreads supple acanthus—   55
a rustic marvel, a wonder to amaze your heart.
To get it, I paid the ferryman of Kalydna⁵ a goat
and a great big cheese of white milk.
And up till now it hasn't touched my lips, but lies
like new. And I'd gladly make you happy with it,   60
friend, if only you'd sing me that bewitching song.
No, I'm not mocking you. Come on, pal. You won't be able
to take that song with you to Hades, where all is forgotten.

Thyrsis

Start, my Muses, start the bucolic song.

I am Thyrsis of Aetna, and the voice of Thyrsis is sweet.   65
Where, yes where were you then, when Daphnis was melting
                                              away, Nymphs?⁶
Was it in the sweet valleys of Peneios or Pindos?⁷

---

5. Kalydna is north-west of the island of Kos, and may thus be an indication that
the poem is set on that island (as is Theocritus 7). Thyrsis, however, comes from Aetna,
and consequently some scholars have tried to locate the poem in Sicily.

6. Daphnis the cowherd is wasting away. But it is only gradually that we find out
why. The gods Hermes (v.78) and Priapos (v.85) at once assume that it is for love.
And the narrative voice of Thyrsis confirms this in v.93. But since Priapos assumes
that Daphnis could gratify his desire if he only wanted to— for the girl is willing
(v.82–85)—we still don't know why he continues to pine away. The answer comes in
Aphrodite's speech (v.97–98), when the goddess says that Daphnis had vowed to defeat
Eros, but has in fact been defeated by him. This suggests that Daphnis either has taken
a vow of chastity (like the legendary hunter Hippolytos, who was likewise tripped up
by Aphrodite), or broken up with the girl mentioned in v.82f. and ruled out the
possibility of reconciliation. In any case, Daphnis dies rather than give in.

7. The Pindos range runs across the north-central Greek mainland and the river
Peneios runs east from these mountains through the region of Thessaly.

For you weren't by the mighty streams of the river Anapos[8]
or Aetna's crags, or the sacred waters of Akis.[9]

Start, my Muses, start the bucolic song.   70

Jackels howled for him, wolves wailed,
even the woodland lion wept for him when he died.

Start, my Muses, start the bucolic song.

And at his feet many cows, many bulls,
many heifers and many calves mourned.   75

Start, my Muses, start the bucolic song.

The first to come was Hermes, [10] down from the mountain,
                              and "Daphnis," he said,
"who's tormenting you, friend, is there someone you want that
                                                              much?"

Start, my Muses, start the bucolic song.

The cowherds came, the shepherds and the goatherds came.   80
And all of them asked him what was wrong. Priapos came
and said, "Poor Daphnis, why are you melting away? That
                                                       girl
roams every spring and every grove—

Start, my Muses, start the bucolic song.

looking for you. What a disaster you are in love, and helpless.   85

---

8. The Anapos flows into the great harbor of Syracuse in Sicily.
9. The river Akis begins south of Mt. Aetna on Sicily and flows east into the sea.
10. Hermes, the messenger of the gods, was also especially connected with herding
and with the trickery associated with cattle-rustling.

They called you 'cowherd,' but now you resemble a goatherd,
for the goatherd, when he sees how his she-goats are mounted,
melts away, weeping that he wasn't born a goat.

Start, my Muses, start the bucolic song.

And you, when you see how the girls are all laughing,   90
you melt and weep that you're not dancing among them."
But the cowherd did not answer them. He bore
his bitter love, and bore his fate till the end.

Start again, Muses, start the bucolic song.

Finally Kypris came; she was laughing with pleasure,   95
secretly laughing, but feigning a heavy heart
she said, "Daphnis, you vowed you would outwrestle Eros,
but isn't it you that obstinate Eros has wrestled down?"

Start again, Muses, start the bucolic song.

Then Daphnis finally answered: "Kypris oppressor,   100
spiteful Kypris, Kypris abhorred among mortals,
you think that my sun has already set.
But even in Hades, Daphnis will be a bitter thorn to Eros.

Start again, Muses, start the bucolic song.

And there's that tale about Kypris, how the cowherd....[11]   105
                              Well then, go to Ida,

---

11. Daphnis deliberately breaks off his sentence, leaving unuttered some presumably
vulgar word indicating that Aphrodite was herself once sexually vanquished by the
cowherd Anchises on Mt. Ida. The child of this union was Aineias.

go to Anchises. There are oaks and cypresses there,
and the bees hum sweetly about the hives.[12]

Start again, Muses, start the bucolic song.

Adonis is also ripe—why, he's not only herding the flocks,
but killing hares and hunting all sorts of beasts.[13]   110

Start again, Muses, start the bucolic song.

Why don't you stroll right up to Diomedes again[14]
and say 'I conquered Daphnis, the cowherd. Come and fight
                                                          me.'

Start again, Muses, start the bucolic song.

You wolves, you jackels, you bears who lurk in the mountains   115
farewell. I, Daphnis the cowherd, won't come to you any
                                        more,
no more will I walk the wood, nor the thicket nor the grove.
                            Farewell, Arethusa,[15]
and rivers who pour your glistening water down from Thybris.[16]

Start again, Muses, start the bucolic song.

---

12. According to Plutarch, it was thought that bees sting adulterers.
13. The beloved of Aphrodite, Adonis was gored in the thigh by a boar during a hunt and died of the wound.
14. In book 5 of Homer's *Iliad*, Aphrodite enters the fray on the Trojan side in order to save her son Aineias. Thereupon the Greek warrior Diomedes—guided by Athena—attacks her with his spear and wounds her so badly that she runs crying from the battlefield.
15. The spring Arethusa, in Syracuse on Sicily, was especially associated with pastoral poetry and came to represent the source of inspiration for that kind of verse. See also n. ad Virgil, *Eclogue* 10.1.
16. A Sicilian mountain or valley of unknown location.

I am that Daphnis who herded his cows here,   120
that Daphnis who watered his bulls and his calves here.

Start again, Muses, start the bucolic song.

O Pan, Pan—whether you're on Lykaion's lofty heights
or roaming about great Mainalos[17]—come to this island
to Sicily. Leave Helike's peak[18] and the soaring tomb   125
of Lykaon's son, which even the Blessed wonder at.[19]

Close now, Muses, come close the bucolic song.

Come, lord, take this pipe—its breath is honey sweet
with fitted wax, its lip is snuggly bound—
for Eros is pulling me down into Hades now.   130

Close now, Muses, come close the bucolic song.

Sprout violets now, you brambles; violets, you thorns.
Let lovely narcissus deck the juniper.
Let all things be reversed: let the pine grow pears
since Daphnis is dying, and the deer drag off the hounds,   135
and the mountain owl serenade the nightingale."

Close now, Muses, come close the bucolic song.

That's what he said, and stopped. And Aphrodite
wanted to raise him up—but all the thread that the Fates

---

17. The mountains Lykaion and Mainalos were in Arcadia in the Peloponnese, a region especially sacred to Pan.

18. Helike was a daughter of Lykaon, the first king of Arcadia. It may be that she is equated here with Kallisto, whose tomb was on Mt. Lykaion. Hence, Helike's peak would be Lykaion.

19. Lykaon's son is Arkas, the eponymous hero of the Arcadians. His tomb was on Mt. Mainalos.

had spun him was gone. And Daphnis went to the stream.   140
                                        The swirl
engulfed the man that the Muses' loved, that Nymphs didn't scorn.

Close now, Muses, come close the bucolic song.

And now, hand over the goat and the cup, so when I've
                                        milked her
I can pour the Muses a libation. Fare forever well,
you Muses, farewell. Another time I'll sing you a sweeter   145
                                        song.

          Goatherd

Thyrsis, may your luscious mouth be filled with honey,
filled with honeycomb, and may you nibble sweet figs
of Agilos, for you sing more sweetly than the cicada.
Here's your cup. Do you see, my friend, how good it smells?
You'll think it was washed in the spring of the Hours.[20]   150
Come here, Kissaitha. Go on, milk her. You nanny-goats,
stop leaping around. You'll get the he-goat up and after you.

          2[21]

Where's my bay leaf? Get it, Thestylis. And where are my
                                        magic herbs?

---

20. The Hours are goddesses associated with Springtime, who confer grace and
beauty on all things.

21. The speaker of the poem is (as we first learn in v. 101) a young woman called
Simaitha—a figure quite unlike women of Archaic and Classical Greek erotic poetry;
for she seems to be neither a *hetaira* nor a slave, but free-born. She has a servant of her
own, Thestylis, and there is nothing mercenary about her amorous relationship with
Delphis. We note, further, that she appears to be under no male supervision (neither
her father nor her mother are mentioned). It has been suggested that her relative

Wreathe the cauldron with scarlet wool
so I can tie him down, that man so hard on me.
He hasn't come these past eleven days,
and doesn't even know if I'm dead or alive   5
and hasn't even knocked, the brute. He's gone another way.
Desire and Aphrodite have made off with his skittish brains.
I'll go to Timagetus' wrestling school
tomorrow to see him, and chew him out for what he does to me.
But now, I'll tie him down with spells. Moon,   10
shine bright. For to you I'll softly chant, goddess,
and Hekate below, whom even dogs shudder at
as she passes over dead men's tombs and black blood.[22]
Hail, terrifying Hekate, be with us till the end.
Make these drugs no less potent than Circe's   15
or Medea's or blond Perimede's.[23]

Jinx, reel in that man to my house.[24]

Barley is the first to melt in the fire. Quick, scatter it on,
Thestylis. You clod, where have your wits flown?
Monster, have I become a laughing-stock even to you?   20
Scatter it on and say: It's Delphis' bones I'm scattering.[25]

---

freedom and mobility are reflections of the altered social circumstances of the Hellenistic
Age, when women's lives came to be a bit less restricted, cf. Introduction p. 7.

22. Hekate is a goddess especially associated with the moon and with magic. Active
especially at night, she is usually thought of as accompanied by dogs and present at
the crossroads, cf. vv.31–32.

23. Simaitha cites the powers of celebrated sorceresses: Circe is the witch in the
Odyssey who turned Odysseus' men into pigs; Medea used her magical skills to help her
beloved, Jason, get the golden fleece. There is greater uncertainty about Perimede. It
has been suggested that she is the same as the sorceress Agamede from *Iliad* 11.740,
who is likewise called blond.

24. We have rendered the Greek *iunx* with "jinx" since the English word may
actually derive from it. The *iunx* was a bird, the wryneck, which was used in love-
spells: it was tied to a wheel which was then spun around so as to draw a lover towards
a particular place.

25. The object of Simaitha's desire, Delphis came (as we learn in v.40) from Myndos,
a town on the coast of Karia in Asia Minor.

Jinx, reel in that man to my house.

Delphis made me suffer. For Delphis I burn
this bay. And as it crackles loudly, catching fire,
and suddenly ignites, and you can't even see its ash,   25
so too may the flesh of Delphis shrivel in the flame.

Jinx, reel in that man to my house.

Now I will burn the bran. You, Artemis,[26] can budge even
                                                        Hades'
adamant and anything else as stubborn—
Thestylis, the dogs are barking in the town.   30
The goddess is at the crossroads. Quick, beat the gong.[27]

Jinx, reel in that man to my house.

Look! the sea is stilled, the winds are stilled,
but the suffering in my breast is not stilled.
I'm all ablaze with him, though he made me his victim   35
instead of his wife—dishonored, deflowered.

Jinx, reel in that man to my house.

As with the goddess' help I melt this wax,
so may he melt with desire right now, that Myndian Delphis.[28]
And as this bull-roarer turns by Aphrodite's power,   40
so may he turn towards my door.

---

26. Simaitha identifies Hekate with Artemis, an identification known also from
cult. It is appropriate, therefore, that she traces the source of her amorous troubles to
a festival of Artemis (cf. vv.64f.).
27. Cf. note on v.13.
28. Cf. note on v.21.

Jinx, reel in that man to my house.

Thrice I make libation, thrice, mistress, say this:
whether woman shares his couch or man,
may he forget them as fast as they say Theseus once   45
forgot Ariadne of the lovely hair in Dia.[29]

Jinx, reel in that man to my house.

Horse-nettle is an Arcadian plant that every
colt and speeding mare goes mad for on the mountains.
I want to see Delphis like that, I want him to come to this   50
                                                    house
like a madman from the gleaming palaestra.

Jinx, reel in that man to my house.

Delphis lost this fringe from his cloak,
which now I pluck apart and toss into the raging fire.
O Eros, torturer, why do you drain the dark blood   55
from my skin, like a leech of the marsh.

Jinx, reel in that man to my house.

I'll crush a lizard and bring him a poison drink tomorrow.
But Thestylis, take these herbs and knead them gently
over his threshold while it's still night   60
and say in a murmer: I'm kneading the bones of Delphis.

Jinx, reel in that man to my house.

---

29. After she had helped him escape the labyrinth on Crete, Ariadne was abandoned
by Theseus. In some versions, this happened on the island of Naxos. Here, it is on the
island Dia.

Now that I'm alone, what will I cry about first in my love.
Where will I start? Who brought me this pain?
Euboulos' daughter, Anaxo, went as basket carrier[30]   65
to the grove of Artemis, in whose honor many
beasts were parading about her, among them a lion.[31]

See, lady moon, where my love began.

And Theumaridas' Thracian nurse, the dear departed
who lived next door, had urged and begged me   70
to go see the parade. And doomed,
I went with her, trailing a fine linen gown
and decked with Klearista's sweeping robe.

See, lady moon, where my love began.

And already half way there, near Lykon's,   75
I saw Delphis and Eudamippos walking by.
Their beards were creamier than helichryse,
their breasts far brighter than you, O Moon,
since they'd just left the gym's sweet exercise.

See, lady moon, where my love began.   80

I saw, went mad, and my poor heart was pierced by fire,
my beauty melted away. As for the parade,
I no longer cared, and how I got back home
I don't know, but a searing fever shook me
and I lay in bed ten days, ten nights.   85

---

30. At a variety of festivals, girls carried baskets containing sacrificial implements.
To be such a basket carrier was considered an honor.

31. Artemis was the "mistress of beasts" and thus it is appropriate that animals were
led in procession as part of her ritual.

See, lady moon, where my love began.

My face went ashen all the time,
the hairs all fell from my head, what was left was only
bones and skin. And whose place didn't I go to,
did I leave out the home of any hag who could cast a spell?   90
But nothing brought relief, and time flew by.

See, lady moon, where my love began.

And so I told my serving girl the truth:
"Go, Thestylis, find me a cure for this agonizing sickness.
The Myndian's[32] got me suffering completely. Go   95
and look by Timagetus' wrestling school.
That's where he always goes, that's where he likes to sit."

See, lady moon, where my love began.

"And when you find him alone, discreetly nod
and say that Simaitha calls you, and lead him here."   100
So I said. She went and brought that glistening
Delphis to my house. But I, when I saw him
crossing the threshold of the gate with nimble step—

See, lady moon, where my love began.

I went all colder than snow, from my brow   105
streamed sweat like drenching dew;
I couldn't speak, not even so much as, in its sleep,
a child might whimper, calling for its darling mother.
But all my shapely body froze like a doll.

See, lady moon, where my love began.   110

---

32. Cf. note on v.21.

And loveless, he looked at me, and fixing his gaze on the
                                                        ground,
sat down on the bed, and sitting told me this:
"Honestly, Simaitha, you outpaced me by no more than I
the other day did handsome Philinos in the race,[33]
inviting me to your home before I came myself."   115

See, lady moon, where my love began.

"For I would have come, I would, by sweet Desire,
with two or three friends at dusk,
bringing apples of Dionysus[34] in my tunic
and, on my head, white poplar, sacred shoot of Herakles,[35]   120
entwined all round with purple bands."

See, lady moon, where my love began.

"And if you'd let me in, it would have been lovely.
The boys all call me quick and handsome.
And I'd have slept only if I'd kissed your lovely mouth.   125
But if you'd turned me away, and the door been barred,
then I swear axes and brands would have joined the attack."[36]

---

33. This is quite a boast, since Philinos, son of Hegepolis, was a famous athlete
from the island of Kos, who won victories at all the panhellenic games. We know in
particular that he was victorious at the Olympics of 264 and 260 B.C.

34. Dionysus is said to have invented apple-growing. Apples are especially appropriate to erotic contexts (cf. Sappho 105a L-P, with note) and were often given as love-
gifts (cf. Theocritus 3.10 and 11.10).

35. Herakles is said to have introduced the white poplar into Greece. Delphis would
be wearing such a wreath because of Herakles' close connection with, and patronage
of, athletics.

36. Delphis says that he would have come to her door as part of a *komos*, a characteristic feature of the ancient erotic scenario: typically, after a drinking party (*symposium*)
one or more revelers would come, attended by slaves, to the door of a beloved and
attempt to gain entrance by persuasion, serenades, threats, force, etc. For other variations on the *komos* cf. e.g. Theocritus 3; Asclepiades G-P 11 = AP 5.64, G-P 12 =
AP 5.145, G-P 13 = AP 5.164; Callimachus 42 Pf. = G-P 8.

See, lady moon, where my love began.

"But now, I see, to Kypris first must go my thanks
and, after Kypris, you next snatched me from the flame,   130
lady, when you called me to this house of yours
half incinerated even so. Yes, Desire often
stokes a flame more fervent than Liparian Hephaestus."[37]

See, lady moon, where my love began.

"And with sick frenzy, he forces the girl from her virgin bed,   135
the bride from the simmering couch
of her man." So he said. And I, too trusting,
took his hand and drew him down on the soft bed.
And quickly flesh warmed flesh, and my brow
grew hotter than before, and we whispered sweetly.   140
Let me not run on too long, dear Moon:
We did the most there was to do, and both reached our desire.
And he had no complaint with me, till yesterday,
nor I with him. But the mother of
our flute-girl, Philista, and of Melixo, came to me   145
today just as the horses were running towards the sky,
lifting the rose red Dawn from the sea.
And she told me, among other things, that Delphis was in
                                                           love.
But whether he's longing for woman or man,
she didn't know for sure, she said, but just that Desire's   150
unmixed cup was what he kept on asking for, and finally
                                                      rushed out
and said he'd deck that house with wreaths.
That's what my friend told me, and she's the kind who tells
                                                      the truth.

---

37. Lipara, where the cult of Hephaestus was especially prominent, is the largest of
a string of volcanic islands (known either as the Lipari islands, or islands of Aiolos, or
even Hephaestiades) just north of Sicily.

And yes, he'd come to me three, four times a day back then,
and he often left his Dorian oil with me.[38]   155
But now I haven't seen him for eleven days.
So, does he have some other joy, has he forgotten me?
But now with these charms I'll tie him down. And if he keeps
                                                                    on
hurting me, I swear by the Fates, he'll beat on the gates of
                                                                  Death.
So deadly are the drugs I keep for him in my chest, I'll tell   160
                                                                    you,
things I learned, Queen, from an Assyrian stranger.[39]
But turn your steeds toward Ocean and farewell,
lady, and I'll bear my longing as I've borne it till now.
Farewell, Moon of the glistening throne, farewell you other
stars, who wait upon the chariot of restful Night.   165

                3[40]

I'm off to sing my love to Amaryllis. My goats
are grazing on the hill, and Tityros is herding them.
Tityros, finest of friends, graze the goats
and drive them to the spring, Tityros. That randy one,
the tawny Libyan, watch he doesn't butt you.   5

O winsome Amaryllis, why won't you peek out from this cave
                                                              any more

---

38. As Dover, *Theocritus: Select Poems* (London 1971), notes (*ad loc.*): "a silent pledge
of return is often more tasteful than verbal assurances." That Delphis left his oil with
Simaitha probably suggests that he expected to be there frequently before or after
working out at the gymnasium.

39. For the Greeks, Assyria and the east were especially associated with magic and
drugs.

40. In this poem, Theocritus takes the normally urban *komos* (in which a reveler
typically goes to the house of his beloved and tries to gain entrance with pleas, serenades,
threats, or any other means) and transposes it to a country setting. The anonymous
speaker is a goatherd; his beloved, who lives in a cave, is a girl called Amaryllis.

and call your darling in? Or do you hate me?
Do I look snub-nosed to you up close,
girl; does my beard stick out? You'll make me hang myself.
Look, I've got ten apples here for you, picked from where   10
you told me to pick them.[41] And tomorrow I'll bring you
                                                            more.
Look at me. Grief is cracking my heart. I wish I were
that bumble bee and could flit into your cave,
slipping through the ivy and fern that hides you.[42]
Now I understand desire. A backbreaking god. He must have   15
                                                            sucked
on a lion's tit, and his mother reared him out in the woods.
He's set me smoldering, cut me to the bone.
O you who peer out sweetly—like pure stone—O dark-browed
girl, hug your goatherd, so I can give you a kiss.
Even in empty kisses there's sweet delight.   20
You'll make me pluck to bits the wreath
I made for you, dear Amaryllis, out of ivy,
twining it with buds and fragrant celery.

O me, what's happening, I'm so helpless. You won't listen.
I'll take off my cloak and jump in the waves up there   25
where Olpis the fisherman watches for tuna.
If I die, at least that ends your fun.
I caught on yesterday, while wondering if you love me:

---

41. For apples as love-gifts cf. Sappho 105a L-P with note, cf. also Theocritus
2.120, 11.10.
42. For the lover's wish that he might be something which has easy contact with
the beloved cf. the anonymous poems *PMG* 900 and 901, Ovid *Amores* 2.15.

the love-grass wouldn't stick when I slapped it on;
it only shriveled on my hairless forearm.[43]   30
And Agroio too, the trusty sieve-diviner,[44] told me
yesterday while cutting grass beside me, that though I
am all yours, you don't waste a word on me.
Truly, I've got a white skinned goat for you, that had twins.
Mermonos, the swarthy spinning-girl,   35
is begging for it. And I'll give it to her, seeing you're so
                                                                    proud.

My right eye's twitching: will I see
her then?[45] I'll lean against this pine and sing.
Maybe she'll look at me. She isn't made of adamant.

Hippomenes,[46] when he wished to wed the maid,   40
took apples in hand and won the race. And Atalanta
saw, went mad, dove deep into love.
Melampos, the seer,[47] drove the herd from Orthrys
to Pylos, and thus into Bias' arms fell
the winsome mother of wise Alphesiboia.   45
And while herding his flock on the mountains, didn't Adonis[48]

---

43. As Dover (*op. cit.*) notes (*ad loc.*), "this was a kind of 'she loves me, she loves me not' divination in which a man smacked a petal or leaf on to the hairless underside of his arm and got his answer from whether it remained stuck to him when the arm was held normally, or curled and fell off."

44. A type of rustic divination. We do not know, however, exactly how the sieves were used.

45. The twitching of the right eye was considered a good omen.

46. Hippomenes won Atalanta as his bride by beating her in a footrace. He was able to do so by dropping apples along the way, which Atalanta could not resist stopping to pick up. For the myth of Atalanta cf. also Theognis 1282–1294 and Catullus 2.

47. This story is known from *Odyssey* 11.287f.: Bias, the brother of the seer Melampos, fell in love with Pero, but her father Neleus would not let her wed unless he was brought the cattle which had belonged to his mother. Melampos undertook to bring this herd back on his brother Bias' behalf. Bias then married Pero and they had a daughter, Alphesiboia.

48. Adonis was the beloved of Aphrodite (here referred to as Kythereia, an epithet coming from the island Kythera, with which she was connected in cult). After he died, he was allowed to return to Aphrodite for a part of each year.

drive lovely Kythereia to the peak of frenzy
so that even when he dies she doesn't put him from her breast?
How I envy that creature of perpetual sleep,
Endymion.[49] I'm also envious, lady, of Iasion[50]   50
who got such things as you uninitiates will never know.

My head is splitting, and you don't care. I'll sing no more,
but lie where I fall, and there the wolves will eat me.
May it be sweet as honey in your throat.

6

Damoitas and Daphnis the cowherd once had driven
their herds to one spot, Aratus. One's chin
amber, the other's beard half-grown. And sitting by a spring
at mid-day in summer, the two of them sang like this.
Daphnis first, since he was first to challenge.   5

Daphnis

Galatea's pelting your flock, Polyphemus, [51]
with apples,[52] and calling you "goat-man" and "lovesick."
And you, poor guy, don't so much as glance at her, but sit there
sweetly piping. Look, again, she's pelting the dog

---

49. The herdsman Endymion was the beloved of the Moon, who made him fall into
an eternal sleep so that she could keep him by her always.

50. A herdsman like Endymion, Iasion was the lover of Demeter. He was punished
for this love by being killed with lightning by Zeus.

51. The love of the sea-nymph Galatea and the one-eyed monster, the cyclops
Polyphemus, was first portrayed in a poem by Philoxenus of Kythera (ca.400 B.C.)
which unfortunately has not survived. The story, with its bold and unheroic reshaping
of the Cyclops story in the *Odyssey*, evidently appealed to the Hellenistic poets, as we
find it also in Theocritus 11 and Callimachus epigram 46 Pf. = G-P 3.

52. On apples in erotic contexts cf. our note on Theocritus 3.11.

that guards your sheep, and it's barking,   10
gaze fixed on the sea, and the bright waves mirror it
as it runs along the softly splashing shore.
Make sure it doesn't leap at the girl's legs
as she emerges from the sea, and slash her lovely skin.
But even from there she preens for you. Like sere thistle-   15
down, when the dazzling summer's roasting,
she runs from her wooer, and if you don't woo, she chases,
and leaves no stone unturned. For in love,
Polyphemus, unlovely has often seemed lovely.

Damoitas then struck up and sang like this.   20

Damoitas

I saw, by Pan, when she pelted my flock,
I noticed her, by my one sweet eye, may I see with it
till the end (that prophet Telemus[53] can take his nasty
                                        prophecies
back home and keep them for his children).
As for me, I sting her by not looking back,   25
and say some other is my wife. And hearing that,
she gets jealous, Paian,[54] starts to melt, and from the sea
looks out in frenzy toward the cave and toward the flocks.
And I set the dog to bark at her. For while I was wooing,
it nuzzled her thighs and whimpered.   30
Maybe when she sees me act this way a lot, she'll send
a messenger. But I'll bar the doors till she swears
to make my bed herself, right on this island.
Truth is, I'm not even ugly, as they say I am,

---

53. Telemus was the seer who prophesied that Odysseus would one day come and
blind Polyphemus, cf. *Odyssey* 9.507f.

54. A reference to Apollo. It may be that the god is invoked as "Paian" in triumph,
or that he is called upon to protect Polyphemus from the affects of Galatea's jealousy.

for yesterday I peered into the sea when it was calm,   35
and handsome my chin, handsome too my single eye
appeared in my opinion, and my teeth's
glint was mirrored brighter than Parian marble.
But to keep clear of envy, I spat three times into my lap,[55]
for so the old crone Kottytaris taught me.   40

When he'd sung this, Damoitas kissed Daphnis
and gave him a pipe, and got from him a pretty flute.
Damoitas played his flute, the cowherd Daphnis piped.
The calves soon gamboled in the tender grass.   45
Victory went to neither, but both emerged unconquered.

7[56]

There was the time when Eukritos and I were going out to
Haleis[57]
from the city, and with Amyntas we were three.
For the harvest festival to Deo was being held by Phrasidamos
and Antigenes, two children of Lykopeus, noblest
of the noble line of Klytia and Chalkon[58]
himself who made the spring Bourina gush beneath his foot,[59]
when he thrust his knee against the rock. And next to it
poplars and elms wove a shadowy glade
decked out above with a roof of green leaves.

---

55. Spitting into one's lap was thought to avert the danger of retribution.

56. The speaker in this poem is called Simichidas, as we find out in v.21. The setting is the island Kos, and the poem contains references to a number of localities on the island.

57. Haleis was a place west of the city of Kos.

58. Klytia was the wife of Eurypylos, a legendary king of Kos, and Chalkon was their son. He is said to have wounded Herakles when that hero attacked the island of Kos.

59. The spring Bourina lay south-west of the city of Kos.

We were not yet half way, and the tomb   10
of Brasilas was not in sight when, with the Muses' help, we
                                              came upon
a traveler, a noble man of Kydonia,[60]
Lycidas by name, and he was a goatherd. No one
who saw him could have mistaken him, for he looked every
                                        inch a goatherd.
On his shoulders he wore the tawny skin   15
of a bristly, course-haired goat, stinking of fresh rennet,
about his chest a timeworn robe held
with a broad belt, and he grasped a crooked club
of wild olive in his right hand. And grinning serenely he
                                          addressed me
with a smiling glance and laughter on his lip.   20
"Simichidas, where are you hiking in the mid-day sun
when even the lizard sleeps in the crannies,
and tomb-haunting larks don't fly about?
Are you rushing to a dinner uninvited, has someone's
wine vat got you scrambling? For as you pass,   25
the pebbles all sing when they bounce off your boots."
I answered him, "Lycidas, my friend, everyone says you're
best by far in piping among the shepherds
and reapers. And it gladdens my heart.
But still, to my mind, I expect I could   30
hold my own. As to our trip, we're off to a harvest festival.
                                          Friends
are holding a feast for Demeter of the fair gown
offering up first fruits. For in her deep generosity to them
the goddess heaped their threshing floor full of good barley.
Come then, as we share both way and time,   35
let's vie in rustic song, and each, perhaps, will help the other.
For I too am a clear voice of the Muses, and all men say
that I'm the finest singer. But I'm not quick to believe,
no by Zeus. For, to my mind, I still can't beat

---

60. Kydonia was a town on the northern coast of Crete.

noble Sikelidas of Samos,[61] or Philitas[62]   40
in singing, but strive like a frog against the locusts."
That's what I said, on purpose. And the goatherd, gently
                                       laughing,
said "I'll give you this staff, because you are
a sapling shaped by Zeus entirely for the truth.
I deeply hate the builder who tries   45
to raise a house high as the peak of mount Oromedon,[63]
and those cocks of the Muses who toil in vain,
crowing against the Chian bard.[64]
But come, let's start our rustic song right now,
Simichidas. And I'll.... but see, friend, if you enjoy   50
this little song I labored over yesterday on the mountain.

Ageanax will have fair sailing into Mitylene[65]
when, as the Kids rise in the evening,[66] the South wind drives
                                  the drenching
wave, and when Orion sets his feet on Ocean,
if, that is, he rescues Lycidas from being roasted   55
by Aphrodite. This hot desire for him is burning me up.
And halcyons will calm the waves, the sea,
the South wind and the East, which stirs the deepest sea-weed,
halcyons, the birds that gleaming Nereids[67]

---

61. Since antiquity, it has generally been assumed that Sikelidas was another name for the early Hellenistic poet Asclepiades of Samos (for a selection of his epigrams cf. above pp. 131–134).

62. Philitas of Kos, who lived in the last quarter of the 4th cent. and first quarter of the 3rd century B.C., was an influential poet and scholar. In addition to this complimentary reference, he was apparently cited with approval by Callimachus in the prologue of his *Aitia*.

63. According to the ancient commentary on this poem, Mt. Oromedon was the highest peak on Kos.

64. This is a reference to Homer, who was widely believed to have come from Chios.

65. Mitylene was a major city on the island of Lesbos.

66. The constellation Haedi (the Kids) rises in the evening in early October.

67. The sea-nymphs known as Nereids were daughters of Nereus, the old man of the sea.

love most, and men whose catch comes from the sea.   60
Since Ageanax desires to sail to Mitylene,
may all be fair, and may he smoothly come to port.
And on that day, wearing a wreath of anise
or of rose or stock about my head,
I'll ladle Pteleatic wine from the jug,   65
lounging by the fire, and on the fire they'll roast me beans.
The couch will be piled elbow-deep
with fleabane, asphodel, and coiling celery.
And lushly I'll drink remembering Ageanax
in the very cups and pressing my lip to the dregs.   70
Two shepherds will pipe for me, one Acharnean,
one Lykopitan. And Tityrus will sing nearby
how once the cowherd Daphnis longed for Xenea,
and how the mountain ached for him, and the oaks
that grow by the river Himera's banks,[68] mourned   75
when he was melting away like any snow beneath great
                                                  Haimon
or Athos, or Rhodope or furthest Caucasus.[69]
And he'll sing how once the ample chest received the goatherd[70]
live, by the wicked rashness of a king,
and how the snub-nosed bees fed him, flying   80
from the meadow to the sweet cedar chest with tender
                                                  blossoms
because the Muse poured luscious nectar on his mouth.
O most blessed Komatas, these were your happy sufferings.
You too were locked in the chest; you too labored through
the spring with honeycomb of bees for food.   85
If only you'd been numbered among the living in my day
so I might have pastured your lovely goats in the mountains

---

68. The reference sets the story of Daphnis in Sicily, for the river Himera flows into the sea on the northern coast of that island.

69. Mt. Haimon is in the wild northern region of Thrace; Mt. Athos on the northern coast of the Aegean; the Rhodope range was in Thrace; and the Caucasus east of the Black Sea.

70. i.e. Komatas.

listening to your voice, while you, beneath oaks or pines,
lay sweetly singing, O sacred Komatas."

So much he said, then stopped. And after him again   90
I spoke as follows: "Lycidas, friend, there are many things
the nymphs taught me, too, while I herded on the mountains,
fine things, that fame may have carried even to the throne of
                                                            Zeus,
but this one best of all by far, and in your honor
I'll begin. Just listen, since you're the Muses' friend.   95

The Loves sneezed[71] on Simichidas, for he,poor fellow,
loves Myrto[72] as much as goats love Spring.
But Aratus, dearest friend in all to him,
has a deep down craving for a boy. Aristis knows,
a noble man and great aristocrat, whom Phoebus himself   100
would allow to take the lyre and sing beside his tripods—
he knows how Aratus burns with boy love beneath the bone.
O Pan, possessor of Homole's lovely plain,[73]
propel the boy uncalled into his loving arms,
whether it's soft Philinos, or someone else.   105
And if you do, dear Pan, may Arcadian boys
not whip you then with squills beneath
your ribs and shoulders when there's scarcity of meat.[74]
But if you're otherwise inclined, may you scratch up your
                                                    whole bug-bitten
body with your nails, and may you sleep in nettles.   110
I hope you get stuck in the Edonian mountains in deepest
                                                        winter

---

71. Sneezing was considered a favorable omen, cf. Catullus 45.
72. A woman's name, unlike the others in Simichidas' song.
73. Pan was the rustic god *par excellence*. Homole was in northern Thessaly.
74. It has been suggested that these lines refer to a ritual comparable to those of many cultures in which a statue of a god is scourged if that god fails to fulfill his normal duties. In the case of Pan, the scarcity of meat will probably refer to game, which belongs to his rural realm.

scanning the river Hebros, close to Ursa Major;[75]
and in summer, herd among the outmost Ethiopians
beneath the rock of the Blemyes, whence Nile can no longer
be seen.[76]

But you, leave the sweet spring of Hyetis   115
and Byblis,[77] leave Oikous, steep abode of blond Dione,[78]
you Loves, like rosy apples,
come drive your arrows into that tempting Philinos,
drive them in for me, since the rascal takes no pity on my friend.
Yet it's clear he's riper than a pear. The women   120
say "Alas, Philinos, your comely bloom is dropping off."
Let's go. Enough waiting here at his door, Aratus,
wearing our feet down. The cock crowing at dawn
can condemn someone else to stupefying numbness.
Let Molon be the one to get throttled in that arena, friend.   125
Let our concern be peace, and may there be some hag
who'll spit and save us from unlovely things.

That's what I said. And, gently laughing as before,
he handed me his stick as a gift from the Muses.
Veering to the right, he set off to Pyxa[79]   130
down the road. But Eukritos and I arrived at Phrasidemos'
with our fair Amyntas, and on thick
beds of fragrant rush we lay
savoring the fresh-cut vine leaves.
Over our heads shook many   135
a poplar and elm. And nearby, sacred water

---

75. The Edonians lived south of the Rhodope range (cf. note on v.77). The river Hebros ran north of that range.

76. The Blemyes were a tribe who lived along the Nile on Egypt's southern border.

77. Byblis was a spring at Miletus on the western coast of Asia Minor. According to the ancient commentary on this poem, Hyetis was likewise a spring in this city.

78. Oikous was a city in Karia. Dione was the goddess Aphrodite's mother.

79. If we may connect some Koan inscriptions, which mention a deme of the Phyxiotai, with the Pyxa mentioned here, the town may have been located south-west of the city of Kos.

from the grotto of the Nymphs fell splashing.
On shady boughs, the scorched
cicadas chattered as they toiled. The tree-frog
in thick spines of bramble murmured from afar.   140
Larks and finches sang, the dove moaned,
whirring bees flew round about the springs.
All was fragrant of richest harvest, fragrant of fruit-time.
Pears rolled by our feet, apples by our sides
in abundance, and sagging towards the ground   145
were branches heavy with wild plums.
And four-year seals were broken on the tops of wine jars.
O Kastalian Nymphs, who hold Parnassus' peak,[80]
was it such a bowl that, in the rocky cave
of Pholos, aged Chiron offered Herakles?[81]   150
And that shepherd by the Anapus,[82]
mighty Polyphemus,[83] who pelted ships with mountains—
was it such nectar stirred him to the dance among sheep-pens,
a drink such as you Nymphs mixed for us that day
by the altar of Demeter at her harvest? Upon her heap   155
may I plant again the great winnowing spade, and she smile
with sheaves and poppies in her hands.

11

There is no other cure for love,
Nikias, not balm nor plaster,

---

80. The reference is to the water nymphs of the Kastalian spring at Delphi. They
are apparently thought of as being present in the sacred water streaming from the grotto
on Kos.

81. The centaur Pholos entertained Herakles with wine given to him by Dionysus
himself. In the version cited here, the noble centaur Chiron was present as well. The
story goes that the other centaurs were drawn to the cave by the smell of the wine, and
a fight ensued in which Herakles defeated the centaurs and accidentally wounded
Chiron.

82. The Anapus is a river in eastern Sicily.

83. For the cyclops Polyphemus as a shepherd, cf. Theocritus 6 and 11.

but the Muses of Pieria: this is something light and sweet
for men—though not easy to find.
You know this well, I think, being a doctor   5
and the special darling of the nine Muses.
That, at least, is how the Cyclops managed best,
my countryman Polyphemus of old, when he yearned for
                                        Galatea,[84]
just as the down came in around his lips and temples.
And he wooed not with apples, nor rose, nor locks of his curly
                                                    hair,   10
but with straight frenzies. The rest he thought irrelevant.
Often the sheep returned to the fold alone
from the grassy pasture, while he, singing of Galatea
alone on the shore, awash in seaweed, wasted away
from sunrise on, in his heart the bitterest wound,   15
fixed in his gut by the shaft of great Aphrodite.
But he found the cure and, sitting upon the rocks
high up and gazing toward the sea, sang thus:

O milk-white Galatea, why reject the one who loves you,
whiter than curd to look at, softer than a lamb,   20
more headstrong than a calf, sleeker than an unripe grape;
and why do you come to me like that when sweet sleep holds
                                                    me,
and slip away again, when sweet sleep lets me go,
and you flee like the ewe when she sees the grisly wolf.
I fell in love with you, girl, when first   25
you came with my mother to gather hyacinth
from the mountain, and I led the way.
And once I'd seen you, from that time on, nor even now
can I stop. But you don't care, by Zeus, no not a bit.

---

84. For the love of the cyclops Polyphemus for the sea-nymph Galatea, cf. our note
on Theocritus 6.6.

I know, you charmer, why you run away: 30
because a shaggy brow spans my whole forehead
one vast brow from ear to ear,
with a single eye beneath, a broad nose over the lip.
Yet, though this is how I am, I tend a thousand head
and milking them, I drink the finest milk.   35
neither summer nor fall do I lack cheese
nor at winter's end—my racks are loaded down.
And I can pipe like no one among the Cyclopes,
singing of you, my honeybunch, and me
often in the dead of night. And I'm rearing eleven fawns for   40
                                                                            you,
all with collars, and also four little bears.
Just come to me—you won't be the worse for it—
and let the foam-grey wave beat against the shore.
Beside me in the cave you'll spend a sweeter night.
There are bays there, there are slender cypresses,   45
there is dark ivy, there's the grape-vine sweet at harvest,
there is icy water that densely wooded Aetna
sends me from the white snow, an immortal drink.
Who would take the sea and waves over these?
And if I seem to you too shaggy,   50
well, I have oak logs and a sleepless fire beneath the ash,
and I'd even let you burn my soul
and my one eye, sweetest thing of all to me.
O why didn't my mother bear me with gills
so I could have dived down to you and kissed your hand,   55
if you won't let me kiss your mouth, and brought you white
                                                                          lilies
or soft poppy with its scarlet petals.
But one grows in summer, the other in winter,
so I couldn't bring you both at once.
But now, little girl, right now, I'll still learn to swim,   60
if only some stranger come sailing here in his ship,
so I can see how sweetly you live in the depths.
Come out, Galatea, and coming out, forget,

170   THEOCRITUS

as I do now in sitting here, to go back home.
Agree to herd with me and milk   65
and set the cheese by adding bitter rennet.
My mother's the one that abuses me, I blame her.
She never told you one nice thing about me,
though she sees me growing thinner by the day.
I'll tell her my head and both my feet   70
are throbbing, so she'll suffer since I suffer too.
O Cyclops, Cyclops, where have your wits flown?
If you'd go weave baskets, cut green shoots
to bring the lambs, you might show a lot more sense.
Milk the ewe at hand; why chase the one that runs?   75
You'll find another Galatea, maybe prettier.
Plenty of girls invite me out for nighttime play,
and they all giggle when I pay attention.
So it's clear that in these parts I'm someone.

Thus Polyphemus shepherded his love   80
with singing, and got along more easily than if he'd payed a
                                                              fee.

HERODAS

Herodas became accessible to us as an author with the British Museum's acquisition in 1892 of a long papyrus containing eight of his so-called "Mimiambs," i.e. mimes written in iambic meter. Nothing whatsoever is known of his life, but references in the poems show that he probably belongs to the first half of the 3rd century B.C. In his Mimiambs, Herodas has (in characteristically Hellenistic fashion) combined two genres which, so far as we can tell, were previously discrete: literary mime, and iambic poetry in the style of Hipponax. Mime traditionally dramatized scenes from everyday life using low characters and colloquial language; Hipponactean iambic also turned to the everyday, but did so in narrative or monologue in a pungent but stylized Ionic dialect and employing a humorous variation on the iambic trimeter known as the "choliamb" or "limping" iamb. It is much debated whether Herodas' mimiambs were performed or were just for reading. Whatever the case, and despite their chatty style, they are written in a deliberately recherché literary language which was doubtless aimed not at a broad public but at the learned Hellenistic elite.

6

Koritto: Sit down, Metro. Get the lady a seat,
           move! Do I have to tell you everything
           myself? You slug, you wouldn't do a thing
           on your own. Why, it's a rock, not a serving-girl
           I've got in my house. But if your barley's being   5
                                     measured out
           you count the crumbs; and if the slightest grain gets
                                                           lost,
           all day your muttering

and fuming strain the walls.
Now you're wiping it off, giving it a shine,
now when we need it, thief? You should thank my   10
                                                guest,
for otherwise I'd have given you a taste of my hands.

Metro: Koritto, dear, you chafe under the same yoke as me.
Day and night I gnash my teeth
and bellow like a dog at these contemptible ciphers.
But the reason I've come to you   15

Koritto: Clear out
and go to hell, you sly beasts, all ears and tongue,
the rest "on holiday."

Metro: Please, no fibs,
Koritto dear: who was it stitched you
that scarlet dildo?

Koritto: Where did you see
it, Metro?

Metro: Erinna's daughter, Nossis, had it   20
two days ago. My word, what a lovely gift!

Koritto: Nossis? Where'd she get it from?

Metro: You won't let on if
I tell you?

Koritto: By my sweet eyes, Metro dear,
no one will hear from Koritto's lips
what you say.

Metro: It was Bitas' wife, Euboule,   25
who gave it to her and said no one should know.

Koritto: Women! The woman will wear me to a frazzle.
I yielded to her pleas
and gave it, Metro, before I'd used the thing
                                                myself.
But she, snatching it up like a windfall, makes it a   30
                                                gift,
and to those she shouldn't. Goodbye and good
                                                riddance, dear,
if that's how she is. From now on she can find

another friend—it won't be me. As a loan to Nossis,
daughter of Medokes (if I grumble louder than a
                                         woman should,
may Adrasteia overlook it)[1] —though I had a   35
                                         thousand,
I wouldn't give her one, even if it was rotten.

Metro: Please, Koritto, don't get mad
as soon as you hear some foolish talk.
An upright woman must put up with everything.
I'm to blame for telling you these things.   40
What can I say? I ought to have my tongue cut out.
But back to what I was really getting at:
who stitched it? If you love me, tell.
What are you smirking at? Are you just now setting
                                         eyes
on Metro for the first time? What's this daintiness   45
                                       of yours?
I beg you, Koritto, don't keep me in the dark.
Just tell me who stitched it.

Koritto: Oh, why beg me?
Kerdon stitched it.

Metro: Which Kerdon, tell me?
For there are two Kerdons: the one is grey-eyed,
the neighbor of Myrtaline, Kylaithis' wife.   50
But that one couldn't stitch a plectrum for a lyre.
The other lives near the boarding house
of Hermodoros, as you head out on the avenue.
He once was someone, now he's gotten old.
Pylaithis, may she rest in peace, had dealings with 55
                                      him.
May her kin preserve her memory.

Koritto: It's neither of those you mentioned, Metro.
He's from Chios or Erythrai (I'm not sure),
runty and bald, you'd say he was the spitting image

---

1. Adrasteia was equated with Nemesis, the goddess of retribution.

of Prexinos, as like him as fig is to fig   60
if you compare—except when he talks you'll know
it's Kerdon, not Prexinos.
He works at home and sells them privately,
for every door now shudders at the tax collectors.
Metro: And the product, how's the product?
Koritto: Athena's   65
workmanship itself, not Kerdon's, you'd say
you were seeing. I myself—for he brought along
                    two of them, Metro—
as soon as I saw, my eyes bulged out.
No man has ever had a cock so very—
we are alone—so very stiff! And not just that,   70
it's soft as sleep, the laces
are like wool, not leather. A kinder cobbler
for a woman, you couldn't find if you looked.
Metro: So why did you pass up the other?
Koritto: Metro, what more
could I do? What lures didn't I use   75
on him? I kissed him, fondled his hairless head,
poured luscious drinks for him, cajoled him,
gave him everything except my body.
Metro: Even if he'd asked for that, you should have gone
                                    along.
Koritto: Of course, but one must have tact.   80
Euboule, Bitas' wife, was right there grinding corn.
Day and night she
grinds our millstone into gravel
so she won't have to spend four obols to grind her
                              own.
Metro: But how did he find his way to you,   85
Koritto, dear? You're not going to keep that from
                    me, too.
Koritto: Artemis sent him, the wife of Kandas
the tanner, she showed him where we live.
Metro: That Artemis is always up to something new.

When it comes to selling sex, she leaves Thallo
                                     far behind.   90
          But since you couldn't salvage the pair,
          you should at least have asked who ordered the
                                                other.
Koritto: I grilled him, but he swore he wouldn't tell.
          For he was taken with her, loved her, Metro.
Metro: That's my exit cue. I'll go see Artemis right now   95
          and find out what kind of a man this Kerdon is.
          Farewell, Koritto. My man is ravenous, and it's time
          for us to go.
Koritto: Shut the door,
          yes you, hen girl, and count
          the hens to see they're safe; toss them   100
          some grains: for I'm sure the bird-poachers
          would steal them right out from your lap.

MACHON

Though known as a playwright of New Comedy, Machon, who flourished around 260–250 B.C., survives chiefly in the "Chreiai." These
"Chreiai," some 460 verses of which are cited by Athenaeus, were
anecdotes or "bons mots" written in the meter and diction of New
Comedy and dealing with that genre's stock characters (e.g. prostitutes,
parasites, gourmands, etc.), though also sometimes with well-known
contemporary personages. They are chatty style in style and often quite
risqué. This particular example concerns the prostitute Gnaithainion
and her mother, Gnaithaina—whose names respectively mean "little
jaws" and "jaws."

17 (Gow) = Athenaeus XIII 581a–582c

A foreigner visiting Athens,
a satrap,[1] very old, about ninety,
saw Gnaithainion at the festival of Kronos[2] going
with Gnaithaina out of a temple of Aphrodite.
And after he'd perused her figure and her movements,   5
he asked how much she'd charge
for the night. Gnathaina, glancing at his purple gown
and spearmen, put the price at a thousand
drachmas. And as though suddenly disabled by a blow, "my
god!,"

---

1. Satraps were governors installed by the Persian king in the various states of the
Persian empire.
2. Kronos belonged to the generation of the Titans and was the father of Zeus, who
supplanted him as the king of the gods. The festival of Kronos (Kronia) was a summer
festival. "Since. . . . 'Kronoi' was a nickname for old dotards, Machon probably chooses
it as appropriate to the satrap" (thus Gow *ad loc.*).

he cried, "you're taking me captive, woman, to get at my war-   10
                                                  chest.
Take five minai, declare a truce
and make the bed for us inside." And she, while the satrap
was still willing to be polite, welcomed him
and said, "Give me what you offered, pops,
for I'm as sure as I can be that,   15
as the night goes on, you'll give it to my daughter twice."

In Athens there was a very handsome coppersmith.
Now Gnaithainion moved in nearby,
and was no longer willing to go with men 'cause of how
sweet she was on Andronikos,   20
the actor. Then, while he was away,
she bore him a baby boy,
and though Gnaithainion didn't want to work
for pay, the coppersmith kept pleading and entreating
till, after spending lots of gold on her, he got her.   25
Now as he was crude and utterly coarse,
he passed the time while sitting at the shoemaker's shop
with some others by slandering Gnaithainion,
saying the only position he had her in
was with her riding on top—five times in a row.   30
Soon after this, Andronikos heard what happened,
when he'd just returned from Corinth,
and getting mad, and bitterly lashing out at her
while they were drinking, he said to Gnaithainion
that, though he'd asked, he'd never gotten   35
her to agree to this position,
while others, vermin, reveled in it.
Then, they say, Gnaithainion replied:
"You fool, it didn't seem right to clasp
a man covered up to his mouth with soot,   40
so I yielded after taking lots of gold,
and had the ingenuity to clasp his body's
very furthest, and smallest, extremity."

Another time, they say, Gnaithainion was once
unwilling to kiss Andronikos while   45
they were drinking, as she'd always done on previous days,
being angry since he wasn't giving her anything,
and so the actor said, "Don't you see, Gnaithaina,
how scornfully your daughter treats me?"
The old woman got upset at her and said, "stupid child,   50
kindly embrace and kiss the man."
But she said, "Mom, how am I supposed to kiss
a good-for-nothing who, under our awning,
expects to have my 'hollow Argos' free?"[3]

Once, on a holiday, Gnaithainion   55
went down to the Piraeus[4] to see some foreign
businessman, a lover. She was well equipped with a litter,
and had, all told, three donkeys,
three slave girls, one young nurse.
Now at a narrow point in the road,   60
a feeble wrestler crossed their path, one of those that always
loses badly in the match.
Unable, then, to get by easily,
and getting crowded into a corner, he said, "You thrice-
                                                            damned
donkey driver, if you don't make way, and fast,   65
out of the road, I'll pin these bitches to the ground
together with the donkeys and the litters."
Gnaithainion replied, "No way, you wimp!
That's something you haven't pulled off yet."

---

3. Argos was called "hollow" because it lay in a valley, cf. Sophocles, *Oedipus at Colonus* 378, 1387.
4. Piraeus is the port of the city of Athens.

THE GRENFELL PAPYRUS

This 2nd century B.C. papyrus is a rare instance of solo song from a "mime," a popular dramatic form which might be in prose or poetry, spoken or sung. While the fragment's meter is influenced by tragedy, the diction is close to "koine," the everyday language of the period and an indication that we are dealing with a popular form of entertainment. The scene, in which a woman stands before her lover's closed door, is a striking reversal of the more common type of *paraclausithyron* in which a male lover is shut out in front of his lover's house. Cf. M.L. West, *Greek Metre* (Oxford 1982) 148–149.

pp. 177–179 Powell = Cunningham, *Herodas* Appendix #1

The choice was made by us both,
we bound ourselves together. And Kypris is love's
security. It's torture
to recall
how he kissed me, when he meant   5
to desert me,
that inventor of double-dealing,
begetter of my love.
Desire gripped me,
I don't deny it, it's on my mind.   10
O beloved stars and lady Night, companions in my desire,
take me to him even now, I'm ready.
Kypris and mighty Eros are driving me there
in their grip.
My guide is the potent torch   15
that's ablaze in my soul.
But this is what hurts me, this is what aches:

that this cheater of hearts,
so proud before, denied my love had sprung
from Kypris,   20
and now can't bear
a chance offense.
I'm going to go mad; I'm so jealous,
so burnt up at being deserted.
I ask only this: throw me the garlands,   25
which, in my loneliness, I'll press to my skin.
Master, don't lock me out and send me off.
Take me. I'm content, I'm eager, to be your slave.
Loving to distraction is a heavy task:
you have to be jealous, conceal, persist.   30
And if you love just one, you just get crazy,
a love for one makes you go mad.
You should know I have a stubborn temper
when I get in a fight. I go mad
if I have to sleep alone, remembering.   35
But you run off to press your flesh to another's.
Look, if we're angry at each other, we'll have to
make up right now.
Isn't this why we have friends,
to tell us who's in the wrong?   40
. . . .

ANONYMOUS SONG
FROM MARISA

This short dialogue-song was written ca. 150 B.C. on a temple door at Marisa in Judaea. It is similar in style to the Locrian song, *PMG* 853.

p. 184 Powell

Woman: I don't know why I put up with you or why I should be
nice.
So I'm sleeping with another guy, when I love you so much?
Well then, by Aphrodite, I'm really glad
that your robe is lying here with me as collateral.

Man: Yeah? Well I'm taking off, I'm leaving you plenty of room.

Woman: Do what you want.
Don't beat on the wall, it makes a racket,
And anyway, my nod beckons you through the doors.

ANONYMOUS EPIGRAMS

"Plato" 9 (Page)

I hold Archeanassa, the courtesan from Kolophon
    in whose very wrinkles wild love sat.
O you poor guys who took her on when she was young
    and new at sailing, through what a pyre you must have come.[1]

Anon. 13 G-P = AP 12.151

Maybe you saw that one of the boys had the most seductive
    bloom? You must have been looking at Apollodotos.
And if you saw him, stranger, and were not mastered by a blaze
    of lust, you've got to be either a god or stone.

Anon. 6 G-P = AP 12.115

I swilled madness—unmixed; drunk on words,
    I'm armed with folly for the long road.
I'll go wooing. What do I care about thunder and lightning?
    If he[2] lets fly—I have love, that impenetrable shield.

---

    1. The epigram's humor is in the *double entendre* "I hold Archeanassa": for Archeanassa is dead, and the speaker is her tombstone. The poem implies that, even in the grave, she is almost too hot to handle.
    2. I.e. Zeus.

Anon. 72 (Page) = AP 5.83

I wish I were the wind and you, walking along the shore,
    would bare your breasts and take me as I blew.

Anon. 11 G-P = AP 12.79

Antipater kissed me, when love was already leaving,
    and fire blazed back from cold ash.
Twice I fell, against my will, in the same flame. Luckless lovers,
    run away, my touch means instant incineration.

MELEAGER

As he tells us himself in his funerary epigrams (G-P 2–4 = AP 7.417–419), Meleager was born in the Syrian city of Gadara, grew up in Tyre and later became a citizen of Kos, where he died. He seems to have flourished around 100 B.C. Meleager is known not only for his many fine epigrams, but for the crucial role he played in the transmission of Greek epigram altogether. For he assembled the first comprehensive anthology of epigram, the so-called "Garland of Meleager." And it is this, together with selections from later anthologies, which made up the anthology of Constantine Cephalas (ca. 900 A.D.)—the basis for the two most important collections that have come down to us today. We have selected a series of epigrams, all of which are about a woman called Heliodora—other series concern Zenophila, and Myiskos. These are the earliest surviving erotic cycles (though earlier ones undoubtedly existed, e.g. Mimnermos' *Nanno* in the 7th cent. B.C.) and one may regard them as a sort of foretaste of the far lengthier cycles the Roman poets wrote on their beloveds.

G-P 41 = AP 5.24

My soul warns me to flee my lust for Heliodora,
    knowing the tears, the former jealousies.
That's what it says, but I have no strength to flee. For even
    as it's warning me, that shameless soul's in love.

G-P 42 = AP 5.136

Fill 'em up and say again, again and again, "for Heliodora,"
    say it, and temper unmixed wine with her sweet name;

lay a wreath soaked in her scent—it's yesterday's,
    but still, it reminds me of her—on my head.
Look! the rose—a lover's friend—is weeping, for it sees
    her elsewhere, not in my embrace.

G-P 43 = AP 5.137

Fill 'em up for my Kypris, my Persuasion, Heliodora;
    and again for her, my sweet-talking Grace:
for she's etched in my gut as all those gods in one, and mixed
    with unmixed wine, I drink her lovely name.

G-P 44 = AP 5.141

Yes, by Eros, I'd take Heliodora's whisper
    in my ears over the lyre of Leto's son.[1]

G-P 45 = AP 5.143

The wreath is withering on Heliodora's head,
    for she's a wreath runs circles round the wreath.[2]

G-P 46 = AP 5.147

I'll weave snowdrop, and I'll weave tender narcissus
    with myrtle, I'll weave laughing lilies,
and I'll weave sweet crocus, and over that I'll weave dark
    hyacinth, and I'll weave rose—the lover's friend,

---

1. Leto's son is Apollo, the god of music.
2. Literally, the second line means "she herself, a wreath, outdazzles the wreath."

so on Heliodora's brow, its curls drenched with myrrh,
a wreath will shower blossoms on her woven hair.[3]

G-P 47 = AP 5.148

I say, one day as she speaks, Heliodora's lilting voice
will top the Graces themselves for grace.

G-P 48 = AP 5.155

Within my heart, Love himself formed lilting
Heliodora, soul of my soul.

G-P 49 = AP 5.157

Heliodora's nail, you were raised by Eros to be sharp,
for her scratch digs right to the heart.

G-P 50 = AP 5.163

Bloom-fed bee, why do you graze the skin of Heliodora,
leaving behind the flowers of spring?
Are you telling me that Love's sweet sting
sticks smarting, bitter in the heart?
Yes, I think that's what you mean. O lover's friend,
buzz off. I got your message long ago.

---

3. It was customary to scatter flowers on a person's head as a sign of honor.

G-P 51 = AP 5.165

Mother of all gods, beloved Night, I beg just this,
     yes I beg, lady Night, my comrade in revels:
if someone's getting hot under Heliodora's
     sheets, warming himself on her restless flesh,
let the lamp go out,[4] may he lie limp
     in her lap, a second Endymion.[5]

G-P 52 = AP 5.166

O Night, and my wakeful longing for Heliodora,
     and the tearful torment of murky dawn,
are there still traces left of my love? Does a kiss,
     a memory, heat her up on the chilly couch?
Does she take tears to bed, kiss an illusive dream
     of me, that she clasps to her breast?
Or is there another young love, a new darling? Never, O lamp,
     look on that. Be guardian of what I gave you.

G-P 53 = AP 5.214

Eros is playing ball with me. It's to you,
     Heliodora, he's pitching my heart; see how it's bouncing?
Come on, make Eros your playmate. If you throw me away,
     he won't brook such unsportsmanlike conduct.

---

4. Here, as in Asclepiades 9, we see that it was customary among the Greeks to make love by lamplight and not in the dark.

5. Endymion was plunged into eternal sleep by the Moon so that she would be able to have him by her always.

G-P 54 = A P 5.215

Eros, I beg, please put my sleepless longing for Heliodora
     to bed, respect my suppliant Muse.
Yes, by your bow that's never been taught to shoot
     at another, but always showers its arrows on me,
if you slay me, I'll leave on my tomb these blood-spattered
     words: "Look, stranger, how Eros kills."

G-P 55 = A P 12.147

Kidnapped! Who'd be dirty enough to fight like that?
     Who'd take arms against Eros himself?
Quick, grab torches. Wait, though....a knock. It's Heliodora.
     Heart, climb back in my chest.

G-P 56 = A P 7.476

Tears for you, Heliodora, down through the earth into Hades,
     I offer you these traces of love,
tears bitter wept. And on your grief-washed tomb
     I pour the memory of longing, memory of kindliness.
Wailing, wailing, I Meleager weep for you, my love,
     even among the dead—an empty thank-you down toward
                Acheron.[6]
O god! where's the girl I long for? Hades plucked her,
     plucked her away, ash stained a flower in full bloom.
But I beg, all-nurturing Earth, cradle my hard-mourned girl
     gently, mother, at your breast.

---

6. One of the rivers of the Underworld.

ROME

CATULLUS

Gaius Valerius Catullus lived from ca. 84 to ca. 54 B.C. Little is known about his life except that he was born in Verona, probably of a prominent family, and came to Rome, where, according to a reference in one of his poems (68.34–35) he made his home. It is widely assumed that the "Lesbia" whom he addresses or mentions in 13 of his poems was Clodia Metelli, a rather infamous Roman aristocrat reviled by Cicero in his oration *Pro Caelio*. The slender Catullan corpus of about 2300 verses is divided into three sections: (1) short poems in various meters; (2) longer poems, mainly in hexameters and elegiacs; (3) epigrams and a few short elegies. Our selection is drawn exclusively from the first and third sections. Whether the order of the poems in the manuscript tradition (which derives almost entirely from a single exemplar) reflects the will of the poet is much debated. Catullus exerted a powerful influence on Virgil, Horace, Tibullus, Propertius, and Ovid, and in many ways is the most versatile of them all. Propertius, writing around 25 B.C., says that because of Catullus' poems, Lesbia is more famous than Helen of Troy (2.34.87–88).

2

O sparrow, darling of my girl,
who she likes to play with, to hold in her lap,
to give her fingertip for pecking,
and arouse to sharp bites
when the dazzling girl of my desire   5
amuses herself with who knows what game
and solace for her sorrow,
I believe, to damp the crushing fire,—
I wish that I could play with you as she does,

and lighten the sad cares of my soul!   10
I like that as much as they say
the racing girl liked the golden apple
that loosened her sash too long tied.[1]

3

Weep, o Venuses and Cupids,
and all the winsome men there are,
the sparrow of my girl is dead,
the sparrow, darling of my girl,
whom she loved more than her eyes,   5
for it was honeysweet and knew its mistress
as well as a girl knows her mother,
and never would wander from her lap,
but hopping about now this way and now that
would keep on chirping for its lady alone;   10
and now it's going down the shadowy road
from which they say no one comes back.
Curses on you, evil shades
of Orcus,[2] who devour all things of beauty,

---

1. Most modern editors detach the last three verses of this poem, considering them
an independent fragment. The manuscript tradition, however, presents them without
a break, and the decision to detach them is related at least partially to the interpretation
of the poem, whose meaning has been hotly disputed by scholars since the Renaissance.
If, as we and many others believe, the speaker is addressing his own penis (= *passer*,
"sparrow"), the sense would be: "that (the way she plays with you) is as pleasing to me
as the apple was to Atalanta," in other words, very pleasing. For a discussion of the
passer in Catullus 2 and 3 (though one that argues against obscenity) see H.D. Jocelyn,
"On some unnecessarily indecent interpretations of Catullus 2 and 3", *AJPh* 101 (1980)
421–441. For the story of Atalanta, see the note on Theognis 1283–1294. According
to Ovid's version (written maybe fifty years after our poem) Atalanta found the prospect
of marriage, and not merely the apples, appetizing (*Metamorphoses* 10.560–680).
2. Orcus is the (god of the) underworld.

you've taken away such a beautiful sparrow.   15
O rotten deed, O wretched little sparrow,
because of what you've done, my girl's eyes
are now all swollen and red with crying.

5

Let's live, my Lesbia, and let's love
and not give a dime³ for all the talk
of overly severe old men.
Suns can set and rise again;
for us, once the brief day ends,   5
we must sleep one endless night.
Give me a thousand kisses, then a hundred,
then another thousand, then a second hundred,
then yet another thousand, then a hundred;
then, when we've had many thousands of kisses,   10
we'll lose track of the number, so we won't know,
and so no one can give us the evil eye
by knowing that our kisses were so many.⁴

6

Flavius, if your darling weren't without charm
and inelegant, you'd want to tell Catullus
about her, and couldn't shut up,
but it's some kind of febrile little

_____

3. Catullus uses the word "*as*," a small copper coin of little value. What with inflation, we have said "dime" instead of "penny."
4. It was thought that excessive felicity could provoke envy (*invidia*: here we have the verb *invidere*), also called "the evil eye." Knowing precise figures or details could supposedly aid anyone wanting to cast the evil eye.

slut you love, so you're ashamed to talk.   5
That you don't spend your nights alone
the bed, though it can't speak, cries out—
and the wreathes, the fragrance of Syrian oil
and the pillows so thoroughly crushed
and the squeaking of the quivering bed,   10
which seems to have gone for a promenade.
So what's the use of keeping silent?
Come on, your loins would not be so fucked out
if you weren't up to some stupidity.
So whatever it is, good or bad,   15
tell me, I want to sing you and your love
to the skies in charming verses.

7

You ask how many kisses of yours,
Lesbia, are enough and more for me.
As many as the number of Libyan sands
near silphium-bearing Cyrene[5]
between the oracle of sweltry Jove[6]   5
and the sacred tomb of old Battus,[7]
or as many as the stars that, when night is still,
gaze at the secret loves of men.
To kiss you that many kisses
is enough and more for crazy Catullus—   10
so that the curious couldn't count them
or put spells on us with evil tongues.[8]

---

5. Cyrene. A town in northwest Libya; Catullus here refers to the province. The word "silphium-bearing" (*lasarpicifer*) occurs only here in classical Latin.

6. The temple of Jupiter Ammon, where there was an oracle, stood on an oasis in the desert, hence Jove is "hot."

7. Battus was the founder of Cyrene. His tomb stood in the agora of the city.

8. See note on 5.13.

8

You're suffering, Catullus, stop being a fool,
and what you see is gone—consider it lost.
Back then the suns shone bright for you,
when you used to go where your girl would take you—
a girl you loved like no girl will be loved—   5
that was the time of all those playful things
that you kept wanting—and she was not unwilling
and the suns really shone bright for you.
Now she's no longer willing; you too: stop wanting (you
                                                    can't),
don't follow a girl who runs away, don't keep suffering.   10
Put up with it stubbornly, be tough.
So long, girl. Now Catullus will be tough,
he won't seek you out, won't ask what you don't want.
But you'll be sorry, when the asking's over.
Bitch. What kind of life have you got left?   15
Who will come to you now? To whom will you seem
                                          beautiful?
Who will you love now? Whose girl will they say you are?
Who will you kiss? Whose lips will you bite?
But Catullus, your mind's made up. Be tough.

11

Furius and Aurelius,[9] comrades of Catullus,
whether he shall go as far as distant India,
where the shore is beaten by the roaring
        Eastern wave,

---

9. Elsewhere Catullus addresses these two only to insult or mock them (cf. poems 15, 16, 21, 23).

or to the Hyrcani[10] or the dainty Arabs,   5
or the Sagae[11] or the arrow-bearing Parthians[12]
or the seas that the seven-mouthed Nile
    discolors,
or if he shall climb the lofty Alps
to see the marks of Caesar's greatness,[13]   10
and the Gallic Rhine and the chilling sea
    of far-off Britain,
—ready to risk all these things with him,
whatever the will of the gods shall bring,
just announce to my girl a few   15
    un-pretty words:
let her live and be well with her fuckers,
whom she clasps three hundred at a time,
loving none truly, but over and over busting
    the balls on them all;   20
let her not look, as before, to my love,
for thanks to her it has fallen like a flower
at the meadow's edge, after it's been nicked
    by a passing plow.

32

Please, my sweet Ipsitilla,
my darling, my charmer,
ask me to come for a noonday snooze,

---

10. The people of Hyrcania, on the south-eastern coast of the Caspian Sea.
11. The Sagae were a Scythian race, living on the Persian border.
12. Parthia was a country of western Asia, below the Caspian Sea.
13. In view of Catullus' brutal invective against Caesar (poems 29 and 57-cf. e.g.
29.11ff.: "Was it for that, O unique emperor, that you went to the furthest island of
the west, so that that fucked out prick of yours could eat up two or three hundred
thousand [*sesterces*]?"), it is unlikely that these references are anything but ironic. They
do, however, allow us to infer that this poem must have been written after 55–54 B.C.,
the date of Caesar's campaigns in these regions.

and if you ask me, add this too:
don't let anyone lock the door;   5
and don't decide you want to go out,
but stay home and prepare for us
nine straight fuckulations.[14]
But if you're in a hurry, ask me over now:
I've lunched, and, lying sated on my back,   10
I'm puncturing my tunic and my cloak.

37

Hopping Inn,[15] and you, the clientele,
nine pillars down from the felt-capped brothers,[16]
you think that you alone have cocks,
that you alone have leave to fuck
all the girls, and to think the rest goats?   5
or because you halfwits sit there all lined up,
a hundred or two, you think I won't dare
plug all two hundred together in the mouth?

---

14. The word we translate here as "fuckulations," *fututiones*, appears to be Catullus' own coinage (it is also used by Martial in the following century). It is derived from the supine stem of the verb *futuere* (to fuck), *futut-*, by adding the substantival suffix *-tio*. To the poet's contemporaries, we suspect, it would have had a learned, and hence slightly comical air, in keeping with the rest of the poem—a parody of the (often pathetic and obsequious) request for amorous favors.

15. Literally, "salacious tavern" (*salax taberna*). The exact nature of the *taberna* is disputed, some seeing a brothel, some Lesbia's home. Efforts to identify the site from the directions in the second verse have confirmed nothing. If Lesbia "has sat down" there, it is presumably not her own home. No reference is made to the presence of other women, neither are we told there are none. At any rate, the speaker inverts conventional procedures for praising places or institutions, formally addressing the tavern throughout most of the utterance, then turning to Egnatius as one would turn to the principal target of praise (vv.7–20). The utterance functions as an abusive implied renunciation of the girl (*puella* v.11ff.), assumed to be Lesbia.

16. The establishment in question, says the speaker, is located nine pillars away from the temple of Castor and Pollux. They are called "the felt-capped brothers" from the headware with which they were often depicted.

Well think again. For all of you,
I'll paint the Hop Inn door with pricks.   10
Because my girl, who ran from my embrace,
the girl I loved as no girl will be loved,
for whom I fought such bitter wars,
has sat down there. And all you fine, successful men
love her, and, what's really a slight,   15
all of you small-time backstreet fuckers.
And you, above all, unique among the shaggies,
son of a Celtiberian rabbit,
Egnatius,[17] handsome with your dark beard
and your teeth, scrubbed down with Spanish piss.   20

41

Ameana, a fucked out girl,
has asked me for ten fucking thousand—
that one with the slimy little nose,
the girlfriend of the bankrupt Formian.[18]
You relatives who care for the girl,   5
call her doctors and her friends,
the girl's insane, she must not be checking
the mirror to see how she looks.

---

17. Egnatius is insulted at greater length in poem 39, where he is reviled for the inappropriateness of his insipidly ubiquitous smile. There we find an explanation (apparently not Catullus' own invention) for the odd method of oral hygiene described here: "Now you're a Celtiberian. In the Celtiberian land each person washes his teeth and rubs his gums in the morning with what he's pissed, so that the more your teeth shine, the more that means you've drunk of the potion" (vv. 16–21). The long hair and beard typical of Celtiberians apparently would have been out of step with the fashions of Catullus and his group.

18. This apparently refers to Mamurra, who was from Formiae, a town on the coast of Latium. In Catullus he is considered Julius Caesar's boyfriend and is reviled in poems 29 and 57; cf. 29.3ff.: "that Mamurra should have what long-haired Gaul and furthest Britain once had," where Catullus suggests that all of Caesar's war-booty has wound up in Mamurra's hands.

42

Come here, hendecasyllables,[19] as many as there are,
all of you from everywhere, howevermany you be,
that sleazy slut thinks I'm some kind of joke
and says that she will not give back
my writing pads, if you can take it!   5
Let's go after her and reflagitate.[20]
Which one is she, you ask. That one, that you see
strutting sleazily, tacky and posturing,
grinning with the snout of a Gallic bitch.
Surround her and reflagitate: 10
"Stinking slut, give back the notebooks,
give back the notebooks, stinking slut."
You don't give a dime? O muck, O whorehouse dregs,
or anything worse that you can think of.
But we must not think this enough.   15
If nothing else, at least let's squeeze
a blush from her steely canine face.
Call out again in a louder voice:
"Stinking slut, give back the notebooks,
give back the notebooks, stinking slut."   20
But we're getting no results, the girl's unmoved.

---

19. Catullus often, though not exclusively, uses an eleven syllable line (the "hendeca-syllable") for invective poetry. In this anthology, all the poems from 2 to 58 except 8, 11, and 51 are written in this meter.

20. We have introduced this word to render the Latin verb *reflagitare*, meaning "to demand repeatedly in a loud voice" (*Oxford Latin Dictionary*). A person could try to recover a debt or other property by vociferously demanding what was due him in a public place, in order to shame the other person into paying the debt or returning the property. A modern example of such "reflagitation" is described in an article entitled "For Spain's Bad Debtors, the Pink Panther Is at the Door" by B. James in the *International Herald Tribune* of 8/12/89: "Some Spanish debt-collection agencies are using ridicule to pressure tardy payers into settling up. The debt collector these days is likely to arrive at the debtor's front door or office in top hat and tails, 18th century wig and court dress or even a Pink Panther costume. The theory is that public shame works just as well as threats and intimidation, and is within the law as well."

You've got to change your method and your mode
if you want to get results:
"O chaste and virtuous maid, give back the notebooks."

43

Hi there, girl with a not so tiny nose,
and not such a pretty foot, and not very dark eyes,
and not so long fingers, and a not so dry mouth,
and hardly an overly elegant tongue,
girlfriend of the bankrupt Formian,[21]   5
the province says you are beautiful?
You are compared with my Lesbia?
O tasteless, witless age!

45[22]

Septimius, holding Akme,
his lover, in his lap, said, "My Akme,
unless I love you madly and am prepared
to keep on loving you ceaselessly all my years
as madly as it's possible to love,   5
then alone in Libya or scorching India
may I meet up with a green-eyed lion."
When he said this, Love, as before on the left,
sneezed his approbation on the right.[23]

---

21. See note on 41.4.

22. The lovers in this poem are executing vows (may I die if I don't love you). Some see a new love here, and no irony; others, the mocking of love-made-new. Cf. 107, 109, and Propertius 3.20.

23. On sneezing as an omen, see note on Theocritus 7.96.

And Akme, lightly leaning back her head   10
and kissing her sweet boy's dazed eyes
with that rosy mouth of hers,
said, "So may we keep on serving this one master,
a much greater, much more poignant fire
blazes within my tender marrow."   15
When she said this, Love, as before on the left,
sneezed his approbation on the right.

Now, starting with good auspices,
both of one mind they love and are loved.
Poor Septimius wants Akme more   20
than all the Syrias and Britains.
In Septimius alone the faithful Akme
takes her pleasure, spends her desires.
Who has seen human beings so happy?
Who's ever seen a more auspicious love?   25

48

If someone would let me keep on kissing
your honeysweet eyes, Iuventius,
I'd keep kissing up to three hundred thousand,
and never feel close to satiety,
not even if the crop of our kissing   5
were denser than the sere fields of wheat.

50

Yesterday, Licinius,[24] at our ease,
we played a lot on my writing pads,
since we'd undertaken to be frivolous:

---

24. Gaius Licinius Calvus (87–47 B.C.), the orator and poet, was apparently a close
friend of Catullus. Only fragments of his work survive.

each of us, writing little verses,
was playing now in this mode, now in that,   5
back and forth, amid laughter and wine.
And I went away from there aflame
with your charm, Licinius, and your wit,
so that, in my distress, I couldn't eat,
and sleep would not veil my eyes with repose,   10
but restless, frenzied, I kept writhing
all over the bed, anxious to see the light,
so I could be with you and talk again.
But after my limbs, exhausted by the struggle,
were lying half dead on the cot,   15
I made this poem for you, my jokester,
so you could read my sorrow here.
Now don't be rash, and don't, I beg you,
scoff at my prayers with those eyes of yours,[25]
lest Nemesis take retribution.   20
She's a violent goddess. Careful, don't offend her.

51[26]

That man seems to me to be a god,
that man, if it can be, leaves gods behind,
who sitting with you over and over
      gazes and hears you

---

25. We have rendered as "with those eyes of yours" the Latin vocative "my little eye" (*ocelle*), a term of endearment found in amorous scenes in Roman Comedy.

26. The first three stanzas are a translation/adaptation of Sappho 31.1–12 (L-P). But there is nothing corresponding to Sappho's fourth stanza (nor to what seems to be the beginning of a fifth) and in its place we have one (which some editors consider an unrelated fragment) wherein Catullus catches himself in mid-revery and reminds himself that he can only indulge in such amorous phantasies because he has nothing better to do. Ovid, later, concurred on *otium* (*Remedia Amoris* 135ff.): "if what you want is an end to love . . . . do things: you'll be safe."

sweetly laughing—which rips out   5
all my senses, for everytime I see you,
Lesbia, nothing is left of me...

        . . . .

my tongue grows slack, a subtle flame
flows through my limbs, my ears echo   10
with their own ringing, double darkness
        covers my vision.
Nothing-to-do,[27] Catullus, is your problem.[28]
With nothing-to-do you go wild with wanting.
Nothing-to-do has already undone kings and   15
        towns that were thriving.

55

I'm asking you, if it's no trouble,
show me these shadowy places where you're hiding.
I've looked for you in the Campus Minor[29]
and in the Circus[30] and all the bookshops,
in the sacred temple of highest Jove.[31]   5
And in great Pompey's portico[32]
I nabbed all the little ladies, friend,
whose faces looked well-satisfied.[33]
"Come on," that's how I dressed them down,

---

27. See previous note. Our "nothing to do" renders the Latin *otium* (leisure, free time).

28. One might be tempted (with Kroll *ad loc.*) to render this phrase (*tibi molestum est*) as "makes you sick."

29. The reference is disputed. Apparently a likely place to find prostitutes.

30. The Circus Maximus, another pick-up spot.

31. The temple of Juppiter on the Capitoline Hill.

32. The Porticus Pompeii, built by Pompey the Great (106–48 B.C.), also a good place to find courtesans.

33. We might also render the verse "and fixed them with a calm gaze."

"give back Camerius, bad, bad girls,"   10
and one of them said, "Have a look...,
he's hiding here in my rosy breasts."
No, putting up with you's a Herculean task,
you keep so proudly to yourself, my friend.
Tell me where you'll be, come on,   15
boldly, out with it, into the light.
Have the milky girls got you now?
If you keep your tongue shut up in your mouth,
you'll throw away all love's fruits.
Venus enjoys a lot of a talk.   20
Or if you like, you can lock your jaw,
so long as you let me in on your love.[34]

58

Caelius, our Lesbia, that Lesbia,
that Lesbia whom alone Catullus loved
more than himself and all his own,
now in the crossroads and alleyways
husks[35] the offspring of heroic Remus.[36]   5

---

34. Reading *vestri sim*. At least as attractive (and just as close to the MSS) is *nostri sis*, which would yield the sense: "so long as I can let you in on my love." On that reading, the speaker wishes to talk about a love affair of his own—a turnaround.

35. A literal rendering of the Latin *glubit*. The verb is used of husking corn and peeling bark off trees. The sense here is disputed. Some think it means merely "robs" (in the sense of "takes for all they're worth"), but it probably refers to pulling back the foreskin in "manual, oral or vaginal stimulation. . . . Catullus provides no clue what form of stimulation he intended. The verb may be deliberately ambiguous. Alternatively it may have had a well-established slang sense which Catullus' readers would have recognized without contextual pointers" cf. Adams p. 168.

36. i.e. Romans; no doubt ironical. Romulus and Remus were the founders of Rome.

70

My woman says there's no one she'd rather marry
   than me, not even if Juppiter himself should woo her.
She says. But what a woman says to her eager lover
   ought to be written on wind and rushing water.

72

You used to say back then you knew only Catullus,
   Lesbia, and that, over me, you wouldn't take Juppiter.
I loved you then not as the mob loves a girl,
   but as a father loves his sons and sons-in-law.
Now I'm on to you. So even if I'm burning out of control   5
   you're worth much less to me, mean much less.
How can that be, you ask. Because that kind of cheating
                            forces a lover
   to be hotter, but less in love.

75

My mind has been dragged down so far, Lesbia, thanks to you,
   and squandered itself so much in its devotion,
that it could no longer love you, even if you were perfect,
   or stop wanting you, no matter what you did.

76

If there is any pleasure for a man when he remembers
   deeds well done and feels he's been upright,
hasn't broken any sacred trust, or in any bond ever abused
   the power of the gods, to trick men,

then many joys await you throughout life, Catullus,   5
    stored up from this thankless love.
Because whatever men can say or do in kindness
    towards anyone, you've said and done.
And all of it has been wasted, entrusted to a thankless mind.
    So why do you keep crucifying yourself?   10
Why don't you toughen your spirit, pull back from there
    and, since the gods say no, stop suffering?
It's hard to put down a long love just like that,
    it's hard, but somehow you must do it.
Only this can save you, this is one you've got to win.   15
    Do it, whether you can or you can't.
Oh gods, if you can feel pity, or if you ever helped anyone
    who was already on the point of death,
look at me suffer, and, if I've lived life purely,
    rip out this plague from me, this ruin   20
that, creeping like paralysis deep inside my limbs,
    has driven happiness from all my heart.
I'm no longer asking that she love me back,
    or—impossible—that she be chaste;
I want to get well, put down this foul sickness.   25
    Oh gods, give me this for what I've done right.

83

Lesbia badmouths me a lot—with her man right there,
    and this, to that fool, is utterly delightful.
Ass, don't you get it? If she'd forgotten me, and said nothing,
    she'd be cured. Now since she rails and snarls,
she not only remembers, but—a far more poignant matter—   5
    she's furious. That is, she's burning, so she talks.

85

I hate and I love. Maybe you ask how I can do it.
    I don't know, but I feel it happen, and it's excruciating.

86

Quintia is beautiful to many. To me she's fair, tall,
    doesn't slouch: these things one by one I'll grant.
But that whole "beautiful"....? No. Because there's no allure
    in that body of hers, large as it is, —not a crumb of wit.
Lesbia is beautiful, and she's not only wholly lovely,   5
    she's stolen every charm from every girl.

87

No woman can say she's been loved so
    truly as you, Lesbia, have been loved by me.
There was never such trust in any bond
    as was found, on my part, in my love of you.

92

Lesbia is always badmouthing me, she never stops talking
    about me. I'll be damned if Lesbia doesn't love me.
How so? It's the same for me. I put her down
    all the time, but I'll be damned if I don't love her.

99

I stole from you, while you were playing, honeysweet
                             Iuventius,
    a little kiss, sweeter than sweet ambrosia.
I didn't get away with it. For more than an hour,
    I remember, I was nailed to the top of a cross,
trying to apologize, but couldn't, for all my tears,   5
    lessen your fury one bit.

For as soon as it happened, you washed your lips
    and wiped them with all your fingers
so that nothing contracted from my mouth might remain,
    like the slimy drool of a sperm-fed whore.   10
Plus, you turned me in to that torturer, Love,
    and wracked me in every way you could,
so that, now transformed from ambrosia, that
    little kiss turned bitterer than hellebore.
And since you offer this penalty for my love,   15
    I won't be stealing kisses anymore.

104

Do you think I could have badmouthed my life?
    —who means more to me than both my eyes!
I couldn't; if I could, I wouldn't be so lost in love.
    But with Tappo you do every unspeakable thing.

107

If ever anything a man wants, hopes for, happens
    unexpectedly, that's really a joy for him.
So this is a joy to me, more precious than gold,
    that you've come back to me, Lesbia, who wanted you.
You've come back to me who wanted, but didn't expect you,   5
                              all by yourself
    you've returned to me—oh what a lucky day!
What living man is happier than I? Or who can say
    there's hope for a better life than this one?

109

This is a delightful love, my life, that you hold out to me,
    one just between us, and forever.
Great gods, make her capable of promising truly,
    of speaking sincerely, and from the heart,
so we can prolong all our lives   5
    this "eternal bond of sacred friendship."

VIRGIL

Publius Vergilius Maro was born in 70 B.C. in Andes, a village near Mantua, in the valley of the Po. He studied in Verona, Milan, and later at Rome. He seems to have spent most of his life between the capital and his villa near Naples, devoting himself to the composition of verse. Maecenas, right-hand man of Octavian (later the emperor Augustus) became his patron and made sure that he was not distracted from this task. His extant works, ten *Eclogues*, the four *Georgics*, and the epic *Aeneid*, produced over a period of more than twenty years, have marked the European poetic tradition about as strongly as anything (including Homer and Dante, between whom he mediates). He died in 19 B.C. In his *Eclogues*, the second and the last of which we present here, he is heavily indebted to Theocritus (see Introduction pp. 37–39).

Eclogue 2

The shepherd Corydon was burning for pretty Alexis,[1]
his master's darling,[2] and so had nothing to hope for.
All he could do was keep coming to the thick shade of the
                                        beech-
tree-tops, and there, alone, would toss off these clumsy
strains to the mountains and the woods, useless exercise.   5
"O cruel Alexis, do my songs mean nothing to you?
Have you no mercy for me? Will you really force me to die?
At this hour even the herds take to the cool shade,
at this hour even the green lizards hide in the thornbushes,

---

1. Alexis is a boy. Contrast the female addressees in Theocritus 3 and especially 11, which provided Virgil with inspiration for this poem.
2. Perhaps a reference to Iollas, the rich lover mentioned in v.54.

and while the reapers lie exhausted by the summer heat,   10
Thestylis crushes garlic and thyme, fragrant grasses.[3]
And all around me, as I search for your traces
in the blazing sun, the shrubbery rings with shrill cicadas.
Wasn't it more than enough to take Amaryllis' fits of rage,[4]
to suffer her pride? or to put up with Menalcas?   15
—though he was very dark, and you are very fair.
Pretty boy, don't trust too much in your color there:
privets fall, though white; dark hyacinths are gathered.
You look down on me, don't even ask who I am, Alexis,
how rich in head, overbrimming with snowy milk.   20
A thousand of my lambs range the Sicilian mountains.[5]
No, fresh milk I don't lack, summer or winter.
And I sing what Amphion used to sing,[6] calling his flocks,
Dircean Amphion, on Aracynthus in Attica.
And I'm not so ugly. I saw myself just now on the shore   25
when the sea was calm, without a breeze. And I'll take on
                                        Daphnis if
you'll be the judge, and if reflections don't deceive.
If only you would live with me on my rugged lands,
in my humble home, shoot deer, and drive
the flock of kids with a switch of green marsh mallow.   30
Together with me you'll take after Pan by singing in the
                                        woods.
Pan first taught how varied reeds are joined
by wax; the sheep and their shepherd mean everything to Pan.

---

3. These are ingredients in a rustic dish called *moretum*, consisting of soft cheese, oil, and crushed herbs.

4. Corydon addresses these questions to himself.

5. These extravagant boasts must be read with a grain of salt if, as seems likely, Corydon is a slave (cf. v.2). See Polyphemus' more credible boast in Theocritus 11.34–37.

6. Amphion, the son of Zeus and Antiope, was a legendary singer who is said to have constructed the walls of Thebes through the power of his song. He is called Dircean because of the river Dirce, which flowed through Thebes, and which came to be virtually synonymous with the city.

Don't be ashamed to rub your lip on the reed.
To learn to do that, what would Amyntas not have done?   35
And I have a pipe of seven reeds fitted together,
seven pitches, that Damoetas gave me long ago
when he was dying, and said, 'You're only the second to have
                                                            this.'
That's what Damoetas said. And Amyntas fell fool to Envy.
Plus, I've two wild kids I found in the valley—   40
risky place—their hide just now sprinkled with white,
that drain a sheep's udders over twice—been saving them for
                                                            you.
For a while now Thestylis has been begging to get them from me,
and she will, since my gifts are dirt to you.
Come on over here, pretty boy. Look, the nymphs   45
are bringing you baskets full of lilies; a gorgeous Naiad,
plucking pale snowdrop and poppy's crowns,
joins narcissus and the blossoms of pungent dill,
and then, weaving in cassia with other fine herbs,
colors the bilberry with yellow marigold.   50
And I shall gather you quince plush white with down
and chestnuts, which my Amaryllis always loved,
and waxy plums (for we must honor this fruit, too),
and I'll pluck you, O leaves of the bay, and myrtle next,
and so put together you'll suavely mingle fragrances.   55
You're a country bumpkin, Corydon. Your gifts mean nothing
                                                        to Alexis.
And, if you could fight with gifts, Iollas wouldn't let you win.
Oh why have I willed this suffering on myself? I let the
                                                        southwind
at the flowers, love-crazed, I let swine into clear springs.
Who are you running from, madman?[7] Even gods have lived   60
                                                        in woods,

---

7. Corydon once again addresses Alexis.

even Dardanian Paris.[8] It's fine for Pallas to dwell
in the cities she has built.[9] Our utmost pleasure shall be the
                                                      woods.
The lioness goes grimly for the wolf; the wolf, for the
                                                      young she-goat;
and it's the clover in flower the lusty little she-goat goes for;
Corydon goes for you, Alexis. Our own desire drags each   65
                                                      along.
Look, the bullocks are bringing back the yoke-hung plows
and the falling sun doubles the shadows.
Yet love still burns me. What measure could there be in love?
Ah Corydon, Corydon, what insanity has gripped you?
Half-pruned, there amid elm-leaves, the vine awaits you.   70
Why don't you at least do something useful—
get ready some withies and rushes for weaving.
You'll find another Alexis, if this one turns you down."

Eclogue 10

Let me fulfill this final task, Arethusa.[10]
I must sing a few strains for my Gallus,[11]

---

8. Paris was shepherding on Mt. Ida when he judged the beauty contest between
Hera, Athena, and Aphrodite. Each goddess tried to persuade him to choose her, but
it was Aphrodite's bribe, the gift in marriage of Helen, the most beautiful woman in
the world, that determined Paris' choice. He thus became a paradigm of those who
value love over all things.

9. Pallas Athena, the virgin goddess, is traditionally the protectress of cities and
keeper of the citadel.

10. In fleeing from the river-god Alpheus (in the western Peloponnese), the nymph
Arethusa passed under the sea and emerged as a spring at Syracuse in Sicily. Here she
is apparently invoked as the Muse of Pastoral song (Theocritus, the inventor of pastoral,
was from Sicily, as was Daphnis).

11. C. Cornelius Gallus (ca.66–26 B.C.) is often considered the inventor of Latin
Love Elegy. He wrote of his love for a woman he called Lycoris—probably the notorious

but ones that Lycoris herself could read. Who'd grudge song
to Gallus?
So, when you glide beneath Sicilian waves,
may the salty sea[12] not mingle its waters with yours,   5
begin: Let's sing the stormy loves[13] of Gallus
while snub-nosed goats clip tender shrubs.
We're not singing to the deaf: the woods echo all.

What groves, what glades held you back, girls?—
O Naiads,[14] when Gallus was dying of an unworthy love.   10
Neither the ridges of Parnassus,[15] nor of Pindus[16]
held you back, nor Aganippe[17] in Aonie.
For him even bay trees, even tamarisks wept.
And for him, as he lay beneath the lonely cliff,
even pine-clad Maenalus wept and the boulders of frozen   15
Lycaeus.[18]
The sheep are standing about. They're not ashamed of us.
And you, celestial singer, shouldn't be ashamed of the flock.
Adonis,[19] too, that beautiful boy, grazed his sheep by the
riverside.
And the goatherd, and the sluggish swineherds came,

---

actress Cytheris, who was also the mistress of Antony. He was a supporter of Octavian (later to become the emperor Augustus) and was appointed prefect of Egypt by him.

12. Literally "salty Doris." Doris was a sea-goddess and mother of the Nereids.

13. Probably a play on Gallus' Loves (Amores), an elegiac poem in four books. Cf. also v.34 and v.54.

14. Naiads are river nymphs.

15. Parnassus was the mountain in Phocis, on whose slopes was the shrine of Apollo at Delphi. The mountain is regularly associated with Apollo and the Muses.

16. Mountains on the border of Thrace and Macedonia, associated with the Muses.

17. A spring at the base of Mt. Helicon, the home of the Muses.

18. Maenalus and Lycaeus are mountains in Arcadia in the central Peloponnese.

19. Adonis was a youth loved by Aphrodite (Venus). A famous Hellenistic lament attributed to Bion tells how Aphrodite mourned for him, and references to the story are common. Still, that Gallus should be compared to Adonis is curious, no doubt playful.

Menalcas[20] came too, drenched from soaking winter acorns. 20
All ask, "Why this love of yours." Apollo came.[21]
"Gallus, what, are you crazy," he said. "Your girl Lycoris
has gone, following another through snows and grim camps of
                                                                    war."

And Sylvanus[22] came wreathed with the meadow's pride,
waving fennel in flower and huge lilies.   25
Pan, the god of Arcadia,[23] came, we saw him ourselves,
stained with elderberries and with vermillion.
"Will there be no end?" he said. "Love doesn't care about such
                                                                    things,
savage love isn't sated by tears, nor grasses by streams,
nor bees by clover, nor goats by shrubs."   30
"But," he said sadly,[24] "still, Arcadians, you shall sing
this to your hills, since only you know how to sing,
Arcadians. O then how lightly my bones would lie
if your reed hereafter told my loves.
I wish that I'd been one of you,   35
a keeper of your flocks, or handler of the ripening grape.
Surely, whether Phyllis were mine, or Amyntas
or some other frenzy—and so what, if Amyntas is dusky,
violets are dusky, too, and orchids are dark—
we would lie together among the willows, under the twisting   40
                                                                    vine.
Phyllis would gather me wreaths, Amyntas would sing.
Here there are cold springs, Lycoris, here there are soft fields,
there's a grove here. Here I could have squandered an age with
                                                                    you.

---

20. Menalcas was apparently a swineherd.
21. Apollo, first in rank among the mourners, tries to talk Gallus out of it: "she's
gone off with another guy, forget about her."
22. Sylvanus was a god of flocks and forests.
23. Pan is a rural god, half man, half goat.
24. Gallus' speech or song begins here and runs to v.69. He begins by addressing
the Arcadians, inhabitants, apparently, of the world of pastoral poetics.

Now an insane love of incessant war[25] keeps me in arms,
in the midst of arrows, in the face of the foe.   45
You, far from home (if I just didn't have to believe it!)
gaze hard-hearted at the Alpine snows, and the frosts of the
                                                        Rhine
without me. I hope the frosts don't hurt you,
that the stinging ice doesn't cut your tender soles.
I shall go, and the songs I've made in Chalchidic verse[26]   50
I'll play on a Sicilian shepherd's pipe.[27]
That's it. I'd rather put up with caves
of beasts in the woods, and carve my loves in young
trees. They'll grow; you'll grow, too, my loves.
Meanwhile, among the nymphs, I'll range over Maenalus,   55
or I'll hunt the wild boar. No frosts will keep me from
sealing off Parthenian glades with hounds.[28]
Already I see myself going over cliffs and echoing canyons,
happily shooting Cydonian arrows from a Parthian bow,[29]
as if this could cure my frenzy,   60
or as if that god[30] could learn to soften at the pains of men.
No, now neither the nymphs of the woods,[31] nor even songs
delight me. Woods, be off again.

---

25. Literally "relentless Mars." It would seem that Gallus has been detained by
military duties.

26. A reference to the Hellenistic poet, Euphorion of Chalkis, who was an important
influence on Gallus' poetry.

27. Sicily was associated with pastoral poetry because its inventor, Theocritus, was
born there.

28. Mt. Parthenius lies between Arcadia and the Argolid, but there may also be a
reference to the Greek poet Parthenius, of whom Gallus was a disciple, and who
dedicated to Gallus his "Sufferings of Love" (Erotika Pathemata), a work summarizing
various love stories from Hellenistic poets.

29. Parthians and Cydonians (in Crete) were famous archers.

30. Love.

31. Literally "Hamadryads," nymphs who were coeval with their trees.

Our labors have no power to alter him,
not even if we drank from the middle of frosty Hebrus![32]   65
or took on the snows and slush of Sithonian"[33] winter,
nor even if, when the seared bark dies high on the elm,
we tended sheep in Aethiopia beneath the sign of the crab.
Love overwhelms all things. We've got to give in to Love, too.

That's enough for your poet to sing, goddesses,   70
while he sits and weaves a basket of slender hibiscus.
Pierian girls, you'll make this the best for Gallus,
for Gallus, my love grows for him hour by hour,
like a green elm shooting up in early spring.
Let's get up. Shade is bad for singers,   75
shade is bad for the juniper, shadows hurt the crops.
Go home, you've had enough. The evening star. Go home, goats.

---

32. The Hebrus is a river in Thrace.
33. The Sithonii were a Thracian tribe; the adjective here is equivalent to Thracian.

HORACE

Quintus Horatius Flaccus was born in 65 B.C. at Venusia, in southern Italy. His father, a freed slave, made sure he got a good education at Rome and then sent him to Athens for further study. After Julius Caesar was assassinated (44 B.C.), Horace joined Brutus' army, later returning to Rome and assuming a modest position in the Roman Treasury. Eventually he was introduced to Maecenas by Virgil, and in time won acceptance to the inner circle and was given a small farm in the Sabine hills. He died in 8 B.C. His works include a book of *Epodes*, four books of *Odes*, and two books each of *Satires* and *Epistles*. In the latter two he furnishes quite a bit of information about his life and personality. Our selection is drawn entirely from the *Odes*, written in meters adapted from Greek lyric poetry.

1.5

What slim boy—beside you on the roses—
soaked with flowing scents, is pressing
    you, Pyrrha, in a pleasing grotto?
        For whom do you bind your yellow hair?   4

—easily elegant. How often he'll weep
over your promises and the shifting gods,
    amazed at the seas rough with black winds,
        the innocent   8

who now enjoys you, believes in your luster,
who thinks you'll never be busy, always
    be ready to love, not knowing the betrayals
        of the breeze. They're fools you dazzle,   12

they haven't tried you. Me, well a votive plaque[1]
on the temple wall tells that I
      hung up my sopping clothes to the god
         who rules the sea.   16

1.23

You shy from me, Chloe, like a fawn
seeking its frightened mother in the pathless hills,
      not without a vain fear
         of the breezes and the woods.   4

For whether the coming of spring has stirred
in the quivering leaves, or the green lizards
      have parted the bramble,
         its heart and knees tremble.   8

But I'm no raging tiger on your track,
a Gaetulian[2] lion out to crush you.
      So come on, stop following your mother
         if you're ripe for a man.   12

1.25

They're stingier now, the rowdy boys, in pitching stones
that rattle your shuttered windows;

---

1. See Introduction pp. 39–40. The speaker vowed to the god that rules the sea (one would have thought Neptune; but it could be Venus, who rules the sea of love and was born at sea; cf. R.G.M Nisbit and M. Hubbard, *A Commentary on Horace: Odes Book 1* [Oxford 1970] *ad loc.*) that if he were saved from shipwreck (a bad love) he would dedicate a plaque of thanksgiving to the god on the wall of his (her?) temple. He now claims to have done so, i.e. claims that he has been saved from love's shipwreck.
2. The Gaetulians lived in north-west Africa.

they don't deprive you of your sleep; and hugging
    the threshold, the door stays shut   4

that used to swing so easily
on its hinges. Less and less do you hear now:
"While I, who am yours, am dying all night long,
    you, Lydia, are sleeping?"   8

You will age, in turn, and, spurned in the lonely alley,
you'll wail at the arrogance of paramours
while the rising Thracian wind[3] rages
    in the dark of the moon.   12

Then you'll feel how the blazing heat
and lust that maddens mares
will rage around your ulcered liver,
    not without a sob   16

that excited boys take more delight
in green ivy than drab myrtle,
and dedicate sere leaves to the eastwind,
    winter's companion.   20

2.5

She's not yet ready to bear the yoke
on her neck, not yet up to the functions
    of a mate, could not bear the bulk
        of a bull rushing into love.   4

The mind of your heifer is in the green
fields, maybe easing in the river
    the crush of summer heat, maybe eager to play
        with the calves in the wet   8

---

3. i.e. a cold wind from the north.

willow grove. Drop your desire
for the unripe grape. Soon Autumn,
    shifting colors, will mark you out
        dark clusters, purple tinged,   12

soon she will follow you. For time runs on
untamed, and will give her the years it takes
    from you; and soon, with headlong
        glance, Lalage will seek a man,   16

the girl you love more than evasive Pholoe,
or Chloris, whose shoulder shines as white
    as a clear moon glistening
        over the night sea, or Cnidian Gyges,[4]   20

who, if you put him in a chorus of girls,
would fool the most perceptive strangers—
    no way of telling—with his flowing
        hair, and ambiguous gaze.[5]   24

2.8

If you had ever suffered at all,
Berine, for your false oaths,
if you'd become uglier by one black tooth
    or one speck on a fingernail,[6]   4

---

4. Gyges is a boy. Cnidos is a town in Caria in the south-west of Asia Minor.

5. Like Achilles who, in order to avoid going to fight at Troy, hid out on Skyros among the daughters of Lycomedes and fooled Nestor and Odysseus (who had come to find him) for a while, Gyges has the beauty of a girl—an ideal in Greek and (by imitation) Roman homosexual poetry.

6. It was an ancient superstition that white specks on the nails meant that someone was a liar.

I'd believe you. But every time you've staked
your perjured head on vows, you glow
lovelier by far, and set forth a public
     problem for the young.   8

You gain from swearing falsely by the buried
ashes of your mother, and the silent stars
of the night, and the whole sky, and the gods
     exempt from icy death.   12

And Venus herself, I say, laughs at this,
the innocent nymphs laugh, and wild Cupid,
forever sharpening burning arrows
     on a bloody whetstone.   16

And a whole new crop of boys is growing up,
a new staff for you, and yet your former slaves
won't leave the home of their lying Lady,
     though they've often threatened.   20

Mothers fear you, for their young bulls,
thrifty fathers fear you; and wretched,
recent brides fear that their men may be
     detained by your aroma.   24

3.9

As long as I was the one you liked
and no better boy was putting
his arms around your dazzling neck
I throve, richer than Persia's king.   4

As long as you blazed for no other girl more
and Lydia didn't come after Chloe,

I, Lydia, my name renowned,
throve, more famous than Ilia of Rome.[7]   8

Now it's Chloe from Thrace that rules me,
who really knows sweet tunes on the harp,
for whom I wouldn't shrink to die,
if the fates spare my girl, let her live.   12

And the one who's scorching me with a two-edged flame,
is Calais, son of Thurian Ornytas,[8]
for whom I'd lay my life down twice
if the fates spare my boy, let him live.   16

What if the old love returns,
and though we broke up, drives us back to the yoke of bronze,
if blond Chloe gets kicked out
and the door swings open for Lydia left behind?   20

Though he's lovelier than a star
and you're lighter than a cork,
and quicker to rage than the Adriatic sea,
I'd love living with you, die with you gladly.   24

3.26

Not long ago I was fit for girls
and fought, not without honor.
        Now my weapons and lyre,
            fallen in action, hang on this wall   4

that guards the left side of
Venus of the waves. Here, put them here, the blazing

---

7. By one account, Ilia was the mother of Romulus and Remus, founders of Rome.
8. Thurii was a city in Magna Graecia in southern Italy.

torches, the crow-bars and bows
    that threatened locked doors.   8

O you, goddess, who rule sumptuous Cyprus and
Memphis,[9] untouched by Sithonian[10] snow,
    queen, with lash aloft,
        just graze proud Chloe once.   12

---

9. The city in lower Egypt.
10. i.e. Thracian.

TIBULLUS

Albius Tibullus, author of 16 elegies in two books, was born in Latium
c. 55 B.C. and died c. 18 B.C. An Eques (knight) he was befriended
by Marcus Valerius Messalla Corvinus (64 B.C.–8 A.D) who was also
his patron. Friend also of Horace (cf. *Odes* 1.33, *Epistles* 1.4), he is,
chronologically, the second of the Latin Elegists, following Cornelius
Gallus (of whom nearly nothing survives). He was slightly older than
Propertius and the relation between their work is a matter of some
controversy, with influence probably running in both directions. In
many senses he provided a model for Ovid, who was about 16 when
Tibullus' first book of elegies came out. Quintilian, the first century
A.D. rhetorician, in a famous passage (*Inst.* 10.1.93), calls him by far
the most "polished and elegant" (*tersus atque elegans*) of the Latin Elegists.

1.4

I hope you'll have a roof of shade, Priapus,[1]
   so neither suns nor snows can hurt you,
just tell me, what's your trick? How do you get beautiful boys?
   Clearly, your beard doesn't shine, your hair's unkempt.
You spend the freezing winter in the nude,   5
   and nude the drought of the seething Dog Star.

---

1. Priapus was the Greek and Roman phallic deity, often presiding, in the form of
a statue or statuette, over gardens. His most characteristic feature was his prominent
phallus. Here the speaker asks him for his secret (1–6), then Priapus responds (9–72),
after which the frame returns and we are apprised of a series of contexts for the
erotodidactic discourse the speaker has elicited from the willing godhead. This poem
is a miniature version of what Ovid was to do (with many a nod to this text) in his
erotodidactic poetry, the *Ars Amatoria* and *Remedia Amoris*.

That's what I said, and the rustic offspring of Bacchus
                                          answered me,
     the god armed with the curving sickle:
"Don't believe the tender throng of boys.
     They all have things you can really love.   10
One you like because he reins his horse in tight.
     Another swims, his white breast thrusting through the
                                          water's calm.
Another gets you 'cause he's brave and bold.
     And that one's fresh cheeks have a virgin blush.
But if at first he should say no, don't let apathy   15
     set in. Little by little, he'll put his neck in the yoke.
It takes a long day to teach a lion to heed a man.
     It takes a long day for mere water to eat away stone.
The year ripens grapes on sunny hills,
     the year directs bright stars with regular motion.   20
Don't be afraid to swear. The lies of love drift useless
     on the winds, over lands and deep seas.
Much thanks to Jove: the father himself ruled null and void
     whatever Love swears foolishly in heat.
Dictynna² lets you promise by her arrows—   25
     and survive; Minerva,³ by her hair.
It's a mistake to be slow. Life will go by—
     and how quickly! The day's not sluggish, won't come back.
How quickly the earth loses its colors of flame,
     how quickly the tall poplar its lovely leaves.   30
And when feeble age, as fated, comes, it lays low
     the horse that once shot out of the Olympic gate.
I have seen a young man, when middle-age was bearing down,
     mourn that squandered days were gone.

---

2. Dictynna was a Cretan goddess identified with Diana (Artemis, in Greek), the
virgin huntress, protectress of animals, goddess of the moon, etc.
     3. The Italian goddess of wisdom, identified with the Greek Athena.

The gods are cruel. A snake sheds the years, renewed.   35
    But fate grants beauty no reprieve.
Only Bacchus[4] and Phoebus[5] are young forever.
    Uncut hair is the right of these two gods.[6]
And you—whatever your boy wants to try,
    give in. Love shall conquer most things just by going along.   40
Don't refuse to go along, though the road is lengthy,
    and the Dog Star's toasting the fields with parching thirst.[7]
Even if, weaving a rusty tinge through the sky,
    a rainbow cloaks the oncoming storm,
or if he wants to skim blue waves in a boat,   45
    you take the oar, stroke quickly through the sea.
And you shouldn't feel ashamed to take on harsh tasks,
    or rub your hands raw on a job they'd never done.
And if he should want to hem in deep valleys with traps,
    if it gets you somewhere, load down your shoulders with nets.   50
If it's fencing he wants, try to play with a weak right hand.
    Offer your naked flank, so he can often win.
Then he'll soften up for you, then you'll be able to take sweet
    kisses; he'll fight back, but will give you the ones you take.
At first the ones you take, then, if you ask, *he'll* offer them,   55
    and then he'll want to wrap himself around your neck.
But O, these times now practice evil arts.
    Even a tender boy usually wants gifts.
But as for you, who first taught that love's for sale,
    whoever you were, may an unlucky rock crush your bones.   60
Love the Pierides,[8] boys, and learned poets,
    and don't let golden gifts outdo the Pierides.

---

4. Bacchus was identified with Dionysus, the god of wine, etc.

5. i.e. Apollo.

6. The passage to adult life was signaled by getting one's hair cut. Bacchus and Phoebus are traditionally portrayed as youths, just on the point of manhood.

7. i.e. in late summer, early fall (when the Dog Star, Sirius, is visible).

8. i.e. the Muses. Pieria was a wood and mountain on the border of Thrace and Macedonia.

It's because of song that Nisus' hair is purple.[9] If there were

no songs,

ivory would not have gleamed from Pelops' shoulder.[10]

Whoever the Muses sing shall live as long as the Earth   65

bears oaks,

the sky, stars, as long as the streams have water.

But whoever doesn't heed the Muses, whoever sells love,

he can follow the chariots of Idan Ops [11]

and fill three hundred towns with his wanderings,

and hack off his worthless sex to a Phrygian tune.[12]   70

Venus herself wants sweet-talk to have its place. She's all for

groveling complaints, tears of unhappiness."

This the god disclosed to me, so I could sing it to Titius,[13]

but Titius' wife won't let him listen.

And he must obey her. But gather around me, your master,   75

all you

who are in the crafty clutches of tricky boys.

Each man has his boast: mine's that lovers who are scorned

should come to me for advice, my door is open to all.

---

9. Pandion's son, Nisus, was king of Megara when it was attacked by Minos. "Nisus died from the betrayal of his daughter. For in the middle of his head he had one purple hair, the removal of which, an oracle warned, meant death. His daughter, Scylla, who had developed a passion for Minos, pulled out the hair." Apollodorus' *Library* 3.15.8, transl. Keith Aldrich (Lawrence, Kansas 1975). Cf. Ovid, *Metamorphoses* 8.1–151.

10. Pelops was cut up by his father Tantalus and served to the gods in a stew. The only god who tasted this stew was Ceres (Greek: Demeter), who was distracted by her grief for her daughter Persephone, and ate a bit of the shoulder. The gods subsequently put Pelops back together and revived him, replacing his shoulder with a piece of ivory. Cf. Ovid, *Metamorphoses* 6.403–411.

11. Ops, a Roman goddess, wife of Saturn, identified here with Cybele, the near-eastern Great Mother. See note on v.70.

12. Phrygia, the region of western Asia Minor, where the goddess Cybele was at home. This goddess was associated with frenzied rites in which worshippers castrated themselves.

13. Perhaps the poet who was a friend of Horace (*Epistles* 1.3.9) and accompanied Tiberius to Asia in 20 B.C.

There'll be a time when, as I discourse on the principles of
love,

    an attentive crowd of boys will walk me home.   80
But O, what a slow love Marathus[14] racks me with!
    My skills fail me, I've run out of tricks.
Boy, go easy, please, so I don't turn into a sorry tale,
    mocked for my hollow mastery.

1.8[15]

I cannot be kept in the dark, what the nods of a lover tell,
    or what light words tell with their mild sound.
It's not that I've got lots, or guts that know about the gods,
    nor does any bird's song sing me what will come.
Venus herself tied my arms in a magic knot   5
    and taught me well, with many lashes.
Don't try to hide it. The god reserves his cruelest fire
    for those he sees are reluctant to submit.
What good does it do you now that you've tended your soft
hair,

    and often adjusted your shifting curls?   10
What good, that you deck your cheeks in bright red,
    what good, that your nails are clipped by a skillful hand?
It's useless to change your clothes, to change your cloaks,
    to pinch your feet in tight-laced shoes.
She looks good even when she hasn't done her face   15
    or coaxed her hair to a skillful shine.
Did some old lady, in the still of night,
    bewitch you with chants, or herbs that made you pale?

---

14. Finally, the name of the speaker's beloved, followed in the next verse by the request.

15. For the interpretation of this poem see Introduction, p 41.

Chanting brings fruit from neighboring fields,[16]
   and chanting stays the sliding of the angry snake,   20
and chanting tries to pull the moon from her car,
   and would, if it weren't for the clashing cymbal's sound.[17]
Why should I wail that chanting has hurt you, or herbs?
   Beauty needs no magic aids.
What hurts is to have touched the body, to have given long   25
   kisses, to have tangled thigh with thigh.
And you, remember, don't be hard on the boy.
   Venus avenges unfriendly acts with torment.
And don't ask for gifts. Let white-haired lovers give them,
   so they can warm their freezing limbs in the silky fold.   30
Dearer than gold's the boy whose smooth face
   shines, in whose embrace no rough beard scratches.
Just put your white arms on his shoulder,
   and look down on the great wealth of kings.
And Venus shall find a way to lie in secret with the boy   35
   when he swells and sows deep into the tender fold;
to give him wet kisses, while tongues tangle and he
   gasps, and fix tooth-marks in his neck.
No gem or crystal can help a woman
   who sleeps lonely in her chilliness, wanted by no man.   40
O, we call back Love too late, too late Youth,
   when white age has stained the old head.
That's when you work on beauty. Then you can change the hair
   so that, tinged with the fresh sap of a nut, it may hide the
                                             years.
Then you can think about pulling white hairs by the root,   45
   taking off the face, and bringing a fresh one back.
So you, while you've got the pristine blossom of your youth,
   use it. It slips away on light feet.

---

16. This was a punishable crime, according to Roman law.
17. Cymbals were supposed to save the moon during an eclipse.

And don't torture Marathus. What glory is there in the
                              conquest of a boy?
    Be rough on old men, girl.   50
But please, go easy on the kid. It's not that he's really sick.
    But too much love stains his body with pallor.
How often, when you're not there, the poor boy sings
                              mournful laments,
    and everything is drenched in tears:
"Why do you scorn me?" he says. "The guard could have been   55
                              handled.
    The craft of deceit is the god's own gift to lovers.
And I know all about furtive love: how breath may be drawn
    lightly, so that there is no sound in the taking of kisses.
And I can slip in even late at night,
    and secretly unbar the doors without any squeaking.   60
But what good are skills, if the girl scorns her poor lover,
    is wild, runs away—from her own bed.
Or when she says she'll come, next thing you know, she goes
                              back on her word,
    and I've got to wait out the night in agony.
And as long as I pretend she'll come, whatever moves,   65
    I think it's the sound of her footfalls."
Stop crying, boy: she hasn't broken down,
    and now your weary eyes are swollen with weeping.
They hate it, Pholoe, I'm warning you, the gods hate pride,
    and it doesn't do any good to put incense on sacred altars.   70
This Marathus here once played those games with unfortunate
                              lovers,
    not knowing that behind his head was an avenging god.
It's even said that he often laughed at the tears of one in pain,
    and lied to keep a hot lover waiting.
Now he hates all pride, now he doesn't like   75
    any cruel doors bolted against him.
And you, just wait, you'll pay if you don't stop being proud.
    Boy, will you beg for this day to come back.

2.4

Slavery and a mistress await me here, I see.
   So goodbye to my old ancestral freedom.
Slavery's what I get, and grim at that. I'm held by chains
   and love never undoes my bonds—
whether I had it coming or did no wrong, it burns—   5
   I'm burning, yow!—take away the torch, cruel girl.
O, if only I couldn't feel such pains—
   I'd rather be a rock amid frozen peaks
or a crag exposed to the crazed winds
   battered by the shipwrecking wave of the vast sea!   10
Now the day is bitter; and the dark of night, bitterer still
   and all my hours are dripping with sorrow's gall.
Elegies are useless, so is Apollo, maker of song.
   She just keeps dunning me for cash with an open hand.
Away, Muses, if you're no use to a man in love—   15
   it's not to sing wars that I till your fields.
I don't tell the ways of the sun nor how, her circle full,
   the moon turns her steeds and gallops off.
What I want from songs is easy access to my girl.
   Away, Muses! if they're worth nothing at all.   20
I've got to come up with some gifts—even by killing, by
                              crime,
   so I won't have to lie in tears at her bolted door.
Or, I could steal precious objects hung in holy shrines.
   But it's Venus above all who I should violate.
She talks me into crime, gives me a money-grabbing   25
   girl: she should feel my sacrilegious hands.
Death to whoever gathers green emeralds,
   and tinges snowy wool with Tyrian purple![18]

---

18. Purple dye was made from the shell-fish, murex, in Tyre on the eastern coast of the Mediterranean.

And Coan cloth's[19] another source of greed in girls
 and sleek pearls from the Red Sea.   30
These things made girls bad: Hence the door first felt the
                key
 and the dog began to guard the threshold.
But if you bring a juicy bribe, the guard's won over,
 the keys won't keep you out, the dog itself is quiet.
Oh whatever god gave beauty to a greedy girl,   35
 what a good turn he did for a bunch of troubles!
Hence crying fits ring out, and fights; that's why
 this god, love, is infamous.
But you, who keep out lovers beaten by the price-tag,—
 may wind and fire wipe out the wealth you've gained.   40
and then may boys watch with glee as your house burns
 and no one bother to throw water on the blaze.
And if death comes to you, there'll be none to mourn
 or toss a gift onto your gloomy rites.
But the good girl who hasn't been greedy can live a hundred   45
              years
 and shall be wept when her pyre is burning,
and some old man, true to an old love,
 shall place a yearly wreath on the heaped-up tomb,
and shall say, when he turns to go, "Rest quietly and well,
 and may Earth be light on your bones, and you at peace."   50
My warnings are true, but what good is truth to me?
 I must worship love by *her* law.
But even if she told me to sell my ancestral estate,
 well, so long! It's "Lares[20] for sale"—and at her command.

---

19. i.e. fine silk from the island of Cos.

20. The Lares were Roman place-gods associated, among other things, with the family household. Here they stand for the home.

Whatever poisons Circe's got,[21] or Medea,[22]   55
    whatever herbs the land of Thessaly[23] bears,
and Horse madness[24]: when Venus breathes desire into wild
                                              herds,—
    the stuff that drips from a hot mare's cunt—
so long as Nemesis[25] looks at me with a calming look,
    those and a thousand other herbs, if she mixes them up, I'll   60
                                              drink.

---

21. Circe was the sorceress, famous from Homer's *Odyssey*.

22. Like Circe, Medea is associated with sorcery. Cf. note on Propertius 2.24b.29.

23. Thessaly was associated with witchcraft, sorcery, etc.

24. Hippomanes, "a mucous secretion discharged by mares in heat" (*Oxford Latin Dictionary*), used in love philters.

25. This is what Tibullus calls his "mistress" of Book Two. More famous is his Delia of Book One. In Ovid's lament on the death of Tibullus (*Amores* 3.9), the two women are imagined arguing at his funeral.

SULPICIA

The *Corpus Tibullianum* includes, in addition to 16 elegies by Tibullus himself, a number which seem to have been written by other poets either under his influence or in a similar style. Among these we find a group apparently by Sulpicia, daughter of Servius Sulpicius (3.16.4). We have included this piece as an example of her art—she is the only woman poet in classical Latin whose work survives.

(Tibullus) 3.18=4.12

May I not now, my light, be as much your flame
    as I think I was a few days ago,
if, in all the follies of my youth, I've done anything
    that I confess I'm sorrier for
than that I left you alone last evening,
    wanting to hide my heat.

PROPERTIUS

If much of Ovid's easy elegance and poise seems to derive from Tibullus, a good deal of his wit can be traced to the Umbrian Propertius (ca. 50–16 B.C.), whom Quintilian admits (*Inst.* 10.1.93) is preferred by some. Difficult for his sometimes baffling forms of expression, Propertius is, like all the major Roman poets, deeply indebted to Callimachus (and not just in the fourth book of the *Elegies*, as has often been said), whom he acknowledges as his master in programmatic poems (which we have not, however, included). The first book of the *Elegies*, called the *Monobiblos*, is generally thought to constitute an organized sequence. For that very reason we have chosen not to excerpt more than a single poem from it, and have turned rather to the splendid second book, which P.J. Enk, arguably the poet's most eminent modern commentator, calls "the most beautiful" (*Sex. Propertii Elegiarum, Liber Secundus* [Leiden 1962] 8) of the four books of *Elegies*.

1.18

This, at least, is a lonely, quiet place for my lament.
    The empty grove belongs to the western breeze.
Here I can wail out stifled sorrows and not catch hell,
    if only the rocks can keep a secret.
Where shall I start, O my Cynthia, to tell the story of your   5
                                           pride?
    What prelude, Cynthia, do you offer to my weeping?
I, who not long ago was counted blest among lovers,
    am now forced to bear a mark because of your love.
Did I earn this? What spells are changing you on me?
    Or was it a new girl that made you harden?   10
Won't you come back?! So help me, no other flimsy girl,
    has placed her pretty feet on my doorstep.

(Though this pain in here owes you lots of bitterness,
    still, my anger will never be so savage
that I'd cause you to rage forever at me rightly, and your eyes   15
    to grow unpretty from spilling tears.)
Or is it that I give insufficient signs, don't grow pale,
    don't proclaim fidelity in a loud voice?
You shall be my witnesses, if trees know any love,
    beech and pine, the darling of Arcadia's god![1]   20
Yes, how often do my words resound beneath your shade!
    how often "Cynthia" is written in your bark!
Or is it that your unkindness has spawned my pains?
    unkindness known only to silent doors.
I've gotten used to taking every order, out of fear,   25
    and not lamenting your haughtiness, though the pain is
                                  shrill.
And for that, I get back these divine springs, this cold cliff,
    a tough sleep on an unkept path.
And whatever story my laments can tell,
    I must say in solitude to shrill birds.   30
But, whatever you are to me, let the woods re-echo "Cynthia"!
    and the lonely rocks not lack your name.

2.5

Is this fair, that you're on the lips of all Rome, Cynthia?
    that you live in open shame?
Is this what I earned the right to expect? You liar, you'll pay.
    And the breeze will carry me, Cynthia, somewhere else.
Out of so many cheating girls, I'll find one   5
    who'd like to become known through my songs,
who won't jeer at me so viciously—it's you she'll
    pick apart. O too late you'll weep that you were loved so long.

---

    1. This is a reference to the rustic god, Pan, who was especially at home in the wild, mountainous region of Arcadia in the central Peloponnese.

Now anger's fresh: now it's leaving time.
    If pain goes away, believe me, love'll be back.   10
The Carpathian waves[2] do not shift in the northwind
    nor clouds veer in the turning southern gusts, as easily
as lovers who are angry change with a word.
    While you can, take your neck from that cruel yoke.
You'll hurt a bit, the first night—but   15
    in love all pain is light if you just bear up.
But you, by the sweet oaths we swore to Juno,[3]
    don't hurt yourself, my life, with your willful ways.
It's not just the bull that gores his foe with hooked horn;
    no, even a sheep, once hurt, fights back the attacker.   20
But I won't tear the clothes from your perjured body,
    my anger won't break your bolted doors,
I wouldn't, in my rage, tear out your braided tresses,
    or dare to hurt you with my powerful thumbs.
A bumpkin may like such filthy quarrels,   25
    whose head the ivy has not wreathed.
So I'll write what your whole lifetime can't delete:
    Cynthia's beauty, great; Cynthia's word, light.
Believe me, though you scorn the murmurs of talk,
    this verse will make you pale.   30

2.8

My girl, loved so long, is being torn from me
    and you, my friend, forbid me to shed tears?
No hatreds are bitter, except those of love.
    Slit my throat; I'll fight it less.

---

2. That part of the Aegean Sea between Crete and Rhodes, named after the island
Karpathos. The area was proverbially stormy.

3. Oaths by Juno seal a union between a man and a woman. They do not necessarily
imply a legal marriage.

Can I see her cocked on another's arm?   5
    Will she not be called mine who was called mine yesterday?
All things change. And yes, love changes too.
    You're conquered or you conquer, this is love's wheel.
Many great leaders have fallen, many great tyrants;
    Thebes has stood its day and Troy's no more.   10
How many gifts I gave, how many songs I made—
    but she, woman of iron, never said, "I'm in love."
Was I such a fool, then, for so many years,
    to put up with you, bitch, and all your house?
Did I ever seem more than a slave to you? or will you keep   15
    firing haughty words at my head?
Is that how you're going to die, Propertius—so young?
    Well die, then: give her a thrill when they lay you in.
She can rail at my ghost, carp at my shade,
    she can dance on the pyre, tread my bones.   20
Why, didn't Boeotian Haemon collapse at Antigone's tomb[4]
    stabbed through the ribs with his very own sword
and mingle his bones with those of his girl,
    without whom he wouldn't go home to Thebes?
But you won't get away with it: you should die with me;   25
    your blood and mine should drip from the same sword.
Though that death of mine will be dishonorable—
    a dishonorable death indeed—but you'll die too.
Left by himself when his woman was dragged away, Achilles[5]
    let his armor just sit in his hut;   30
he had seen the Argives strewn in flight along the shore,
    and the Dorian camps broil to the torch of Hector.

---

4. Haemon killed himself at the side of his betrothed, Antigone, when his father
Creon had her killed because she had dared to violate his interdiction against burying
her brother, Polyneices.

5. It was because Agamemnon stole his mistress, Briseis, that Achilles chose to sit
out the Trojan war. Propertius, embellishing on Homer, makes it seem as though
Achilles came back into the fight only once Briseis had been returned; in the *Iliad*,
however, it is the warrior's rage over the death of his companion Patroclus that finally
drives him to re-enter the fray.

He had seen Patroclus disfigured, stretched out huge
     on the sand, and his hair lying splattered with gore,
and he bore all this because Briseis was beautiful: 35
     so great a pain rages over a love torn away.
But when the captive girl was returned—atonement too
                                        late—,
     he dragged the mighty Hector with his Haemonian team.[6]
Since I'm far inferior in my mother and my arms,
     is it a wonder if Love beats me down?   40

2.9

What that guy is, I often was; but maybe, someday,
     when he's been dumped, another will be dearer.
Penelope could live untouched for two decades,
     woman worthy of so many suitors,
could put off the match with her deceiving skill,   5
     unwinding by nightly craft what she wove each day.
And though she never hoped to see Ulysses,
     she stayed put, got old, waiting for him.
And didn't Briseis embrace the dead Achilles,
     and lash her lovely face with frenzied hands,   10
and though a captive, weep and wash her bloodied lord,
     laid out in the golden shallows of Simois,
and befoul her hair, and bear the body, Achilles'
     great hulk in her little hands,
since neither Peleus nor your sea-blue mother was there for   15
                                        you,
     nor Deidamia of Scyrus, her bed bereft.[7]

---

6. Haemon was the father of Thessalus, the eponymous hero of the region of
Thessaly. Thus "Haemonian" = Thessalian.

7. When Achilles was a boy, his mother knew that if he went off to Troy he would
be killed. She therefore dressed him as a girl and gave him to the king of Scyrus to care

So that Greece rejoiced, then, in its trueborn girls,
  then decency prospered, even among arms.
But you couldn't be idle for a single night,
  beast, or remain alone a single day.   20
Why you even slurped down drinks, laughed a lot,
  —and maybe there was nasty talk of me.
And you're chasing that guy, who left you before,
  Now that you're caught, I hope to god you enjoy him.
Is that what I get for the vows I took for your health   25
  when the Stygian waters were stirring around your head
and we (your friends) stood at your bed weeping ...?
  Where was he then?!—oh gods!—you lying woman!—or
                                        who was he?
What if I were a soldier kept in the distant Indies,
  or if my ship were stuck in the Ocean?   30
But concocting lies and snares is easy for you.
  That's one skill a woman always learns.
The Syrtes do not change under shifting gusts,[8]
  nor leaves begin to tremble in the wintry southern blasts,
as quick as a woman's bond fails to stand fast in wrath,   35
  whether the cause is grave, or whether it's slight.
Now, since that's how you feel, I'll give up:
  I beg you, boys,[9] take out still sharper arrows,
see who can peg me best, undo my life:
  my blood will be your biggest prize.   40
I call the stars to witness, and the morning frosts,
  and the door slyly opened to my begging hand.
Nothing's more welcome in my life than you,
  and won't be now either, no matter how nasty you are.

---

for. But Achilles slept with the king's daughter, Deidamia, who bore Achilles a son:
Pyrrhus.
    8. The greater and lesser Syrtis were two flat and sandy regions between Carthage
and Cyrene, surrounding respectively the gulf of Sidra and the gulf of Gabes.
    9. i.e. Cupids.

No mistress will ever leave tracks on my bed, 45
    I'll be alone, since I'm not allowed to be yours.
But I pray, if I've lived my years well,
    let that man turn into stone in the heat of the act.
The Theban commanders didn't fall more willingly for their
                                      kingdom
in grim combat gear, their mother between them, 50
than I would, if I could fight with my girl between us:
    I wouldn't run away from death, so long as you die.[10]

2.12

Whoever that guy was who painted Love as a boy,
    don't you think he had amazing hands?
He first saw that lovers lack sense
    and that great goods are squandered on trivial concerns.
And it was no slip that he added breezy wings 5
    and made the god fly from the human breast:
for it's true, we get battered by one wave after another,
    and a good wind won't stay put in any quarter.
And he did well to arm the hand with hooked arrows
    and lay a Cnosian[11] quiver on both shoulders: 10
since he strikes before we (seemingly secure) even make out
                                our enemy,
    and nobody walks away healthy from that wound.
His weapons have stuck in me, his boyish image has stuck,
    but it's obvious he's lost his wings,
since, oh boy, he never flies out of my chest, 15
    and wages constant warfare in my blood.

---

10. On the analogy of Eteocles and Polyneices, the Theban commanders and brothers, who killed each other, though their mother tried to hold them apart, the speaker
is willing to die as long as his rival dies too.
    11. Cnossos was the ancient capital of Crete.

What kicks do you get out of living in dry marrow?
    If you have any shame, shoot your weapons elsewhere.
Better to go after those your poison hasn't touched—
    it's not me, but my thin shade that's taking the beating.   20
And if you kill it, who will there be to hymn such things?
    —this slender muse of mine is your big boast—
to sing the girl's face and fingers and dark eyes,
    and how suavely she walks along.

2.22a

You know that yesterday lots of girls stirred me alike;
    you know, Demophoon, that lots of trouble is coming my
                                                way.
If by chance a haughty one denied me something in her   11
                                                glance,
    a chill sweat covered my forehead.   12
Every public place I go, it never fails,   3
    and the theater, O god, was born to be my downfall:
Whether some dancer stretches his arms in a supple gesture,   5
    or plays varying melodies with his mouth,
all the while my eyes are seeking to wound themselves,
    in case a dazzler's sitting down with her breast exposed,
or her floating hair wanders across her perfect brow,
    slipped out from the pearl clasp atop her head.   10
You ask, Demophoon, why I am so ripe for them all?   13
    No love has that "why" you're asking for.
Why does anyone gash his arms with sacred knives,   15
    and hack himself to the crazed rhythms of a Phrygian
                                                flute?[12]
Nature granted a vice to each of its creations:
    to me Fortune gave this: always to be a bit in love.

---

12. The Great Mother (Magna Mater) was a Phrygian goddess worshipped with wild
dances and self-mutilation.

Even if the fate of that singer Thamyras[13] pursues me,
  I will never—you're jealous, I know—be blind to beautiful   20
                                        girls.
And if I seem to you scrawny and slender of limb,
  you are deceived: Venus isn't worshipped with sheer
                                        strength.
You can ask around: often a girl has found from experience
  that my service lasts out the night.
Juppiter stopped the Bears in their tracks for Alcmena,   25
  and twice at night the sky was without its king,[14]
but he did not therefore come languid to the lightning bolts.
  Love does not, of itself, strip itself of its strength.
Yes, and when Achilles would go from the embrace of Briseis,
  did the Phrygians run the less away from Thessalian   30
                                        weapons?
Yes, and when savage Hector rose from the bed of
                                        Andromache,
  were the Mycenaean rafts unafraid of battle?
Either of them could demolish ships and walls:
  In this field I'm the son of Peleus, here I am the savage
                                        Hector.
See how by turns the sun and the moon serve in the sky?   35
  So for me, one girl just isn't enough.
Let another hold me and warm me in her eager arms,
  if this one doesn't have time.
Or if she should become enraged at my messenger,
  she should know there's another who wants to be mine.   40
Because two ropes protect a ship better,
  and it's safer for an anxious mother to suckle twins.

---

13. Thamyras boasted that he could sing better than the Muses, and challenged them to a contest. The Muses struck him blind for his arrogance and made him forget his song-craft (cf. Homer, *Iliad* 2.594ff.).

14. Juppiter came to Alcmena disguised as her husband, Amphitryon, and to prolong their pleasure made the night twice as long. The ancients called the Big and Little Dipper "the Bears."

2.22b

If you're cruel, say no; if you're not cruel, come.
    But what's the point of saying words that mean nothing?
For a lover this is the most jagged pain of all:
    when a girl suddenly says she's not coming.
How many sighs toss him all around the bed,   5
    when he says he won't receive a girl who hasn't come,
And pesters his messenger to repeat what he's already heard,
    and makes him find out what he's afraid to know.

2.24b

Is this what you were beckoning me to enjoy back at the first?
    That you, so formly, should be so fickle—aren't you ashamed?
One or another night barely spent in love,
    and I'm already called a burden to your bed.
Why it was just now: you were praising me, you were reading   5
                          my poems;
    this love of yours turns its wings that quickly?
He should take me on in genius, take me on in skill,
    but most of all he should learn to love in just one house.
If you like, he should fight the Hydra of Lerna[15]
    and bring you the apples of the Hesperian dragon,[16]   10
guzzle foul poisons with gusto, get shipwrecked and gulp
                        brine,
    and never refuse to be wretched for your sake
(o my life, I'd like you to try me out in these tasks!):
    and soon this hero of yours will be one of the meek,

---

15. The Hydra of Lerna was a many-headed dragon which was slain by Hercules as one of his labors.
16. This dragon, likewise overcome by Hercules in the course of his labors, guarded the apples in the garden of the Hesperides.

though now he's come boasting into your overblown favors.　　15
　　Watch: next year you'll break up.
But me, the whole span of Sibyl won't change me,[17]
　　or the labor of Hercules, or death's black day.
You'll gather my bones and say, "Your bones, Propertius,
　　these are yours? Ah, you were true to me.　　20
You were true, yes, though your grandfather's blood
　　wasn't blue, and you were never all that rich."
There's nothing I won't take. Your cheating never changes
　　　　　　　　　　　　　　　　　　　　　　me.
　　I don't think it's a burden to put up with a beautiful girl.
I believe that not a few have died over that figure,　　25
　　I believe it, but not that many have kept faith.
Theseus didn't love the daughter of Minos for very long,[18]
　　Demophoon dropped Phyllis[19]—both were bad guests.
You know about Medea, and her trip on Jason's keel[20]—
　　she was left alone as soon as he'd been saved.　　30
It's a callous girl who fakes love to a lot of men,
　　who pretties herself for more than one.
Don't compare me to the rich and famous.
　　There's hardly a one who'll gather your bones on that final
　　　　　　　　　　　　　　　　　　　　　　day.
That's what I'll be for you. But I pray that you be the one　　35
　　to wail for me with naked breast, your hair undone.

---

17. The Sibyl of Cumae was a priestess of Apollo and the mouthpiece for his oracles. The god granted her to live a thousand years—though he did not grant her eternal youth (cf. Ovid, *Met.* 14.132f.).

18. After she'd helped him escape the labyrinth, Theseus abandoned Ariadne on the island of Naxos.

19. Demophoon, the son of Theseus, abandoned Phyllis, daughter of the king of Thrace, after he'd stayed with her on his way back from Troy.

20. Medea, the princess of Colchis, fell in love with Jason and helped him, by means of sorcery, to steal the golden fleece from her father. After they got home safely on their ship, the Argo, Jason left her for another woman.

2.27

Still, you mortals try to find out the uncertain hour
    of your demise, and what way death will take,
and you try to find out from the clear sky (a Phoenician
                                          trick)[21]
    what star's propitious for men, what star is bad.
Whether we chase the Parthians[22] by foot or Britons by boat,   5
    by sea or land you can't see the perils of the way.
And again, you weep that your head's exposed to the mob
    when Mars whips up two wavering bands of men,
and also that your house could burn or just collapse,
    or that poisoned cups could come to your lips.   10
Only the lover knows when and by what death
    he'll die, and isn't afraid of battle or the northwind's blasts.
Let's say he's already perched at the oar amid Stygian reeds,[23]
    eyeing the eery sails of the hellcraft,
if but a breeze from his crying girl call him back,   15
    he'll make the journey that no law concedes.

2.29a

Yesterday, my light, I was wandering—drunk in the night,
    and no group of slaves was guiding me,
and a band of I don't know how many little boys[24] appeared
    in my path (fear kept me from counting them)
and some of them had torches, others arrows,   5
    and a bunch of them seemed to be readying chains for me.

---

21. The Phoenicians were credited with advances in astronomy.
22. See note on Catullus 11.5.
23. The Styx was the principal river of the underworld.
24. i.e. Cupids.

And they were naked. And one of them was naughtier than
                        the rest:
   "Grab him," he said, "you recognize him;
This is the guy that angry woman gave us the contract on."
   That's what he said, and the knot was around my neck.   10
Then one of them said to push me into the middle, and then
                       another:
   "He should die, since he doesn't believe we're gods.
She waits for you for hours, and you're not worth it,
   while you, you dolt, go asking at any old door.
And when she's untied the nocturnal laces from her Sidonian   15
   headband,[25] and fluttered her weary eyes,
the fragrances that waft upon you won't be from Arabian
                       herbs,
   but ones that Love has made with his own hands.
Go easy now, boys,—now he'll swear true love;
   and anyway we've come to the house she told us: look."   20
And so they threw my cloak back around me and said:
   "Now go. And learn to spend your nights at home."

2.29b

It was morning and I wanted to see if she was sleeping
   alone. And Cynthia was alone in her bed.
I was amazed: she'd never seemed more beautiful,
   not even when she was dressed in purple
and went to tell her dreams to virgin Vesta[26]   5
   so they wouldn't do any harm to her or to me.
And that's the way she looked, just stirring from sleep.
   O, the dazzling power of beauty just in itself.

---

   25. Sidon is a city on the eastern coast of the Mediterranean.
   26. That is, Cynthia got dressed up to go to the temple of Vesta (the Roman goddess
of the hearth) to tell her bad dreams and thereby avert any possible evil consequences.

"What are you some kind of morning girl watcher?" she said.
    "Do you think I have your ways?   10
I'm not so easy. One lover will be enough for me—
    you or someone else who can be truer.
There are no traces that the bed's been crushed,
    no signs that two have squirmed about.
Look, no aroma rises from my whole body,   15
    signaling adultery."
That's what she said. And fending off kisses with her right
                        hand,
    without fastening her sandals, she lept onto her feet.
And so I, keeper of so sacred a love, have been made a fool of.
    Since then I haven't had a happy night.   20

3.6

Tell me what you feel's the truth about my girl,
    and I hope, Lygdamus, your lady's yoke is lifted from you.
You're not puffing me up, are you?—tricking me with empty
                        joy,
    telling me what you think I want to believe?
All messengers should speak without falsehood,   5
    and a slave, being afraid, must be even truer.
Now if you've got some news, begin from the top
    and tell me. I'll drink it up with pricked ears.
So you saw her crying with her hair undone
    and the drops were falling heavy from her eyes?   10
You saw no mirror, Lygdamus, on the bed?
    The bedside vanity was closed?
Gloomy clothes hung on those beautiful arms?
    Not an ornament? Not a gem on her snowy hands?
The house was sad, and her servants sadly   15
    worked the daily wool, while she spun by the hearth?

And she'd press her eyes to the wool to dry them
    as she told about our fight in a mournful voice?
"You were witness, Lygdamus—is this the boon he promised me?
    It's wrong to break faith, even if the witness is a slave.   20
So he can leave me?!—wracked, though I've done nothing,
    and keep a little (I won't say what she is) at home?!
He likes it that I melt away here on this lonely bed.
    If he wants to, Lygdamus, he can dance on my corpse.
The witch, she's beaten me with herbs, not personality.   25
    He's led about by the rhombus with its whirling thread,
dragged along by the portents of the swollen bush toad
    and the dried bones of choice snakes,
and the screech owl's feathers, found on a neglected tomb,
    and woolen ribbons worn on the couch of death.   30
If the voice of my dreams doesn't lie, Lygdamus, I swear
    he will be at my feet—a late but full retribution.
A foul spiderweb will be woven in that unused bed
    and Venus herself shall sleep through their nights."
If the girl really meant it, complaining to you like that,   35
    run back the same way you came
and tell her that I told you with many a tear
    "There may be anger in my love, but I do not cheat."
Tell her: "that I am twisting in the same fire."
    I'll swear I've been pure these past twelve days.   40
And if, from so big a war, I get a prosperous peace,
    as for me, Lygdamus, you'll be set free.

3.8

That fight yesterday by lamplight was a pleasure for me,
    so many curses, your voice enraged,
when, crazy drunk, you thrust the table away
    and threw full winebowls, your hand insane.
Come on, be bold, attack my hair,   5
    mark up my face with your lovely nails,

threaten to take a torch and burn out my eyes,
    tear off my shirt, leave my chest bare.
I am, it's clear, being given signs of a true heat.
    No female feels pain for a love that's not intense.   10
Any woman whose rabid tongue splatters abuse
    is writhing at the feet of buxom Venus.
Say, on a walk, she rings herself with herds of chaperones
    or, like a stricken Maenad,[27] runs down the middle of the
                                      road,
or frenzied dreams are always frightening her,   15
    or a girl in a painting moves her and she's sad.
I am a soothsayer for all such torments of the soul.
    I have learned that, often, these are the marks of a real love.
No love is sure that you can't turn into a fight.
    Girls who couldn't care less I leave to my foes.   20
Let the boys see the bites and bruises on my neck,
    let black and blue marks indicate my girl's been with me.
In love, I want to feel pain, or listen to someone in pain,
    to see tears, either mine or yours,
like when you send a guy a message hidden in your glance   25
    or trace with your fingers unutterable signs.
I hate dreams that are never punctuated with sighs.
    May I always go pale for a girl who gets angry.
The flame was sweeter for Paris when, in delicious warfare,
    he could take pleasure in his Tyndarid.[28]   30
Whether the Greeks were winning, or Trojan Hector was
                             standing firm,
    he was waging the biggest war in Helen's lap.
I'll always be fighting—with you or with my rivals
    for your sake. With you, I want no peace.
Be happy that no girl is as beautiful. You would be sorry   35
    if one were. Now you can be rightly proud.

---

27. A maenad (literally "a maddened woman") was a female devotee of Dionysus.
28. Helen was the daughter of Tyndareus.

And as for you,[29] who wove your nets in our bed,
    may your father-in-law and your mother live with you
                               forever.
If you've been given the chance to steal one night,
    she gave it, hurt by me, not hot for you.   40

3.20

Do you think he can still remember what you look like?—
    that guy you saw set sail from your bed?
Tough man, who could trade a girl for lucre.
    Was all of Africa worth your tears?
But you, foolish girl, imagine his empty words are sacrosanct.   5
    He's probably grinding his chest against another girl.
You have a potent beauty, the arts of chaste Pallas,[30]
    and your learned grandfather's sparkling fame reflects on
                               you.
Your home would be happy, if only you had a faithful friend.
    I'll be faithful, girl, come running to my bed!   10
And you,—who drive the summer's flames too slow,—
    Phoebus, shrink the span of this lingering sunlight.
My first night has come; the first night's hours are mine.
    Moon, linger longer over this first embrace.
I must draw up a treaty first, seal vows,   15
    write a law for love made new.
Love himself will bind our pledge with his seal
    and the starry goddess' woven wreath will be witness.[31]
How many hours shall expire in my negotiations

---

29. In the last four verses of the poem the speaker addresses another man. What he says, however, is directed to Cynthia as well.

30. The arts of Pallas are the feminine domestic skills of spinning and weaving.

31. A reference to the constellation of Ariadne's Crown. Ariadne was found by Bacchus on the island of Naxos, where she had been abandoned by Theseus. He promised to marry her and, as a token of his love, made her marriage crown a constellation.

before Venus whips up her sweet warfare! 20
For when an affair's not enforced by a bond of trust
    no deity avenges nights spent waiting,
and lust soon loosens the bonds it had imposed.
    So these first omens must sustain our bond.
Whoever wrecks the altar where he's sworn a pact 25
    and sullies the wedding rites in a new bed
may he suffer all the usual pains of love
    and provide the plot for saucy gossip.
Though he weeps, may his lady's window never open.
    May he love forever, forever lack love's fruition. 30

OVID

Ovid was born on March 20th, 43 B.C. in Sulmo. He was an Eques (a knight), and enjoyed the privileges of that rank: he was sent to Rome as a boy to study rhetoric and toured Athens and the Greek east. Though he may originally have had senatorial aspirations, he soon gave these up for a literary career. Many believe he brought Latin elegy to its most technically refined and elegant form. His *Amores* (or "Loves")—from which our selection is drawn—was an early work which first appeared in five books but was subsequently revised and pruned down to three. Central to this work is a woman named Corinna. After writing his *Heroides* (letters from legendary heroines to their lovers or spouses) and the epic *Metamorphoses*, Ovid's career went into a sudden tailspin when the emperor Augustus took offense at his *Ars Amatoria* ("Art of Love") and at something else that Ovid never specifies. In 8 A.D. Augustus banished the poet to the city of Tomis on the west coast of the Black Sea, where he languished until his death in 17 A.D.

1.5

It was sweltering, and the day had reached midafternoon.
    I laid my limbs in the middle of the couch to relax.
One part of the shutters was open; the other, closed.
    Nearly the kind of light you see in the woods,
or like the twilight that shimmers when the sun is fading,   5
    or when night's gone, but the day's not yet arisen.
That's the kind of light you should offer to shy girls,
    where bashful modesty can hope to hide.
And look, Corinna comes in wearing a loose gown,
    her parted hair covering her dazzling neck,   10

just as shapely Semiramis is said to have come
    to her chambers;[1] and Lais, loved by many men.[2]
I took off the gown; it was thin, and didn't really hurt,
    but still she kept struggling to keep it on.
But since she struggled like a girl who doesn't want to win,   15
    she was easily undone by her own betrayal.
When she stood, uncovered, before my eyes,
    in her whole body there was no imperfection.
What shoulders I saw and touched, what arms!
    The beauty of her breasts—how fit for squeezing.   20
And beneath her firm chest, a stomach so smooth!
    What sides! How ample! What youth in those thighs!
Why go into details? I saw nothing I couldn't praise,
    and pressed her naked body to my own.
Who doesn't know the rest? Both exhausted, we lay together.   25
    May I have many afternoons like that.

2.10

You were telling me, yes it was you, I remember, Graecinus,
    that a guy can't love two girls at the same time.
Deceived by you, disarmed by you, taken unawares,
    I'm disgracefully in love—at the same time—with two girls.
Each is shapely, both are devoted to elegance,   5
    there's no telling which one's superior in skill.
One is prettier than the other; the other's prettier, too.
    One appeals to me more, but so does the other one.
I wander like a skiff driven by warring winds.
    These two loves have me split in two.   10

---

1. Semiramis was a legendary queen of Babylon, famous for her beauty.
2. Lais was a celebrated *hetaira* of Corinth in the 4th cent. B.C.

Why, Erycina, are you doubling my unending pains?[3]
    Wasn't one girl enough to worry about?
Why add leaves to the trees, stars to the full sky?
    Why collect water and add it to the high seas?
Still, better this than that I lie without love.   15
    I'd wish that on my enemies—the stern life.
Let my enemies sleep on a lonely bed,
    and stretch their limbs out wide in the middle.
As for me, let raging Love wreck my useless sleep;
    I don't want to be the only weight on my bed.   20
Let my girl destroy me unrestrained;
    if one is enough, fine; and if she's not, then two.
I shall suffice. My limbs are slender but not without strength.
    My body lacks bulk, not energy;
and pleasure will nourish and reinforce my trunk.   25
    No girl's been disappointed by my services.
Often I've spent the hours of the night at lusty play,
    and still been useful and vigorous in the morning.
Blessed is he whom the wargames of Venus destroy.
    May the gods make that the cause of my demise.   30
Let the soldier impale his chest on enemy spears
    and buy an eternal name with his blood.
Let the greedy man seek wealth, get shipwrecked and drink
    with his perjured mouth the waves he's thrashed with oars.
For myself, I'd like to fade out in the motion of Venus.   35
    When I die, let me slacken in the middle of the act.
And let someone in tears at my funeral say,
    "That death of yours was becoming to your life."

---

3. Erycina is Venus, so called because her cult was brought to Rome from Mt. Eryx in Sicily.

2.15

Ring, about to wreathe the finger of a lovely girl,
    in whom only the giver's love should be weighed,
go, gift, give pleasure. May she take you gladly
    and slip you right over her knuckles.
I hope you fit her as well as she fits me,   5
    and cozily rub her finger, your circle just right.
Lucky stiff, you'll be handled by my mistress, ring,—
    what a jerk! I already envy my gift.
I wish I could suddenly turn into my present
    by the arts of the Aeaean[4] or the old Carpathian.[5]   10
Then I'd want you, lady, to touch your breasts
    and dip your left hand[6] inside your clothes.
I'd slip off your finger, though I'd been clinging tight,
    slacken with amazing skill and slide down your lap.
Also, so I could seal secret writing tablets   15
    and not get my dry jewel caked with wax,
I'd first touch my lovely girl's moist lips;
    But please, no letters that hurt my case.
And when she tries to put me in her jewelbox, I won't come
                                             off
    but tighten my circle around her finger.   20
May you never, my life, be ashamed of me
    and your slender finger refuse to bear my load.
Wear me when you bathe your body in warm water,
    the gush will not erode the inlaid rock.
But with you naked, I think, my member shall leap with lust   25
    and I, a little ring, shall play the man's part.

---

    4. A reference to Circe, the sorceress famous from Homer's *Odyssey*, who lived on
the island Aeaea.
    5. Proteus lived, according to some authors, in the Carpathian sea. He was famous
for being able to change his shape at will.
    6. The left hand was traditionally thought especially good for sexual manipulation.
The epigrammatist Martial calls it the *manus fututrix*, i.e. "the fuck-hand" (XI 22.4).

Why say "shall" uselessly? Go, little gift,
    she should feel I'm bound—by giving you—to her.

2.19

If you feel no need to guard your girl, fool,
    guard her for my sake, so I'll love her more.
If you can have it, who wants it; if you can't, it burns hotter.
    Only a man of iron loves what another lets him.
We lovers should fear as much as hope.   5
    The odd rebuff should be your opening to woo.
What good is luck that never lets you down?
    I don't love what couldn't ever hurt me.
Cunning Corinna saw this weakness of mine,
    a tricky girl, she knew how I could be caught.   10
How often, when she was fine, she'd fake a headache
    and tell me to leave, while I lingered, heavy footed.
How often she feigned guilt, and—as much as an innocent
    girl can—offered me the semblance of a cheater.
That way, when she'd wrecked me and stoked the cooling fire,   15
    again she'd be kind, responsive to my desires.
How many sweet nothings she told me, what sweet words she
                               cooked up.
    How many kisses, O mighty gods, what kisses they were!
And you, too, who not long ago ravished my eyes,
    always fear an ambush, when I ask you, always say no.   20
And let me lie prostrate at the threshold of your door
    and suffer an extended chill in the frosty night.
That way my love will be firm and grow through the long
                               years.
    That gets me off, that is my spirit's food.
A love that's sluggish and puts up turns boring for me   25
    and, like over-sweet food in the gut, can make you ill.

If a bronze tower had not housed Danae,
  Danae would never have been made a mother by Jove.[7]
While Juno was guarding Io transformed by horns,
  Jove found her even sweeter than he had before.[8]   30
Whoever wants what he can have, what's easy,
  should pick leaves off trees, drink the water of major rivers.
A girl who wants to rule long should trick her lover
  (god forbid I be racked by my teachings).
Come what may, readiness puts me off.   35
  What follows, I flee; what flees I follow.
But you, you're too sure of a beautiful girl.
  Begin now to bolt the door at nightfall.
Begin to ask who's furtively treading your threshold
  so often, why your dogs are barking though the night is   40
                                               still;
why her clever handmaid is bringing and taking letters,
  why she so often wants to sleep alone.
That girl should obsess you sometimes, eat at your marrow.
  Give me scope and material for my tricks.
Steal sand from the shore when no one's there: 45
  that's what it is to love the wife of a fool.
I'm telling you now: if you don't begin to guard your girl
  she'll begin not being mine.
I've long put up with a lot, often I hoped that maybe,
  if you'd guard her, I could fool you good.   50
You're slow, you take things no man should take.
  I've just about had it with love that's handed over.
Alas, shall I never be kept from going to her?
  Will the night be mine forever—unavenged?

---

7. Danae was locked in a bronze chamber by her father, Acrisius, because he had received an oracle that she would bear a son who would kill him. Juppiter, however, fell in love with Danae and, turning himself into a shower of gold, slipped through the roof and into Danae's lap.

8. Juno changed Io into a cow so as to keep her from Juppiter, and set her under guard.

Shall I have nothing to fear? Dream without sighs?   55
    Won't you give me one reason to wish you dead?
What do I want with an easy—a pimp of a—husband!
    Your quirk is wrecking our joy.
Find another guy, someone who likes your patience.
    If you want me to be your rival, tell us "No!"   60

3.7

Well, was she not beautiful? not an elegant girl?
    Was she not—I believe—often the object of my prayers?
Yet it was she that I limply and uselessly held;
    rather, I lay like a crime, a burden on the idle bed.
And I couldn't—though I wanted, and the girl was wanting it   5
                                                    too,—
    enjoy the help of my lifeless loins.
Yes, she encircled my neck with her ivory
    arms, whiter than Sidonian snow,
and, with her eager tongue, stuffed me with wrestling kisses
    and slid her lusty thigh beneath my thigh,   10
told me sweet nothings, called me her master,
    and other common phrases that people like.
But, as if struck by icy hemlock, my member
    would not budge, deserted my desire.
I lay there, an inert trunk, a mirage, an idle weight,   15
    and it wasn't clear whether I was a body or a shade.
What will my old age be like, if it ever comes,
    if my youth isn't up to the task.
I'm ashamed of my age: what good are manhood and youth
    if my girlfriend didn't feel my manhood or my youth?   20
A priestess of chastity, about to approach the eternal flames
    gets up like that,—or a sister honored by her beloved
                                            brother.

Yet not long ago, two times Chlide the redhead, three times
                                        Pitho,
    and three times Libas rode my service through.
And I remember that, in one brief night, Corinna   25
    demanded—and I bore up—nine times in a row.
My body's not limp from being bewitched by some Thessalian
    poison, is it?[9] It's not spells or herbs that are hurting me?
A Phoenician sorceress hasn't carved my name in wax
    and stuck a little pin in my liver, has she?   30
Ceres, when spellbound, withers into barren weed;[10]
    spellbound, springs run out of water.
Under spells, acorns fall from the oak, grapes from the vine,
    and fruit floods down, though no one moves the tree.
Who says magic spells aren't causing this slump in my   35
                                        powers?
    Maybe that's why my crotch feels nothing.
Add to this the shame of the thing. Shame itself got in the
                                        way,
    that was the second cause of my weakness.
What a girl! yet I was merely looking and touching—
    even her tunic touches her like that.   40
At her touch the elder from Pylos[11] could get young again
    and Tithonus[12] feel sturdier than his years.
She was mine, but no man was hers.
    What line can I think up now to win her again?
I think the great gods are ashamed of the gift they gave me, 45
    since I made such shameful use of it.
I wanted to be let in; I was let in;
    take kisses, I took them; be next to her, I was.

---

9. Thessaly was especially associated with magic and witchcraft.
10. The goddess Ceres here stands for the fruit of the field.
11. Nestor, the elder statesman of Homeric epic.
12. Like Nestor, Tithonus was proverbially associated with old age. He was the
beloved of the Dawn, who carried him off and begged Juppiter to give him eternal life.
The god granted the request, but the Dawn had forgotten to ask also for eternal youth.

But where did such great luck get me? What's a kingdom you
                                        can't use?

So did I hold that treasure like a wealthy miser?   50
That's how that broadcaster of secrets thirsts in the middle of
                                           waves

and "has" apples he can never touch.[13]
Who, I ask, rises in the morning from the bed of a winsome
                                          girl

ritually clean, ready to approach the holy gods?
But didn't she squander sweet kisses on me, the best   55
  of kisses, stir me up with every trick?
She could have moved massive oaks, hardest diamond,
  could have moved deaf rocks with those sweet words.
She was worthy, yes, to move men, living men,
  but I was neither living nor man, as I was before.   60
What good does it do for Phemius to sing to deaf ears?[14]
  What good's a painting to Thamyras?[15]
Yet I silently envisioned every form of ecstasy,
  imagined the layout of every position!
But my member, as if it were about to die, lay   65
  shamefully, limper than yesterday's rosebuds.
And now here it is, inopportunely vigorous and strong.
  Now it wants action, wants to go straight to the front.
Won't you lie still there, have some shame,—O worst part of me!
  I've been taken before by your promises.   70
You failed your master; disarmed by you, I was caught
  and suffered great shame and bitter losses.

---

13. Because he had served a sacrilegious meal to the gods, Tantalus was punished
by having to spend eternity in a pool of water, which would recede as soon as he bent
to drink it, and next to an apple tree whose branches would veer away whenever he
reached for them.

14. Phemius was a singer in the house of Odysseus in Homer's *Odyssey*.

15. Thamyras was a singer who boasted that he could outsing the Muses themselves,
and challenged them to a contest. For this, the Muses struck him blind and made him
forget his song-craft.

And my girl didn't even disdain to incite you
    softly with the motion of her hand.
But when she saw no skill could make you rise,   75
    that you just lay there, mindless of her,
"Why are you toying with me?" she said. "Who told you to
                              come, you nut,
    if you didn't want to, and dump your balls on my bed?
Either a poisoner from Aeaea[16] has bewitched you with binding
    threads, or you've come to me slack from another love."   80
That was it, she jumped up, wearing her tunic still untied
    (beautiful, racing off in her bare feet)
and, so her girls wouldn't find out I hadn't touched her,
    she tried to disguise the disgrace by rinsing with water.[17]

3.11a

I've long put up with a lot. But crimes have crushed my
                              patience.
    Leave my exhausted breast, you sleazy love.
Yes, I've freed myself and fled my chains,
    and I'm ashamed of what I put up with without shame.
I've won, defeated love, and tread him underfoot.   5
    Horns have sprouted, though late, upon my head.[18]
Endure it, be tough. Someday this pain will prove a benefit.
    Often a bitter juice brings strength to the sick.
How could I, so often driven from the door, have laid
    my tender body on the rough ground?   10

---

16. Cf. note on 2.15.10.
17. It was customary for women to rinse themselves after intercourse (cf. Ovid *Ars Amatoria* 3.96, 620; Martial VII 35.7) and by doing so here, the woman wants to make others think that she did in fact make love.
18. Horns traditionally signified strength.

How could I, because of some guy whom you were holding in
                                             your arms,
   have slept like a slave in front of your bolted door?
I saw, when the tottering lover walked out of your gate,
   carrying his useless, discharged body home.
But better this than that I should be seen by him: 15
   let that disgrace befall my enemies.
When did I not patiently cling firm at your side?—
   I myself your guardian, your man, your follower.
Yes, and people liked you when you were escorted by me.
   My love for you caused many to love you.   20
Why should I mention the dirty lies of your treacherous
                                         tongue,
   and the gods you swore by falsely—to my harm?
Why mention the silent nods of young men at parties,
   and the words hidden in coded signs?
I was told you were sick. I raced over, frantic: 25
   I got there, and you weren't sick for my rival.
Often I endured all this, and more that I won't tell.
   Find another guy instead, who'd like to take that stuff.
Now my ship, crowned with a votive wreath,[19]
   listens unmoved to the swelling waters of the sea.   30
Cut the sweet talk, stop wasting those words that once
   controlled me. I am not the fool I was before.

3.11b

Love and hate are wrestling, pulling my weak heart
   this way and that; but love is winning, I think.
I flee your depravity; your beauty drags me back from flight.
   I recoil from your vices, your body I love.
So that I can't live with you or without you   5
   and seem to have forgotten what I swore.

---

19. Ships were crowned with garlands when they got home safely after a voyage.

I wish you were less shapely or less slutty:
  Such lovely shape doesn't mesh with wicked ways.
Your feats deserve hating, your face urges love.
  I'm in a fix, *she* outweighs her crimes.   10
Go easy, by our lovers' oaths, by all the gods
  who often lend themselves to your perjury,
and your beauty, like a deity to me,
  and by your eyes, that stole my own.
Whatever you'll be, you'll always be mine; just you choose   15
  if you want me willing, or to love you under constraint.
I'd rather raise my sails to favoring winds,
  and want to love you; though I'd have to anyway.

3.14

I don't, since you're beautiful, insist you not cheat,
  but I don't need to suffer from knowing.
My morality doesn't order you to be true,
  but rather asks that you try to pretend.
A girl who can say she hasn't cheated isn't cheating;   5
  it's just the confession of guilt that sullies your name.
What madness! to tell in the light what's hidden in shadows,
  and openly narrate what you secretly do.
A whore, before hooking her body to an unknown citizen,
  slips the bolt and shuts the people out;   10
and shall you then lay your faults out before the public
                                                                                          tongue?
  Shall you rehearse the evidence of your crime?
Think better of it. At least be like faithful girls,
  and, though I know you're not, let me think you're true.
What you do, do it. Just say you haven't done it,   15
  don't be ashamed to speak modestly in public.
There's a place that requires naughtiness. Fill it with all
  pleasures, and let shame be far away.

As soon as you leave there, all your lasciviousness
 should vanish. Leave your sins in your bed.   20
There you should not be ashamed to strip down to the skin
 or to entangle thigh with thigh.
There the tongue should be plunged into flaming lips
 and desire fashion love into a thousand poses.
There sweet sounds and words should never cease   25
 and the bed should shake with the motion of lust.
But put on, along with your clothes, a sin-fearing look,
 and let some shame deny the dirty work.
Fool people. Fool me. Let me be stupidly wrong
 and let me enjoy my credulous folly.   30
Why must I so often see messages coming and going?
 And why is the bed so crushed?—not just the middle: the
                                                                 sides!
Why must I witness your hair tangled by more than sleep,
 and bitemarks on your neck?
You do all but parade the crime before my eyes.   35
 If you won't spare your name, spare me.
My brain stops and I die each time you say you've cheated,
 and an icy fluid rushes through my limbs.
Then I love you, but hate what I must love,
 then I'd really like to die—along with you.   40
I won't even ask, and what you go about hiding
 I won't seek out. Fooling me will be like a gift.
Even if you get caught in the middle of the crime
 and I've seen your sins with my own eyes,
say I didn't see what I saw too well,   45
 my vision will be outweighed by your words.
An easy win: to beat a guy who wants to be beaten,
 if your tongue can just remember to say, "Did not"!
Since you can vindicate yourself with just two words,
 you'll win, if not on the merits, then 'cause the judge is   50
                                                                 yours.

SUGGESTIONS
FOR FURTHER READING

For a general treatment of Greek and Roman poetry we refer readers to the relevant sections of *The Cambridge History of Classical Literature vol.1: Greek Literature*, P.E. Easterling and B.M.W. Knox, eds. (Cambridge 1985) and *vol.2: Latin Literature*, E.J. Kenney and W.V. Clausen, eds. (Cambridge 1982), as well as those in *Civilization of the Ancient Mediterranean*, 3 vols., eds. M. Grant and R. Kitzinger (New York 1988).

Archilochus: M.L. West, *Studies in Greek Elegy and Iambus* (Berlin 1974); J. Henderson, "The Cologne Epode and the Conventions of Early Greek Erotic Poetry," *Arethusa* 9 (1976) 159–179; G. Nagy, "Iambos: Typologies of Invective and Praise," *Arethusa* 9 (1976) 191–205; A.P. Burnett, *Three Archaic Poets* (London 1983); J.M. Bremer, A. Maria van Erp Taalman Kip, and S.R. Slings, *Some Recently Found Greek Poems*, Mnemosyne Suppl.99 (Leiden 1987).

Alkman: D. Page, *Alcman: the Partheneion* (Oxford 1951); A. Griffiths, "Alcman's Partheneion: the morning after the night before," *QUCC* 14 (1972) 7–30; C. Calame, *Les choeurs de jeunes filles en Grèce archaïque* (Rome 1977); L. Rissman, *Love and War. Homeric Allusion in the Poetry of Sappho* (Meisenheim 1984).

Mimnermos: H. Fränkel, *Early Greek Poetry and Philosophy* (New York 1973) 207–214; M.L. West, *Studies in Greek Elegy and Iambus* (Berlin 1974) 72–76.

Sappho: G.W. Most, "Fr.16.6–7 L-P," *CQ* 31.1 (1981) 11–17; E.S. Stigers, "Sappho's private world" in *Reflections of Women in Antiquity*, ed. H. Foley (New York 1981) 45–61; J. Winkler, "Gardens of nymphs: Public and private in Sappho's lyrics," *ibid.* 63–89; *idem, The Constraints of Desire* (New York 1990) 162–187; B. Gentili, "The Ways of Love in *Thiasos* and Symposium" in *Poetry and Its Public in Ancient Greece* (Baltimore 1988) esp.72–89; J.M. Snyder, "Sappho of Lesbos," in *The Woman and The Lyre* (S. Illinois Univ. Press 1991) 1–37.

Ibycus: H. Fränkel, *Early Greek Poetry and Philosophy* (New York 1973) 280–291; B. Gentili, *Poetry and Its Public in Ancient Greece* (Baltimore 1988) 99–104.

Anacreon: H. Fränkel, *Early Greek Poetry and Philosophy* (New York 1973) 291–303; G. Kirkwood, *Early Greek Monody* (Ithaca 1974) 150–177; L. Woodbury, "Gold

Hair and Grey, or the Game of Love: Anacreon fr.13: 358 PMG, 13 Gentili,"
TAPhA 109 (1979) 277–287; S. Goldhill, "Praying to Dionysus: re-reading fragment 2 (301 Page)," *LCM* 9 (1984) 85–88; B. Gentili, *Poetry and Its Public in Ancient Greece* (Baltimore 1988) 89–99.

Theognis: M. Vetta, *Theognis. Elegiarum Liber Secundus* (Rome 1980); M.L. West, *Studies in Greek Elegy and Iambus* (Berlin 1974); Th. J. Figueira and G. Nagy, *Theognis of Megara. Poetry and Polis* (Baltimore 1985); E.L. Bowie, "Early Greek Elegy, Symposium and Public Festival," *JHS* 106 (1986) 13–35; O. Murray, ed., *Sympotica: The Papers of a Symposium on the* Symposion, *Oxford 1984* (Oxford 1990).

Hipponax: M.L. West, *Studies in Greek Elegy and Iambus* (Berlin 1974), R.M. Rosen, "Hipponax, Boupalos, and the Conventions of the Psogos," *TAPhA* 118 (1988) 29–41.

Pindar: H. Fränkel, *Early Greek Poetry and Philosophy* (New York 1973); F. Nisetich, *Pindar's Victory Songs* (Baltimore 1980); K. Crotty, *Song and Action. The Victory Odes of Pindar* (Baltimore 1983); D.S. Carne-Ross, *Pindar* (New Haven 1985); G.W. Most, *The Measures of Praise*, Hypomnemata 83 (Göttingen 1985).

Bacchylides: M. Lefkowitz, *The Victory Ode* (Park Ridge 1976); A.P. Burnett, *The Art of Bacchylides* (Cambridge Mass. 1985).

Ischia Cup: K. Alpers, "Eine Beobachtung zum Nestorbecher von Pithekussai," *Glotta* 47 (1970) 170–174; A. Heubeck, "Schrift," in *Archaeologica Homerica* III, 10 (Göttingen 1979) 109–116; J. Latacz, *Homer* (Zürich 1985) 80–84. On the iambic meter of v.1, see M.L. West, *Greek Metre* (Oxford 1982) 40 n.28.

Asclepiades: S.L. Taran, *The Art of Variation in the Hellenistic Epigram* (Leiden 1979); A. Cameron, "Asclepiades' girl friends" in *Reflections of Women in Antiquity*, ed. H. Foley (New York 1981) 275–302.

Callimachus: P. Bing, *The Well-Read Muse. Present and Past in Callimachus and the Hellenistic Poets* (Göttingen 1988); L. Coco, *Callimaco Epigrammi* (Rome 1988).

Theocritus: C. Segal, *Poetry and Myth in Ancient Pastoral* (Princeton 1981); D. M. Halperin, *Before Pastoral: Theocritus and the Ancient Tradition of Bucolic Poetry* (New Haven 1983); H. Berger, "The Origins of Bucolic Representation: Disenchantment and Revision in Theocritus' Seventh Idyll," *CA* 3 (1984) 1–39; S. Goldhill, "Framing and Polyphony: Readings in Hellenistic Poetry," *Proc. Cambr. Philol. Soc.* 212 (1986) 25–52; *idem* "Desire and the figure of fun: glossing Theocritus 11," in *Poststructuralist Classics*, ed. A. Benjamin (New York 1988) 79–105; *idem*, "Theocritus and Hellenistic Poetics," in *The Poet's Voice* (Cambridge 1991) 223–283.

Herodas: I. C. Cunningham, "Herodas 6 and 7," *CQ* 14 (1964) 34f.; J. Stern, "Herodas Mimiamb 6," *GRBS* 20 (1979) 247–254; G. Mastromarco, *The Public of Herodas* (Amsterdam 1984).

Catullus: D.O. Ross, *Style and Tradition in Catullus* (Cambridge, Mass. 1969); K. Quinn, *The Catullan Revolution* (London 1959, rev. ed. 1969); *idem. Catullus: an Interpretation* (London 1972); T.P. Wiseman, *Catullus and his World: A Reappraisal* (Cambridge, 1985).

Virgil: M.C.J. Putnam, *Virgil's Pastoral Art* (Princeton 1970); E.W. Leach, *Virgil's Eclogues: Landscapes of Experience* (Ithaca 1974), R. Coleman, *Vergil: Eclogues* (Cambridge 1977) 1–36; J. Van Sickle, *The Design of Virgil's Bucolics* (Rome 1978); P. Alpers, *The Singer of the Eclogues: A Study of Virgilian Pastoral* (Berkeley 1979); J. Griffin, *Virgil* (Oxford 1986); D.M. Halperin, "Bucolic Poetry" in vol. 3 of *Civilization of the Ancient Mediterranean*, eds. M. Grant and R. Kitzinger (New York 1988) 1467–1475.

Horace: E. Fraenkel, *Horace* (Oxford 1957); S. Commager, *The Odes of Horace* (New Haven 1962); R.G.M. Nisbet and M. Hubbard, *A Commentary on Horace, Odes I* (Oxford 1970) xi–xxxviii; M.S. Santirocco, *Unity and Design in Horace's Odes* (Chapel Hill 1986); D. Armstrong, *Horace* (New Haven 1989).

Tibullus: F. Cairns, *Tibullus: A Hellenistic Poet at Rome* (Cambridge 1979); R.O.A.M. Lyne, *The Latin Love Poets* (Oxford 1980) 149–189.

Sulpicia: M.S. Santirocco, "Sulpicia Reconsidered," *CJ* 74 (1979) 229–239; J.M. Snyder, "Sulpicia of Messalla's Circle," in *The Woman and The Lyre* (S. Illinois Univ. Press 1991) 128–136.

Propertius: M. Hubbard, *Propertius* (New York 1975); J.P. Sullivan, *Propertius: a critical introduction* (Cambridge 1976); R.O.A.M. Lyne, *The Latin Love Poets* (Oxford 1980); J.P. Hallett, "The Role of Women in Roman Elegy," in *Women in the Ancient World: The Arethusa Papers*, J. Peradotto and J.P. Sullivan, eds. (Albany 1984) 241–262; H-P. Stahl, *Propertius: "Love" and "War"* (Berkeley 1985).

Ovid: J.C. McKeown, *Ovid: Amores* vol. 1 (Liverpool 1987); S. Mack, *Ovid* (New Haven 1988); E.J. Kenney's introduction in A.D. Melville (transl.), *Ovid: The Love Poems* (Oxford 1990).